A
Writer's
Companion

❖❖❖

A
Writer's
Companion

THIRD EDITION

Richard Marius

Harvard University

McGraw-Hill, Inc.

*New York   St. Louis   San Francisco   Auckland   Bogotá
Caracas   Lisbon   London   Madrid   Mexico City   Milan
Montreal   New Delhi   San Juan   Singapore
Sydney   Tokyo   Toronto*

This book was developed by
STEVEN PENSINGER, Inc.

A Writer's Companion

This book is printed on acid-free paper.

5 6 7 8 9 0 DOC DOC 9 0 9 8 7

ISBN 0-07-040526-3

This book was set in New Baskerville by ComCom, Inc.
The editors were Steve Pensinger and David Dunham;
the production supervisor was Diane Ficarra.
The cover was designed by Jo Jones.
R. R. Donnelley & Sons Company was printer and binder.

Library of Congress Cataloging-in-Publication Data

Marius, Richard.
    A writer's companion / Richard Marius.—3rd ed.
      p.   cm.
    Includes bibliographical references (p.   ) and index.
    ISBN 0-07-040526-3
    1. English language—Rhetoric.   2. Exposition (Rhetoric)
I. Title.
PE1429.M27   1995
808'.042—dc20   94-4025

About
the Author

*R*ichard Marius directed the Expository Writing Program at Harvard University for sixteen years, teaching students and creating the philosophy for the only course required of all Harvard undergraduates. That philosophy is embodied in this book. He is the author of three novels, biographies of Thomas More and Martin Luther, and several textbooks on writing, including the *McGraw-Hill College Handbook* which he wrote with Harvey Wiener. His articles have appeared in publications as diverse as the medieval journal *Traditio* and the nonmedieval journal *Esquire*. He reviews books for many periodicals, including *The New York Times*, and he writes a regular book review column for *Harvard Magazine*. He was one of the editors of *The Yale Edition of the Complete Works of St. Thomas More*, and with Keith Frome, he has edited the *Columbia Anthology of Civil War Poetry*. He now teaches English and Religious Studies at Harvard and is at work on a fourth novel and a large book on Martin Luther. In 1993 he was awarded the Harvard Foundation Medal for his contributions to minorities at Harvard.

For
Willis C. Tucker
and
John Lain
Beloved Professors
The School of Journalism
of
The University of Tennessee

Contents

Preface

Scarcely a week goes by that someone does not say to me, "I've always wanted to write" or "I'm going to write a book someday." Most people who say such things to me are older, successful in their work, and armed with experiences and thoughts that they should share with others. Sometimes I am so interested in their ideas that I batter them with demands that they get busy and get on paper the stories they have to tell.

I have also pushed my own students in the same literary direction, and after more than thirty years in the college classroom I am proud of the many books and articles my students have written and of the notes of appreciation I have received from them both privately and in the acknowledgment pages of their works.

My original plan for this book was to set down in a conversational way the things I try to teach my students. In writing the first edition, I tried to talk into the page the way I talk with my classes and with the many students who come into my office to sit with me at my long, cluttered table and to go over their papers.

In that respect I have tried to duplicate the advice and the kindness and generosity that marked my relations with the men to whom this book is dedicated, Willis Tucker and John Lain, who taught me in journalism school at the University of Tennessee when the world was young. And I have never had far from my mind the open-mindedness and the aversion to formality and rules that marked the teaching style of the late Sydney Ahlstrom, who taught me in graduate school at Yale. If there is a heaven, I hope that these three and I can put our feet up on a cloud somewhere and talk for ten thousand years about all the languages of the universe.

The response to the two earlier editions of the book lets me think that readers have taken it in the spirit that it was written. I have received more correspondence about *A Writer's Companion* than about anything else I have ever written, and now and then somebody calls me up long distance to say, "I love your book." I love it, too. It has been a joy to write. And as best I can tell, the only continent where it has not found readers is Antarctica.

I teach regularly out of the book myself so that to me it is something alive and continually changing as living things do. Steve Pensinger, the indefatigable friend and gentle editor of this and other writing books of mine, thought we needed a third edition. I have worked at it for more than a year, and here it is.

As in the second edition, I have made major revisions, always aiming at greater clarity and usefulness without making the book so heavy that it should come slipcased with a wheelbarrow. I have compressed some things, expanded others.

Above all, I am interested in answering this question: "What is American English today as we encounter it in the essay?" How do successful writers achieve their effects in this marvelous language of ours?

The philosophy of the book remains simple: We learn to write by writing and by thinking about what we have done. I have never found any utility in grammar drills. I ask my students to make notes, to share their notes with me, to write short preparatory exercises that allow them to think about their evidence and to organize their thoughts. Then I like them to write a draft of a complete essay. I comment on those drafts, trying above all to help student writers discover what they want to say and then to say it well. I read as many drafts of papers as my students care to write during a term. I must write things again and again before I get them right; I try to give my students the same opportunity, and I have written this book to help all of us along our way.

A fundamental conviction motivating this book is that writers must think logically about their own premises and about evidence if they are to write well about anything. I don't care much for sappy personal writing where writers tell me what they feel about things rather than what they know about things. We seem awash nowadays in the rhetoric of dramatic personal experience, where writers gush over their emotions about the commonplaces of life. I suppose some little demon down inside most of us tells us that some enterprising producer will make a movie of our lives whereby we are elevated above the common herd by how much we have suffered and how much we have felt. And, of course, our tradition includes some great autobiographical writing.

But autobiography is not the writing most in demand in our society, and in my experience most writers do not do it well. I recall a few years ago canoeing with a friend down the Ardeche River in France to enjoy the experience of seeing its gorgeous canyon and shooting its thrilling rapids. To our astonishment, after emerging upright out of the foam and roar of our last rapids, we discovered ourselves paddling a long, calm stretch of the river that ran through a nudist colony. I observed that most people look better clothed than naked, that indeed only a few have a natural talent for nudity. I feel that way about autobiography. Most of it is self-indulgent and self-serving, and few people have a gift for doing it.

To take part in a democratic society, to have a true liberal education that, as the word *liberal* implies, makes us free, we need to know experiences beyond our own. Despite the difficulties of being objective about anything, we need to cultivate dispassion and to make decisions on reasoned knowledge rather than on the blind emotions of the moment, no matter how noble those emotions seem at the time.

Societies stand or fall on their ability to know the world and come to terms with it. We have to learn facts, consider our assumptions about those facts, and wrestle them into meanings that can be apprehended by the human community around us. We have to ask questions, look for contradictions, find the puzzles, and admit it when we cannot resolve all our problems.

I regularly teach an undergraduate seminar in Shakespeare's English history plays. I tell my students that if they tell me what happens in the play they are writing about and if they solve all the problems, they will get a C. Only if they locate puzzles in the texts and take them into account in their essays will I consider giving them an A or a B. The most honest kind of writing about serious matters never claims to possess all knowledge or to answer all the interesting questions.

I have designed this book primarily for writers of academic essays or feature articles in journalism. But even those people who write autobiographically, taking their own intimate experience as the major text, should learn to ask questions of themselves. Do their memories play tricks on them? Do other people who shared their experience remember it differently? Are they being honest about their own motives? I believe it was George Orwell who said that he never trusted an autobiography unless the writer turned out to be a scoundrel at least once in the piece.

As the examples in the book show, I have tried to see how good writers—those widely read and appreciated by the community of educated men and women—achieve their effects. I have quoted from many modern American writers and from a few writing in Great Britain. As in the second edition, I have taken some examples from *Modern American Prose,* edited by John Clifford and Robert DiYanni and now in its third edition. Those who want to use the two books together can do so easily. But the examples stand on their own, and I am confident that the principles advanced in this book can be verified by consulting any anthology of modern English and American nonfiction prose.

As always, I owe debts to many friends and friendly readers. Steve Pensinger remains not only a canny editor but also fun to be with, and since he has now moved to Boston, I can see him without having to fly across the continent.

David Dunham has gallantly shepherded my manuscript into print. Willis C. Tucker, my ever patient and generous journalism professor emeritus from the University of Tennessee remains, at age 85, both friend and adviser. He made many suggestions about the second edition that I have incorporated in the third. Michael Hennessy, Southwest Texas State University; Barry M. Maid, University of Arkansas at Little Rock; and Thomas Recchio, University of Connecticut, reviewed the first draft of the manuscript for this edition and made dozens of thoughtful suggestions, most of which I have incorporated into the book.

My colleagues in the Expository Writing Program at Harvard make me think every day about what we do and why we do it. I am especially grateful to Linda Simon, Nancy Sommers, Stephen Donatelli, and Gordon Harvey for their ever delightful talk about writing. Rod Kessler at Salem State here in Massachusetts and Nancy Anderson of Auburn University in Montgomery, Alabama, continue to share with me their experience of using the book in the classroom, and we have talked and laughed away many an evening together. Paul Doherty at Boston College has made several helpful suggestions.

Others from the past remain in beloved memory—my late and dear mother, a dauntless newspaperwoman in the second and third decades of this century when the profession was not thought ladylike, a woman who read her children the King James version of the Bible every day and set its soaring cadences indelibly in our hearts; Bill Bayne, editor of the *Lenoir City News,* who suffered my early prose and even paid me for it when I attended college classes in the morning and worked for him in the afternoon; John Lain, who, with Willis Tucker, made himself the enemy of my adjectives when I wrote for him at the University of Tennessee.

I also had the very good fortune to fail Latin as a freshman at Lenoir City High School in Tennessee back in 1948. Sent off in disgrace to live with an aunt that summer in Philadelphia, I took Latin from Myron V. Harrison at Simon Gratz High School and discovered suddenly that I loved it. And Myron Harrison, at age 92, remains a dear friend.

My wife Lanier Smythe, and my sons Richard, Fred, and John sustain me by their love and their good talk and their laughter. My brother John and my friends Ralph and Connie Norman, Milton and Margaret Klein, David and Jean Layzer, and John and Judy Fox endure through the decades.

Richard Marius

A
Writer's
Companion

❖❖❖

One

First Principles

Writing is never easy, and no book can make it so. It is one of the most mysterious and complicated things we do. As we sit at our desks, pencil in hand, or at our keyboards, we bring together muscles and brain, memory and desire, and a rhythm of motions and subconscious forces much as we do when we dance or sing or talk or play baseball or ride a bicycle. It is a solitary occupation with deferred rewards. Perhaps that is one reason I have known so many people who want to be writers but so few who like to write.

At last, our work is exposed to readers who judge us by what they find on the page. We will never see most of them; most will never see us. For them, we are the words they read. We are not there to tell them what those words mean, to smile, to frown, to gesture, to explain when they do not understand. They construct an image of us from what we write, and if they don't like us, we fail—at least with them. No wonder most good writers approach writing with just a twinge of terror in their bones.

Writing is risk and adventure. In June 1993, at the end of a 500-mile bike trip, I topped Logan Pass in Glacier National Park and looked down a switchback road with snow on naked mountains above and a deep green chasm below. Snowmelt washed across the narrow highway, and for long stretches no roadside barrier existed to keep a windblown bicycle and its rider from plunging into the abyss. But what a ride! Many of us in our group went singing down the mountains.

So it is with writing. Some people publish and perish. But to be read and appreciated is one of the greatest joys on earth, a triumph heightened by the danger we risk when we put words on paper. Some writers say they don't care what anyone thinks of their work. They lie. We all care. My favorite baseball writer, Roger Angell, of *The New Yorker,* had this to say about the late William Shawn, the distinguished editor of that magazine for more than three decades:

Journalists like to think of themselves as tough birds, old pros. It's a business, this writing game, and when you finish this piece it's time to go on and knock off the next one. But Shawn, who was as tough as manganese-molybdenum in some ways, knew better. He had somehow perceived that writers are desperately in need of praise for their work—wild for it. The hard creative process, even when it's only getting things down on paper for a magazine, isn't just another line of work but also represents the writer's semineurotic need to rearrange the world and set it out in more orderly and appetizing forms. It's something a child would do, and children can never get enough praise, particularly if it comes in the form and person of an adult who will give them full attention: attention beyond measure. Praise makes them grow and go on, and those who bestow it are remembered vividly, even after they are gone.[1]

Writing is performance. A writer being read and appreciated is like a pianist receiving a standing ovation, a pitcher throwing a no-hitter in the World Series, a swimmer winning a gold medal in the Olympics. The crowd cheers; the performer is in ecstasy.

Like all the performance arts, writing requires discipline. If you don't *want* to write and love to write enough to spend time writing and rewriting, you can never write well. Like playing a piano or fielding a baseball, writing demands ceaseless work as the writer seeks to master the fundamentals and find something worth writing about and words worth reading.

Many steps in the writing process are simultaneous. While the hand moves, the brain selects from many options, memory informs, and some vague sense of what is appropriate crowds into our heads. In this book I consider the elements of writing separately, in the same way that a batting coach might give special attention to a player's wrists in swinging the bat without assuming that the rest of the batter's body remains still while the wrists snap. You put the elements together when you write, and if you write enough, you begin to handle all those elements at the same time.

My advice is descriptive, not prescriptive. That is, I show how many published writers create their effects. Writing has few rules, and most can be broken now and then. Writing does have principles, created by those who have written and read the English language over centuries. I have tried to define some of those principles from my reading of writers I like and who appeal to large, educated audiences today. Test them by your own reading.

The French critic Roland Barthes has said that we can never write without taking into account what has been written. Writing takes place within a community of writers and readers and as part of an unfolding tradition. Saul Bellow has a fine phrase to describe writing—"breaking bread with the dead." Readers approach any text with expectations picked up from a lifetime of reading authors living and dead. They are frustrated when these expectations are not met. They may tolerate a few lapses—a long, swirling sentence here, a misspelled word there, a breakdown in diction somewhere else, occasional blandness, even some confusion. But frustrate them too often and they will give up. The writer's job is to create an audience and keep it to the end.

Writing must *communicate;* that is, it makes a community. In some ancient societies, writing was considered a sacred act because it had so much authority in the community, and thus only priests were allowed to do it. In its various forms, writing is still the strongest cement of the social order. Both writing and speaking follow conventions about the meanings of words, the forms of sentences, the shapes of various kinds of discourse, the standards for evidence, and so on. Conventions are habits built up over centuries.

Since my first real job was as a reporter on a semiweekly newspaper, I always assumed that writing was to be read. If people in Lenoir City, Tennessee, could not understand what I wrote about the garden club or high school commencement, they told me about it—quickly and sometimes vehemently.

But then I became a professor! Alas! Lots of professors—and far too many students—seem to pride themselves on turning out prose that scarcely anybody can understand and that nobody can read for pleasure. This professorial attitude seems to be something like this: "Hey, I'm superior; I'm elite; I don't write for a bunch of slobs. I write only for those superior folks like me, and I like it when only a few of them understand what I'm talking about."

A teacher on my staff, fresh out of a graduate school that shall remain nameless in these pages, said to me one day in awakening wonder, "Oh, you want student writing to be *read.*" "Yes," I said in pathetic gratitude. "Oh yes, yes!" This new and astonishing concept struck her like a rock from heaven. She had been immersed for years in literary theory and its incomprehensible jargon, and she thought that writing should indicate mastery of an almost private language.

But to be read by whom? All of us belong to several "discourse communities," groups with shared knowledge and interests within which we communicate—communities where our language makes sense. The largest of these discourse communities consists of those who speak English, especially American English. Within that community we don't have to define words like *table* or *chair* or *dog*—unless we happen to be talking about some special example of each of these objects.

Within that huge community of English speakers are multitudes of subgroups—computer users, students of the sixteenth century, baseball fans, and legions more. Each community has its special language. The definition of a *discourse community* is that its members share terms that may be meaningless to those outside the community. Members of discourse communities don't have to have every technical word explained to them.

If I write that the Red Sox beat the Yankees in the last of the ninth last night on a suicide squeeze, every serious baseball fan finds a world of meaning in that statement. Nonfans find the sentence opaque. Suicide squeeze? Did a Red Sox player kill himself so the team could win?

Fans have no problem here. For starters, no long-suffering Boston fan can imagine that any Red Sox player would make a personal sacrifice for the team. The sentence rather tells us that the teams were playing at Fenway Park in Boston, that the game was tied in the last of the ninth inning, that the Sox were batting with a runner on third with no more than one out, that the Boston manager ordered the batter to bunt, and that the runner on third started for home plate as soon as the pitcher committed himself to throwing the ball. If the batter had missed the bunt, the catcher could have easily tagged the runner out. But the batter made contact with the ball, hit it slowly along the ground in front of the plate, just out of the catcher's reach, and the runner scored, ending the game.

Can a nonfan understand even this expanded explanation? Perhaps not. But any baseball writer who set out to explain every term in every story would quickly lose her job. Baseball writers address fans who know a lot about baseball—a discourse community. They try to make sense within that community, using what readers know (here the rules and language of the game) to report something new (how the game came out last night).

What does your audience know? Ask yourself that question every time you write. It has no easy answers. The community of language users is so large that its members never completely agree on the definitions of all the words. New words pour into the language; old words dry up and blow away. How all this happens is mysterious. The task of the writer is to sort out effective usage from ineffective usage, to choose words that communicate rather than words that don't, and to answer the questions of the audience he or she has chosen.

I hesitate to speak of "good" usage or "bad" usage, for "good" and "bad" imply a moral judgment of language that I do not share. Having grown up in rural Tennessee, I know that you are not stupid or immoral if you say "ain't" or "between you and I" or "he don't." But these usages do not conform to the expectations of educated readers. These readers are likely to assume that you don't belong in their group if you write such things. Foolish? Unfair? Perhaps. But that is the way groups are. Baseball fans would howl if they heard somebody wonder if the home team might punt in the last of the ninth. Such usage would tell them that he is pretending to be a member of a group to which he does not belong. They would also howl if a baseball writer explained the term "home plate" on the sports pages of the morning paper. Any writer who did such a thing would obviously have no sense of what baseball fans know and don't know. Groups can be cruel to such people.

"Ain't" and "between you and I" are fairly obvious offenses against the discourse community of the educated. But most questions of usage exist in a gray zone of uncertainty. No language is like the geometry of Euclid, a logical system based on unbreakable laws flowing in perfect harmony from primary assumptions. Too many books and too many teachers have tyrannized beginning writers with rules. Many of these teachers are modern puritans, convinced that our corrupt world is about to topple and only stern discipline and their infallible wisdom can save us.

In his angry and foolish book *Paradigms Lost* (the title is a heavy-handed play on Milton's *Paradise Lost*), critic John Simon asks why language changes. His answer: "Language, for the most part, changes out of ignorance."[2] Simon's fierce pages burn with denunciations of the "permissiveness" that descriptive books like this one inculcate in the young, and in a typical passage he assaults the National Council of Teachers of English (an organization to which I belong) as "a body so shot through with irresponsible radicalism, guilt-ridden liberalism, and asinine trendiness as to be, in my opinion, one of the major culprits—right up there with television—in the sabotaging of linguistic standards."[3] Frenzied rhetoric like this makes Simon sound a little like a puppy yapping at the mail carrier.

For at least a couple of centuries, doomsayers have predicted that civilization was about to collapse because good English was dying; a grammatical Chicken Little is always somewhere predicting that the sky will fall. In *Grammar and Good Taste,* Dennis E. Baron tells us of the amusing frustration of the English grammarian Robert Lowth, who in 1762 wrote a book intended to provide a scientific understanding of good English style. Lowth conjured up a set of rules for writing—and then complained that Shakespeare, John Donne, John Milton, and the translators of the magnificent King James version of the Bible had violated the rules and had therefore fallen into poor writing![4]

That is the fate of any frantic quest for proper English usage carved in tablets of stone by the moving finger of God. Look around just a bit, and you will find good writers who violate these commandments. Like the Puritans of old, our latter-day linguistic purists find evil everywhere, even in authors known to be superb. Poor John Simon mentions several writers he considers exemplary—but then, like Lowth before him, cannot resist the temptation to point out their errors. In the end, his book presents us with a man who must get sick every time he reads a book. No wonder he sounds so grouchy!

Language is art, not science. It has "standards," but they change with life. Classical Greek and Latin don't change much nowadays; the people who used them are dead. They changed a great deal while the Greeks and Romans lived. From Homer to Plato, Greek changed, and from Plato to the New Testament it changed yet again; living Greek has changed a great deal more in the past two thousand years.

In our society, the most important umpires of language are the editors who decide what will be published and what will not. Editors want to publish readable writing that others will buy. Editors who publish unreadable stuff get fired. Editors who can judge what the public will read keep the publishing business alive and themselves comfortable. Editors decide who will be our "professional writers"—writers who get paid for writing and who make editors look good to publishers.

The flexible standard for this book is the work of professional writers published by editors. I call it "editors' standard," and I have tried to describe what works most of the time. Nothing works all the time. Every writer occasionally breaks the rules, and every writer occasionally fails. If your audience likes your work when you break the rules, you win. But if you break too many rules, no editor will publish your work. The real "rules" of language are the expectations of readers as these expectations are defined by editors.

Writers must respect readers. Reading is hard work. The written words lie there, as Socrates told Phaedrus in a famous dialogue, without the help of a living person to explain them. They must speak for themselves. If we misunderstand them, no voice speaks out of the writing to correct our mistakes. Words have histories; they have shades of meanings; they have contexts. Times change, and readers of different generations read into words thoughts that differ from what the writer may have intended. In Anthony Trollope's delicious nineteenth-century novel *Barchester Towers,* the slimy hypocrite Obadiah Slope "made love" to the virtuous Eleanor Bold in a carriage. Trollope meant that Slope proposed marriage to her. Today we are likely to be somewhat startled by coming upon this phrase in such a context with such a proper couple.

Less striking changes also overtake words. Readers bring their own experiences to every text. The same reader may see one thing in a text in youth, another in the same text in middle age, and yet another in old age—and all the interpretations may make sense. All this complicates the writer's task. Readers bring their own experiences to any text they read, and they can easily be confused or come away with an impression different from what the writer intended. Good writers know how easily they may be misunderstood, how quickly they may fatigue readers, and how hard they must work to convey the meaning they intend. Good writers also know that readers have other choices. No reader has to read my work. I'd better try to be interesting, or else my readers are gone.

Most modern writing has a conversational tone. It is not stuffy and formal. When read aloud, it sounds almost like someone talking. But speaking is always easier than writing. Speakers can misuse words and still be understood because of their tone of voice, their gestures, and their expressions. They can repeat themselves until we get the point. Speaking is a democratic art; nearly everyone does it well enough to communicate.

The movies, radio, and television have inundated us with speaking by all sorts of people who might find it difficult to write an essay. We hear their words, their tones, and on TV talk shows see their carefully informal and humble grins. Often the spoken words of celebrities do not mean much of anything; confronted with a TV camera and an audience of millions, they lunge after expression in bursts, like a child hopping down the street on a pogo stick. Even so, out of such talk we construct understanding because we can see the people talking, and often someone comes on afterward and explains to us what has been said.

We are also accustomed to seeing speakers wander from one point to another, break off thoughts in midutterance, say confusing things, and contradict themselves. But we put up with such things on late-night talk shows, perhaps because we are looking at celebrities and they are amusing and perhaps because we don't have the energy late at night to do anything but sit there and look passively at the tube.

Writing and reading are far more demanding. Readers construct meanings from texts. Texts do not have body language and intonations. They stand alone. Writing represents more extended and more complicated thought than the thought expressed in most conversations. The writer develops ideas in chains, one thought carefully linked to what has come before it. That adds difficulty, for readers must remember what has come before, be aware what is there now, and anticipate what will come in the next paragraph or on the next page. Reading puts a strain on short-term memory: We have to remember the beginning throughout the piece. We have to be reminded continually where the writer has been and where that writer is taking us. The good writer helps the reader's memory hold on to the entire piece of writing as it unfolds under the reader's eyes.

On the bike trip I took in June 1993 through the Pacific Northwest, the organization in charge painted yellow arrows on the roads so the bikers would not get lost. At any intersection where we might take a wrong turn, a small, bright-yellow arrow on the pavement told us the right way to go. And sometimes even on a long stretch where we did not turn, we were glad to see one of those arrows that said, in effect, "Yes, you're heading in the right direction."

The generous writer provides arrows all through his or her prose to orient readers and to keep them on track. The limitations of our short-term memory and the purposes of reading require that written language be much more precise and better organized than spoken language. Professional writers succeed in taking readers to a destination; the best writers give pleasure along the way. How do they do so? Here are some principles to keep in mind.

1. Professional writers conceive of their writing as a story to be told.

They try to interest readers in their story—a story about something that has happened or the story of their thinking or the thinking of others on a subject. They set out to tell that story as engagingly as possible, asking themselves always this question: How can I make my readers turn the next page? Of course, good writers want to be correct—just as the pianist wants to hit all the right notes. But professional writers—like professional pianists—never assume that being correct is enough.

The shape of stories has evolved by custom. Let's take a look at what happens in a familiar story. Here is the beginning of a story we all know:

> Once upon a time, a little girl named Red Riding Hood lived on the edge of a great forest. On the other side of the forest lived her grandmother, and in the forest lived a big, bad wolf.

Any 5-year-old knows that somehow the forest, the grandmother, and the words are going to come together in the story that follows. It will be a story that the child will relive step by step in the imagination generated by the telling. Many beginning writers and a great many professors have trouble with this concept. Write to make a reader *relive* a story, relive my thoughts? It's too much trouble. Why not just summarize the facts and lay them out there for readers to pick up if they need them? So we get papers like this in composition courses and in academic journals:

> In the following paper, I am going to tell the story of a young woman named Little Red Riding Hood who got into trouble with a wolf in the forest. I shall tell how she started through the forest to deliver some cakes to her grandmother. I shall tell how she encountered the wolf, together with some details about the wolf's trickery and his ugly disposition. Finally, I shall tell how Little Red Riding Hood and her grandmother came to a bad end.

Or we have writers who think their intentions are more important than their story. So we get the sincere version, inspired perhaps by public figures who suppose that no matter how dishonest and incompetent they are, they will be forgiven if only they seem sincere.

> It is a sad fact that human beings encroaching upon the environment, especially the forest, have created unpleasant and aggressive attitudes in the animals who ordinarily might live there peacefully with their human brothers and sisters. Wolves, for example, have been proven to be harmless and even friendly to human beings in the wild. But when their habitat is harmed by improper lumbering activities, usually in the interest of those manufacturing paper towels and toilet paper in the mindless human world, disastrous consequences ensue. We see how far ecological damage to the environment may go as we study the story of an unfortunate and innocent young woman when she encountered an equally unfortunate and innocent young wolf in a forest that had been unforgivably damaged by those out to make a profit rather than serve nature.

Or we get the essay shaped by the conviction that a piece of writing must be the consequence of a deduction, that it must contribute to a great truth already certified by noble and established authority stretching back for centuries.

> From the dawn of time, forests have been the preserve of wild animals often dangerous to human beings, especially to children, and numerous indeed are the tales of bloody encounters between wild beasts and little girls and boys. Let us look at one example of this oft-repeated drama in history by examining an old fairy story in which a young woman, armed only with a basket of cakes, encounters a wolf in the forest, with results that in most versions of the tale were extremely unpleasant for the little girl involved. First, let us survey the geography of the environment where the story takes place.

The original version of the story gets right to the point. It combines elements that are in a certain tension with each other—a little girl, a forest, a big, bad wolf, and a grandmother. Just to put them together signals danger to the little girl. We know that something threatening will happen. We assume that somehow these elements will come together and that the tension will be resolved. We might write the story like this:

> Once upon a time, a little girl named Red Riding Hood lived on the edge of a great forest. On the other side of the forest lived her grandmother, and in the forest lived a big, bad wolf. Now one day Little Red Riding Hood's mother gave her a basket of cakes and said, "Little Red Riding Hood, take these cakes across the forest to your grandmother's house." And so the little girl started through the woods. But then she met a talent scout from the Dallas Cowboys, and he said to her, "Little Red Riding Hood, you don't want to waste your life here in the forest. You want the bright lights, the big city. Come with me to Dallas and become a cheerleader for the Cowboys, and you will be on TV every Sunday afternoon." So Little Red Riding Hood threw down the basket of cakes and left the forest forever.

Any 5-year-old hearing the tale told in that way would ask immediately, "What about the wolf? What about the grandmother?" The beginning of a story makes a promise. It introduces elements that must come together somehow as the story goes along. Just like a story, an essay or an article begins with elements out of balance with each other and an implied promise that the writer will put those elements together and that we as readers will live in the writer's mind as he or she works out the story of how this unbalance is resolved. Or, as writer Rosellen Brown has said, "All fiction, to some extent, depends on the entry of disorder, or the threat of disorder, onto the scene."[5]

Much the same can be said for the good essay. Like a story, a good essay or article begins with elements in tension. Something is out of order, or something threatens. If you don't have tension, you don't have a story—or an essay. The story imposes order on reality by establishing connections and making some resolution. A story or essay may not solve the problem presented by the introduction. But at least it sets it in a context, allows us to understand something about it, and provides a sense that we have come to an ending, that a climax has been reached.

It is a linear process, though at times, like a railroad winding over hill and dale, it may seem to wander. When we get to the end of the story, we see that everything included in it has had a purpose and that purpose is to work out the tension presented at the beginning. A good opening makes us wait for something to happen; then that "something" happens at the climax to which the story—or the essay—goes. If you don't have a climax, you don't have a story—or an essay. Facts piled on top of one another without a climax don't make a story or an essay; they only make a mess on the page.

Therefore, when you begin to write, look for the story—the elements in tension with each other, the puzzle, the threat, the challenge that cries out for some resolution or explanation. Look for the tensions in any topic you choose to write about.

Good writers are infinitely curious. They ask questions all the time about what they experience, what they see and hear, what they read. Many questions that arise in good writing are about unbalanced elements. Why did President George Bush win such a spectacular victory in the Gulf War and yet lose the next election? Why does a Stephen King novel make us so afraid when we know it is fiction? How can we clean up the environment while the world economy is sagging? What happens to children when their parents are divorced?

The first impulse of good storytellers is not to prove that they are more intelligent than anybody else or that they don't make mistakes or that they are on the right side of this or that moral issue. Their first impulse is to tell the story so that hearers—or readers—are swept up in it, made part of a community that asks, "How does this all come out?" If you tell the story well, you can trust your audience to believe in you.

Find the story in your data and tell it. Everything else in your writing will then fall into place. In the next chapter, I have some important things to say about the difference between an essay and a report. But both are based on finding the story.

2. Professional writers are efficient.

They use as few words as possible to say what they want to say. They use short words rather than long ones when the short words express their meaning just as well. They get to the point quickly. A doctor complaining about the obscurity of writing in the medical profession sent me the following example of prose that no editor of a popular magazine would allow to see print. The writer is trying to show how the treatment of cancer affects community hospitals.

> The cancer burden and its financial ramifications have escalated to enormous proportions on the community level. Early diagnosis with open com-

munication to the patient and cost containment are dominant in the perspective of community medicine. Bed space, operating room facilities, and therapy units are in desperate need of expansion but are curtailed by certificates of need. The burden of creative and imaginative utilization of existing advantages is projected back to the physician, and his personal role in directing a diagnostic maneuver, informing the patient of results, and accomplishing therapy is intensified.[6]

A professional writer would have revised to condense.

The burdens of cancer have become enormous for community medicine. We want to diagnose the disease early, communicate honestly with the patient, and contain costs. We are short on hospital beds, operating rooms, and therapy units; and we lack the money to expand. The physician must take responsibility for using what is available for diagnosis, for telling the patient the results, and for directing the therapy.

In the second version, I have reduced ninety-one words to sixty-six. I do not think I have cut anything essential from the first version, although I cannot understand parts of it. (What does the writer mean by "certificates of need"?) Professional writers prune away the nonessential as they revise their early drafts.

"Efficient" does not mean bland or simple. If you have complicated thoughts, you must sometimes use complicated language to express them. But always ask yourself if the complicated language is necessary. Unfortunately, many writers believe they must write obscurely to be taken seriously. I found the following sentence in an academic journal that shall remain nameless. It is professorial writing at its worst:

Individuals with a strong home-defense orientation in living areas noted for multiple instances of criminal behavior in urban regions are most likely to practice the acquisition and continued possession of firearms.

The writer *means* that in urban neighborhoods where crime is common, people buy guns to defend themselves. Why not say that?

Efficient prose may not even mean brevity. Sometimes a longer version of a thought is clearer—and therefore more efficient—than a shorter version. The shorter version may abbreviate ideas so much that readers have a hard time following them. Here is a sentence from an article in a recent scholarly journal. The article analyzes what various groups of white people believe about opportunities for blacks in our society.

The category of persons who see black opportunity as average and not greatly improved appears to contain a subtype who seem to be saying that opportunity for blacks has always been equal, denying the existence of past inequality of opportunity.

After reading the rest of the article, I think this sentence can be translated as follows:

Some people think opportunities for blacks are about equal to those for whites and that there has been no great increase in opportunities for blacks in recent times. Some of these people seem to think that blacks have always had equal opportunity and that inequality of opportunity never existed.

The second version is longer, but it is more efficient because it is easier to understand. Efficient prose allows readers to move through a piece of writing without having to back up and read it again. Efficient prose does not have to sound as if it belongs in a first-grade reader.

3. Professional writers are direct.

They begin most of their sentences with the subject and tell us quickly what the subject does—or what happens to the subject. They do not write many long, looping, dependent clauses between subjects and verbs. They usually put direct objects immediately after the verbs.

We read silently now; only a couple of centuries ago it was common practice to read everything aloud. Then readers could modulate their voices and emphasize phrases in such a way that the audience could understand, more or less, even the long sentences common at the time.

We also read quickly. Even a slow reader absorbs about 250 words a minute. Hardly anyone can speak that fast. We read more easily if subjects are close to verbs and verbs close to direct objects. Direct writing is more conversational; that is, the sentence patterns are much like those in the sentences we use in speaking to one another.

In *The Philosophy of Composition*, E. D. Hirsch, Jr., illustrates the increasing directness of English style by giving several translations of the same text from Giovanni Boccaccio, the greatest of the fourteenth-century storytellers in Renaissance Italy. Hirsch shows that as the English translations come forward in time, they are both shorter and more direct. Here is a version from the sixteenth century:

Saladin, whose valliance was so great that not only the same from base estate advanced him to be Sultan of Babylong, but also thereby he won diverse victories over the Saracen kings and Christians; who through his manifold wars and magnificent triumphs, having expended all his treasure, and for the execution of one exploit lacking a great sum of money, knew not where to have the same so readily as he had occasion to employ it. At length he called to remembrance a rich Jew named Melchizedech, that lent out money for interest in Alexandria.[7]

An eighteenth-century version reads like this:

Saladin was so brave and great a man, that he had raised himself from an inconsiderable person to be Sultan of Babylon, and he had gained many victories over both the Saracen and Christian princes. This monarch having in diverse wars and by many extraordinary expenses, run through all his treasure, some urgent occasion fell out that he wanted a large sum of money. Not knowing which way he might raise enough to answer his necessities, he at last called to mind a rich Jew of Alexandria named Melchizedech, who lent out money on interest.[8]

An even more recent and direct translation is the following:

Saladin, who was so powerful that he rose from an ordinary man to the rank of Sultan of Babylon and won countless victories over Saracen and Christian rulers, found that he had exhausted all his wealth, both in war and in the exercise of his extraordinary munificence. Now, by some chance, he felt the need of money, and a lot of it, too, and not knowing where he could get it as quickly as he wished, he thought of a rich Jew called Melchizedek who was a moneylender in Alexandria.[9]

We can understand the first version only if we read it slowly aloud. It is littered with cumbersome dependent clauses and participial phrases that come between subjects and verbs. We can understand the second version fairly well by reading it silently, and we can comprehend the third version even more readily. We could probably design an even more direct version.

Saladin was so valiant that he rose from ordinary status to become Sultan of Babylon and won countless victories over Saracen and Christian rulers. He found that he had spent all his money, both in war and extravagance. Now he needed a lot of cash and needed it quickly. Not knowing where else to get it, he thought of a rich Jew called Melchizedek who was a moneylender in Alexandria.

One of the best ways to revise your own writing is to go over and over it, seeing how few words you can use to convey the information and get the effects you want to give your audience. Computers make this process much easier than it once was.

4. Good writers engage readers.

They stimulate the imagination, the image-forming ability of the mind. The children of my generation listened to radio dramas and made pictures in their heads of what they heard. Ages before that, a bard singing the epic tales of the tribe by the fire at night summoned up pictures in the minds of the circle of silent listeners.

These pictures are painted by the experience of the readers and listeners. A good writer describes a scene, providing a few telling details, and readers understand because these details remind them of parts of their own experiences. I tell a story and interest you because somehow my story stimulates a flood of your own memories.

Our most vivid memories are of sense experiences, objects we saw or heard or tasted or felt or smelled. Good writers develop a knack for calling on these memories when they write. Here is the opening paragraph of a story from a recent *New Yorker* about the political terror in Ethiopia under a Marxist dictatorship that overthrew the Emperor Haile Selassie in 1974:

> Outside Akaki Prison, in central Addis Ababa, one rainy July dawn, some thirty women stood huddled under umbrellas, waiting to be searched by a prison guard. A dog moved among them and sniffed at their feet. Most of the women were members of the Ethiopian royal family or of the nobility. All were dressed in black, and some wore veils. They wore no jewelry except tiny gold crosses hanging discreetly on gold chains.[10]

The writer, Mary Anne Weaver, provides a flood of details that stir up various kinds of memories. We have not seen *this* prison, but we have seen some prisons—perhaps in the movies—so that the word calls up in our minds impressions of bleakness. The rain, the dawn in July, the umbrellas, and the sniffing dog all recall our memories of such things; and the tiny gold crosses on "discreet" chains not only call up memories of gold crosses we have seen but also make a contradiction between our ideas of wealthy and bejeweled "royal" families and "nobility"—ideas we may have picked up through the movies or television or children's books—and the reality that Weaver presents. Our memories give us the scene and show us immediately that there is something wrong here. Although few of us have been to Ethiopia, these details activate our minds and make us feel that we can see this scene.

Weaver could have written, "A group of women stood outside a building in an Ethiopian city." Instead, she put together words and phrases rich with sensory images that we could imagine because they activated fragments of our memories. She makes us recombine our memory of those experiences and become engaged with the experience she describes.

When teachers say "Be concrete" or "Be specific," they mean you should use the solid, sensory words good writers use to call up some memory, some experience, something readers have seen and heard and felt and smelled and tasted. Our most vivid memories are of sense experiences—a rumble of thunder on a stormy night, the sharp blue sky of a wintry day, the taste of mustard, the smell of perfume, the feel of sandpaper. Use sensory words in your writing, and readers respond.

You do not have to convey sense experience in every sentence, and you may write more abstractly if your audience already knows a lot about your subject and has an intense interest in it. You can be less vivid because you can assume a high degree of interest in your readers. For this reason, many articles in specialized journals seem dull to outsiders; they are addressed to people already deeply interested in the subject and knowledgeable about it. Cancer researchers want to get quickly to the point in a technical article about cancer; they do not have time for vivid descriptions. But when they read other things, cancer specialists are like the rest of us: They appreciate being engaged by lively writing addressed to sense experience.

Even articles in specialized journals should use vivid examples now and then. Too many writers forget to keep the minds of readers alert and responsive. A few years ago one of my students used the word *relationship* fourteen times in a three-page essay. When we talked about the paper, I suggested that she vary her writing a little more. The word *relationship* recalled no sharp memories of sense experience. My student disagreed. "It makes sense," she said. "It's grammatical. I don't see why you criticize me when it's correct."

She had been taught that the aim of writing is only to be correct, to obey the rules of grammar and syntax. No one had made her reflect on her own attitude when she reads, the swift judgments she makes as she decides whether a piece of writing is worth her time. I doubted that she would have been willing to read her essay if it had been written by someone else. Her attitude was, "It's correct! Take it or leave it!" Confronted with that sentiment, most readers will leave it.

So much for my first principles. I hope this book will help you win readers to your writing as many of my students now happily publishing their work are winning readers to theirs. If you read it carefully and apply its precepts to your prose, you can write more efficiently and vividly and you may gain some other rewards as well. People will respect you for your writing, and you will be happier doing it. You may even get to the point where writing becomes an addiction. Let me know if that happens. I answer all my mail.

A final piece of advice: Read. Read everything you can. Read day and night. Good writers are good readers. When they like a piece of writing, they try to decide why; when they dislike something, they ponder their aversion. If you make reading a lifelong habit and try to imitate in some way the writing you like best, you will be on the way to writing well.

Two

The Writing Process

No writer I know gets it right the first time. Most of us have to write and rewrite to write anything worth reading. Readers nowadays are in a hurry. They will seldom struggle to understand difficult writing unless they are forced to do so. Samuel Johnson, the great eighteenth-century writer, said, "What is written without effort is in general read without pleasure." Today, what is written without effort is seldom read at all.

Writing takes time—lots and lots of time. Good writers don't dash off a piece in an hour and go on to other things. They do not wait until the night before a deadline to begin to write. Instead, they take notes. They plan. They write first drafts. They revise. One writer I know types laboriously on a typewriter and, in revision, cuts his manuscript up with scissors and tapes the parts together again in an order he finds suitable. Even after a second draft, most writers look over their work and rewrite. The computer allows us to make revisions swiftly—tightening sentences, shifting paragraphs around, or cutting them out altogether. But even small writing tasks may require an enormous investment in time; and computers don't finally do the work. You do.

So it is with all worthwhile disciplines. A good athlete can run a hundred-yard dash in less than ten seconds; but to prepare for those ten seconds takes weeks of training. If you want to be a writer, you must be serious about the job and willing to dedicate hours to your work, revising it again and again.

Most of us sometimes suffer writer's block. We can't get started or, once started, lose sight of our destination; our brains go dead, as if the power had gone off in a house at night. If you suffer writer's block, you're in good company.

Writer's block is seldom a matter of sitting at a desk while words fail to come. Usually it is a consequence of impatience with the task. The words seem not to be there. We surrender. We tell ourselves we will write for a while and go to a movie; then we decide we will go to the movie and write afterward; later we decide to go to bed and write in the morning. We put off writing as we put off a visit to the dentist.

The best way to avoid writer's block is to sit down at your desk and stay there, fingers on the keyboard or wrapped around a pen or pencil. Years ago, B. F. Skinner, the behavioral psychologist, rigged a clock to a light over his typewriter. When he sat down to write, he turned on the light, automatically starting the clock. When he stood up for any reason, he turned the light off, stopping the clock. He spent four hours a day writing. The clock told him when he had completed his task. Mechanical? Yes. But it worked. His clock drove him to concentrate on spending real time on real work, and he was an astonishingly prolific writer, turning out books and articles until he died in August 1991 in his eighties.

The first rule of writing is this: Sit down and do it. Stay there. Keep going. We all get discouraged—especially before the mountain-climbing task of writing the first sentence of the day. We have trouble organizing our thoughts. We decide to make another cup of coffee. We think of a magazine we have not read, a telephone call we have not made.

Finally, we write a sentence or a paragraph or a page, and immediately we need to change it. Writers love new beginnings, clean slates, unblemished pages. We think a new start will get it right. But when we begin and begin and begin again, we deceive ourselves. We are only looking for an excuse not to get on with it. The habit of starting again and again quickly makes us give up for the day, saying, "I'll do it tomorrow. I've made myself so nervous by all these false starts I can't go on today." So the game is lost.

Most writers have one or two favorite places to work. I love to work in my cluttered study here on the second floor of my house or in my equally cluttered study in the main library of my university. When I walk into either place, something inside me says, "You are here to write." The Southern writer Thomas Wolfe was large and tall; he wrote in longhand while standing up, using the top of his refrigerator as a desk. Ernest Hemingway often wrote standing up at a little portable typewriter. William Faulkner sat at his kitchen table in his rambling frame house on the edge of Oxford, Mississippi. Make a workplace for yourself, and commit yourself to spending three or four hours there every day at your writing.

I've always tried to write whole drafts of a book or an article as soon as possible. As I say to my students, once you get a work "in being," there on your desk as a pile of paper or there on the hard disk of your computer, to be summoned up at will, you can start revising. In writing this edition of *A Writer's Companion,* I worked through the entire book, putting it on my hard disk, and I then called it up every day, adding, subtracting, sharpening, and rethinking. Once you have a text in front of you, you can do all sorts of things with it. I always tell my students that if they plan too much before they write, the planning sometimes takes the place of writing.

But although I'm a believer in getting a first draft together as quickly as possible, I do *not* always write the draft in the order that the piece will appear. Very often I think of the middle or the end of a book or an article before I'm clear on the beginning. I don't put off writing what comes to mind, even if it means that I write the middle before I write the beginning. Put off writing out an idea, and it may be lost. You may discover, as many writers do, that the beginning is the last thing you write.

When you have your draft before you, the real fun begins—revision. With my first draft before me, I am confident that I have something to say. I can then set myself to the task of sharpening every sentence, choosing the right word, adding a paragraph here or there, slashing out whole pages, changing the order of my writing, examining connections and transitions to be sure my readers know where I'm taking them (painting those bright yellow arrows on the road), examining my conclusions, tightening the organization so that it holds together and says what I think it should.

Revision requires that you read your own work again and again. Inexperienced writers find that task hard. Too many new writers deliver their first drafts with the air of weary coal miners eager to shed their dirty clothes at the end of the day. In the Army's basic training program, sergeants regularly warn recruits about the unfired rifle in combat. Many soldiers in the thick of a fight refuse to fire their weapons, seemingly afraid of attracting hostile attention. A similar caution curses new writers who refuse to reread their work when it is done. They are afraid they will find something wrong. They want to get rid of their work as soon as possible.

It may be a comfort to know that professional writers suffer similar pangs. If anything, their unhappiness is greater because they make a living from writing, and their first drafts may persuade them that they need to find another job or face starvation. Battle-hardened professionals do not see a first draft as final. Rather, they expect it to be like a blob of clay that a skilled potter flings onto a spinning potter's wheel. Potential beauty resides in the blob; it can be brought out by the skilled and careful touch of the potter's hand.

All writers must reconcile themselves to slow improvement rather than instantaneous perfection. Now and then, all habitual writers have sudden revelations. A sentence or an idea leaps unexpectedly into the writer's mind like a gift from God. More often, however, the writer labors steadily on details that add up to a book or an article as bricks laid carefully on top of each other finally make a wall. It's worth saying again that writing well is like preparing for a musical concert or an athletic contest; you work at every detail so that the final performance will make you one with your audience.

Preparation for Writing

But let's take a step back. How do we get to the moment where we sit down and start putting words on paper? First, we have to have something to write about; we have to know something. Two parts of the writing process are inseparable: knowledge and finding a subject to write about—a step we call "invention." You have to know something before you can write an essay; deciding what to write depends on the stories you find in your knowledge.

Battered old writing teachers curse their fate when they read papers filled with sweeping generalizations and preachy assertions of opinion. Such papers betray student writers who have not looked anything up, not read any books or articles, not asked any questions.

Hardly anyone can write about a subject that has not been written about before. Writers are obligated to have at least a rough idea of what has been written before about their topic. I love to write surrounded by my books, and I sometimes tell my students to write their first drafts in the huge, quiet reference room of our main library. When they want to check a date, a spelling, a historical fact, a quotation, or the plot of a book or a play, they can easily find it. Now that library catalogs are on line and accessible by computer, no writer has an excuse for not knowing if something has been written before on the topic that he or she addresses.

As you read about a topic, you find data falling into what lawyers call "fact patterns." That is, the facts start indicating conclusions. For example, to prepare to write a paper on Hamlet's friend Horatio, you may read every speech Horatio gives and the attitudes expressed about him by other characters in the play. You may also recall that Horatio was the name of the legendary Roman soldier who stood valiantly at a bridge over the Tiber, defending Rome single-handedly from its enemies. The name Horatio is also, for anyone who knows the classics (as Shakespeare certainly did), a synonym for faithfulness. The facts begin to add up to a conclusion: Horatio may be the only unambiguously unselfish and loyal person in *Hamlet*. When that thought strikes you, you have a standard by which to measure the morality of the other characters.

Write about what you know; that is a familiar piece of advice to writers. The backside of this aphorism is that you cannot write well about anything you *don't* know. Many inexperienced writers can write fairly well about themselves. The reason is simple: They know a lot about themselves, and the subject interests them. Autobiography has its place in literature, but it is not the kind of writing most college courses require, and demand for autobiography in the world beyond college is limited. Most people read to learn facts and what the facts mean. The most sought-after writers are experts in subjects beyond their intimate experiences. You can be an expert about several subjects if you're willing to work at it. As writer David

Halberstam loves to say, writers succeed not only by writing but by doing "legwork"—getting out in the world, reading, conducting interviews, looking up facts.

Keep notes on your reading and your observations—not merely factual notes but notes about what you think about those facts. When I have to write something, I begin by filling notebooks. I live surrounded by them. I carry one or two in the shoulder bag that goes back and forth with me on my daily bicycle commute between home and my office. Whenever I go somewhere—even across Logan Pass on a bicycle—I have a notebook close at hand. I am always scribbling ideas, trial sentences, random observations, questions. Like a prospector digging through mud and sand for gold, I sift through my notes for facts and thoughts that may go into a finished work.

Find your own writing process. Mine is wrapped up in my notebooks, and I urge the process on you. A notebook is portable, durable, and efficient since you are not likely to lose pages out of it. A friend of mine carries a small pack of 3 by 5 cards wrapped with a rubber band in his shirt pocket. The cards are hard on his shirts but good for his mind and memory. The great Russian-American novelist Vladimir Nabokov wrote his books in pencil on such cards, and later someone typed his manuscripts from them. He revised his manuscripts, and his typist did them again. You can take your notes on cards and later arrange them in the approximate order of your essay and write from them.

Don't be afraid to let your notebook get messy and disorganized. It's your private property, your fenced-in garden—or pigpen—where you can play with your thoughts or wallow in them. No one else will see it. Professional photographers throw away fifty shots for every one they keep. You can toss away the ideas you jot down but decide not to use. You will find that the habit of writing keeps your mind working, seeking, playing; and out of all that will come some things you can use in your final drafts of articles or essays.

Learn to paraphrase and summarize information. The best reading is done with a pen or pencil in hand and a notebook open beside the book or magazine on your desk. A *summary* condenses information. A *paraphrase* puts in different words the thoughts of a source. Summarize when you want a ready reference to the contents of a book or an article. A summary should be as brief as you can make it. You can waste time by trying to include every detail of your source in a summary. Barbara Tuchman, one of our most popular historians, gives her view of taking notes (and provides a process different from my dependence on notebooks):

> As to the mechanics of research, I take notes on four-by-six index cards, reminding myself about once an hour of a rule I read long ago in a research manual, "Never write on the back of anything." Since copying is a chore and a bore, use of the cards, the smaller the better, forces one to extract the

strictly relevant, to distill from the very beginning, to pass the material through the grinder of one's own mind, so to speak.[1]

Paraphrase when the source text is difficult, perhaps written in an old or foreign language. Paraphrasing give you a chance to interpret the source as you read it, and you may use your interpretation in your later writing.

Thomas More, the English scholar and saint who died as a martyr to his Catholic faith in 1535, wrote vigorously against Protestants when they entered England during the reign of Henry VIII. Here is a text from one of More's works:

> I here also that Tyndale hyghly reioyceth in the burnyng of Tewkesbery/but I can se no very grete cause why but yf he reken it for a grete glory that the man dyd abyde styll by the stake when he was fast bounden to it. For as for the heresyes he wolde haue abiured them agayne wyth all hys harte, and haue accursed Tyndale to, yf all yt myghte haue saued hys lyfe. And so he gaue counsayle vnto one Iamys that was for heresye in pryson wyth hym. For as Iames hath synnys confessed / Tewkesbery sayed vnto hym, saue you your self and abiure. But as for me bycause I haue abiured byfore, there is no remedy wyth me but deth. By whych wordes yf he had not ben indyspayre of lyfe / it well appereth he wold wyth good wyll haue ones abiured, and ones periured agayne.[2]

As you can see, this text, written in sixteenth-century English, would be difficult to copy in a notebook word for word. One can, however, paraphrase it and, in reviewing it in one's notebook, recall More's thoughts. Here is a paraphrase:

> Protestant William Tyndale, translator of the New Testament into English, praised martyrs to Protestant faith in England, but More mocked Tyndale's praise, saying of a man named Tewksbury, who had been burned at the stake, that the only thing heroic and praiseworthy about his death had been that once bound to the stake, he stayed there. Tewksbury, More says, had been accused of Protestant beliefs once, had renounced them, and had returned to the Catholic faith, and therefore saved himself from burning. But then he had gone again into Protestantism and had been arrested again for heresy. English law held that a person convicted the second time of heresy had to be put to death without mercy. More says Tewksbury would gladly have recanted if he could have saved his life again but that Tewksbury knew this was not possible. However he did advise another accused Protestant whom More calls James to recant and save his skin. James later gave testimony to the authorities about Tewksbury's statement. More's point is that a Protestant "martyr" died because he had no choice, not because he bravely sacrificed himself for his faith, and so he could not be claimed by Tyndale as proof of faith unto death.

Note that the paraphrase is a little longer than the source. The paraphraser, a student of More's work, explains what is going on in the source—good practice for any researcher.

A summary would be even shorter.

> More mocked Tyndale for claiming one Tewksbury as a martyr. Tewksbury would have saved his life if he could have, says More. But he had already been condemned once as a heretic; a second condemnation brought an automatic death sentence under English law. Tewksbury advised a fellow prisoner, condemned only once, to recant and save his life.

We might imagine this summary in even a shorter form: "More mocks Tewksbury's martyrdom after Tyndale had praised it."

For both paraphrase and summary, in doing research note down the page number and title in More's works where the text appears. You can easily look it up again if you have some questions from your own notes, but if you have taken the notes carefully, you will probably not have to do so. In my own work on Thomas More, many paraphrases I made in studying his work made their way almost unchanged into the biography I published in 1984. I have often found that as I summarize or paraphrase from a source, pen or pencil in hand, ideas pop into my head that I have not thought of before. I jot them down, and sometimes I use them in interpreting the texts I am writing about.

Summaries save time for you and your readers. Now and then we all must quote word for word from a source in order to capture a colorful phrase or an important meaning. But never quote if you can summarize or paraphrase accurately *unless* the text is so rich that you cannot do without quoting it. In his biography *Truman,* David McCullough tells the story of President Harry Truman's fierce letter to music critic Paul Hume after Hume had panned a concert given by the President's daughter, Margaret, who fancied herself an opera singer. Truman wrote to Hume, "Some day I hope to meet you. When that happens you'll need a new nose, a lot of beefsteak for black eyes, and perhaps a supporter below!"[3] One cannot summarize such a comment; McCullough quoted that line and the whole letter—and he did the right thing. But use a direct quote only if it is necessary to express either the information or the mood you find important in the quotation.

When you copy a source word for word, use quotation marks in your notes. When you summarize, make a note of the source to use later on in your footnotes or endnotes. Plagiarism—the most serious offense a writer can commit—may result from poor note-taking. Take care to avoid even the appearance of stealing ideas and language from others. To avoid confusion and plagiarism, some people write direct quotations, summaries, and paraphrases on one page and their own comments, thoughts, and questions on the facing page. I put a little arrow (→) next to my own thoughts to distinguish them from summaries and paraphrases of my sources.

Comment as you read and take notes. Make a list of questions about any subject you want to write about. Part of knowledge is the recognition of ignorance. Unanswered questions drive you to seek more information, and if after a search you still cannot find an answer, you will have learned something important about the limits of knowledge about your topic.

Finding a Topic

What will you write about? Students told to write a paper for a course are sometimes terrified by this question. I offer two broad answers: Write about things you know that your audience does not, or write about the puzzles you find in your evidence. Even if you write merely to convey information, you must provide some sense of why that information is important. Therefore even a factual article should have in it an element of tension, of something out of balance that must be put right.

Aristotle taught his students certain "common topics" that could be subjects for speaking or writing. He said that we can write about what kind of thing something is; that is, we can define a thing or describe its parts. We may compare something with something else, pointing out similarities and differences. We can discuss relations such as cause and effect, oppositions, and contradictions. We can speak or write about circumstances— whether something is possible or not, whether or not something happened in the past. Or we can provide our reasons for accepting a theory or belief that we cannot prove beyond the shadow of a doubt.

All these "common topics" may help us write. I have frequently asked my students to define terms such as *reason,* as it is used by Martin Luther or Thomas More, or *honor,* as it is used by characters in Shakespeare's plays. They can take these or other important words in our texts and define them as one person uses them. They can then put that definition in relief by comparing it with someone else's definition, including their own, and discuss the causes that made these persons define these words as they do. They can show the contradictions in how one person or several used the words. They can argue perhaps that it is impossible to be consistent about a word like *honor* and provide examples of inconsistency, in say, Shakespeare's play *Henry V.* Finally, they can argue that one part of the definition seems more important than another.

Any time you find a key word like *reason* or *honor* or *democracy* or *liberal* or *conservative* or anything else, you can use Aristotle's "common topics" to write a paper about it. As I wrote earlier in this book, many great and frequently used words are abstractions. They do not create pictures or other sensory images in our memories. They do not mean the same thing to everybody. We may define them only by the context in which people use them, and nearly everyone uses them in a special sense.

For Shakespeare's Henry V, "honor" seems to be a willingness to fight to the death without fear. The young king talks fervently about "honor" the way saints talk about faith. In the stirring battle scenes of the play *Henry*

V, we see this abstraction applied to the world where people live and die. By examining his language and his conduct, we see what honor means to the king. We can see its parts, seek its causes, compare it with the "dishonor" of other characters, speculate about whether Henry's definition is satisfactory, comment on the circumstances of his times and Shakespeare's that made such a definition popular then, ask whether his way of speaking about honor allows him to be a worthwhile character. Like most teachers, I am delighted when my students hand in papers in which they have used these Aristotelian "topics" to analyze an important word in a text. And my students are delighted when they discover how many questions they can ask a text, using ancient Aristotle as a guide.

Use your notebooks to work your way through your reading and your ideas. Trust yourself. Most people have interesting thoughts, but they usually do nothing with them. A major difference between creative and noncreative people is that creative people take their idle musings seriously enough to make something of them.

In writing an essay, choose a limited problem, one you can define precisely. You cannot do an elaborate psychological analysis of Henry VIII in five pages. You cannot use the simple title "Luther" for a ten-page library paper. Limit your topic to a story you can tell in the space at your disposal and prove to readers that you have become expert in that subject. Yes, you have time to be an expert in a limited subject; believe that, and you can be a writer.

Write titles that describe your work. Good titles are essential to good writing, but I'm surprised at how seldom students think of them until the last minute. Try different versions of a title in your notebook.

The following suggestions may help you find topics in your reading and your observation:

1. Be a close reader—or a close observer.

In looking at people, we ask, What qualities give this person his or her identity? In looking at a painting, we say, How is this painting different from anything else I have ever seen? In looking at a written text, this question becomes, What exactly do the words say? Why is this paragraph or these lines essential to the whole? How dependable is this source? What bias did this writer have in putting down this account? What can I read between the lines of this source?

A close reading is the first step toward understanding written texts. I sometimes give my students sources of the battles of Lexington and Concord, fought in Lexington and Concord, Massachusetts, in April 1775 to open the Revolutionary War. I say to them, "Tell me the story of the battles." The sources come from both the British and the Patriot sides. Some were written immediately after the battle, some, years later. Naturally, contradictions abound.

Among the sources is the story Paul Revere wrote about his famous "midnight ride." Most of us have read Henry Wadsworth Longfellow's poem, which portrays Paul Revere making plans for his midnight ride, speaking to a friend who was to place lanterns as a signal in the tower of Old North Church. Says the Revere of the poem:

> And I on the opposite shore shall be
> Waiting to ride and spread the alarm
> Through every Middlesex village and farm.

Longfellow gives us several verses showing Revere doing just that—standing by his restless horse, waiting impatiently to see the lanterns gleam out through the dark across the Charles River to signal that British troops are on the march along the country roads of Middlesex County in Massachusetts to seize arms and gunpowder the Patriots have stored at Concord.

The first time I gave this assignment, one of my students, a biology major (who eventually went to law school!), in reading Revere's recollections, saw that Revere had ordered the lanterns posted *before* he had himself rowed across the Charles to his waiting horse. He had learned the direction of the British troops before he slipped out of Boston. But Revere feared that the British might catch him as he was crossing the river to the Cambridge side. He had the lanterns posted to warn others who might carry the lanterns in his place. Most of us have taken our idea of Revere's ride from Longfellow; my student took it from Revere himself—a superior source.

Students commonly believe that all possible truth has been squeezed out of familiar texts. In fact, a delight in scholarship lies in the power of texts to yield new truths to those who study them diligently. Read carefully, and you may well discover that previous students have missed something. Their interpretations may therefore be wrong. It is seldom enough to read a text once. Good thinkers read a text a dozen times, coaxing their minds to see it anew. They are like the fictional detectives Sherlock Holmes or Hercule Poirot, who find clues that suddenly reveal a truth the casual observer has overlooked entirely.

Always ask how dependable your sources are. In my assignment on the battles of Lexington and Concord are two accounts giving the number of British troops in the expedition. The diary of a British officer says there were 600; a minister who witnessed the skirmish at Lexington preached a sermon a year later on the anniversary of the battle saying there were from 1200 to 1500 British soldiers involved. My students sometimes have trouble seeing that an officer marching in the British force and writing the day after the battle is a much more reliable source for the number of soldiers with him than a minister watching from a distance and preaching on the subject a year later, when Lexington and Concord had already become legendary.

Defining, sorting out, examining causes and effects, and comparing events in your own experience serve much the same purpose as examining a text carefully. It is a close reading of the self that may lead to revelation for yourself and others.

2. Look for patterns in the evidence.

Many writers return to the same themes over and over again, perhaps using the same words to describe them. Pay attention to the obvious. When you see the same words or themes or incidents again and again, ask what they mean. William Faulkner, the Mississippi writer and Nobel Prize winner, wrote about families in many of his books and stories. How were these families alike and how not, and how do his families differ from common conceptions about the family today? One answer is that in Faulkner's world, divorce was rare. What did that mean for the family? Martin Luther talked about "faith." What did he mean by "faith"? Faith in what? Karl Marx wrote frequently of the "bourgeoisie." What was it? Did he use the word in the same way all the time?

Listen for silences in the evidence. What did Franklin D. Roosevelt say about blacks, about Jews, and about women in his speeches? Almost nothing. Why? What did American political figures say about Hitler's hostility to Jews during the 1930s? Why did Luther seldom speak of hell when he spoke of his fears before God? The silences are clues to the larger world view of the writer.

3. Use inferences when you write.

Inference is one of the surest ways to originality. We'll consider inference again when we talk about argument. But let's consider it here because we can scarcely avoid it in any kind of writing.

When we infer, we use previous knowledge and experience to help us understand something new. Inference is basic to all reasoning. It is the skill of Sherlock Holmes on a murder case and the skill of the medical researcher looking for a cure for breast cancer or AIDS. Without inference, we merely report facts.

Inference suggests what the facts mean. We see smoke and infer fire. We see a woman smile and infer that she is happy; we see a child cry and infer that he is unhappy. We see two men shouting and shaking their fists at each other in the street, and we infer that they are angry. Past experience tells us that people smile when they are happy, cry when they are not, and sometimes shout at each other when they are angry.

We infer from statistics. Eighty-three percent of the men who die from lung cancer are cigarette smokers; we infer that cigarette smoking causes lung cancer.

We infer from texts. "The Lord is my shepherd," reads the Twenty-third Psalm. "I shall not want. He maketh me to lie down in green pastures:

he leadeth me beside the still waters." We infer that the writer of these words lived amid sheep and shepherds and that the first people who heard his song understood him because they were children of a life among pastures and herds in the open air.

The more we know about a subject, the more reliable our inferences. If a scholar has carefully read again and again the thousands of pages left to us by Sir Thomas More, I trust his inferences more than I do the claims of someone whose only knowledge of More comes from the Hollywood movie "A Man for All Seasons" or the pictures of More drawn or painted in his lifetime.

Our inferences may be wrong. That is why some students and other inexperienced writers fear to infer. Nobody likes to be wrong. Yet knowledge advances as we test inferences. And it is almost impossible to write an interesting essay without inference. Without inference you only report evident facts, and you do not try to make sense of them.

Suppose a teacher asks you to write a 2000-word essay on Shakespeare's *Hamlet*. You will bore her into a trance if you summarize the plot. She's read the play a hundred times. She's seen it on the stage and in the movies. She knows what happens to all the characters, and she has probably memorized many of the lines. If you tell her only what she already knows, your paper is doomed to be as forgettable as last year's TV sitcom.

The assignment is to write an essay. We write essays to tell readers something they don't already know or else to make them see in a new way what they do know. We write to share our reasoning, our thinking. By summarizing the play, student writers make a subtle and lethal change in the assignment: They make it an examination. We take examinations to prove to others that we know something. We read examinations only because our jobs force us to read them. Not many readers sit down in their easy chairs at night and say, "Well now, I think I'll relax and improve my mind by reading a few examinations."

When you begin to infer, you start thinking; and if you think, some readers will be interested in what you write about your thoughts. For example, look at these words from Hamlet's famous soliloquy:

> To be, or not to be: that is the question:
> Whether 'tis nobler in the mind to suffer
> The slings and arrows of outrageous fortune,
> Or to take arms against a sea of troubles,
> And by opposing end them? To die: to sleep;
> No more; and, by a sleep to say we end
> The heartache and the thousand natural shocks
> That flesh is heir to; 'tis a consummation
> Devoutly to be wish'd. To die, to sleep;

To sleep: perchance to dream: ay, there's the rub;
For in that sleep of death what dreams may come,
When we have shuffled off this mortal coil,
Must give us pause.

We have all heard these lines a thousand times. But what do they mean? Why is Hamlet not sure that there is life after death? The church of his time taught that eternal life in heaven or in hell was the fate of every mortal. Why does Hamlet not profess that faith? We may infer that the faith in an afterlife was being eroded, that to people of Shakespeare's day death appeared more final, heaven and hell much more uncertain, than they had appeared in medieval thought and that Shakespeare's world view may have been distinctly unchristian.

A geologist observes a boulder resting on the naked granite of a mountain in New Hampshire and sees that the boulder is unlike the granite and unlike any other stone in New Hampshire but that it is like the stone in a part of Canada to the north. She infers that the strange boulder has been carried to this place by the ice sheets that once covered New England, pushing huge loose stones down from the north. Since no one in historical memory ever saw these huge layers of ice cover New England, the entire theory of an ice age rests on the inferences of geologists. A particular inference stands until someone can come up with one that seems more valid.

Inference is a powerful tool. Be brave enough to infer when you write, and be aware of your inferences when you make them.

4. Ask the journalistic questions.

Writers ask questions and answer them. The writer who asks the best questions usually writes the best and most original piece.

Journalists are trained to answer these five questions in every story they write: Who? What? Where? When? Why? When we read, we want to know the answers to all these questions. We hear that a friend has had a wreck. What happened? Who was driving? Who was hurt? Who was responsible? When did it happen? When did the police get there? When did the ambulance come? Where did it happen? Where were the injured taken? Why did it happen?

By asking these questions you can scan any subject you want to write about and fill out a paper with answers. These questions can help you see a text more clearly and help you define topics for a paper. For example, when you read the short story "A Rose for Emily" by William Faulkner, you can ask the question, Who is Miss Emily Grierson? The answers might run like this:

She is a woman grown from beautiful youth to ugly old age in a changing Mississippi town.

She is the only daughter of a protective and tyrannical father.

She is a member of a family that takes pride in its reputation.

She is a woman with little money.

She is lonely.

She is unloved.

She is a monument and a curiosity in the town.

She is a failure in all her personal relations except that with a black servant.

She is a murderer.

The list can go on. As you write down every response you can think of to the question "who?" you begin to see details and meanings that you might easily have overlooked in a first reading. The same process works for the four other questions. As you write the answers to these questions, you begin to see other questions you have not thought of before.

Asking these questions does not end your writing process. You must find ways to weave your answers into an essay. While you are doing that, you may discover that some answers are unimportant or that they do not fit your purposes. But at least with the questions before you, you have some raw material to work with.

5. Make connections between what you observe and other things you know.

When you read any text, ask yourself how you can bring your experience, your knowledge, to bear on your reading. If you write for an English class, think of ways to bring to your paper things you learned in history, in philosophy, in physics, in economics, or whatever to your paper. Creative people have a mental scanner in their heads that plays across the entire range of their knowledge when they study any subject, illuminating it by everything that is part of their lives.

This connective quality overlaps the ability to infer things. You may read Hemingway's 1940 novel, *For Whom the Bell Tolls,* and look carefully at the strong woman character Pilar, wife of Pablo, the guerrilla leader in the hills during the Spanish civil war of the late 1930s. If you have read other Hemingway novels and short stories, you may compare Pilar with women in those works. Or you may compare her with women portrayed by other authors. How does she compare with the women in Faulkner? With women in the fiction of Henry James? What would a modern feminist say about Pilar?

As I have noted, comparison is one of the "common topics." By comparing one thing with another, you may see both things more clearly. You integrate your own experience and understand it better. You may know vaguely that you like Faulkner's women better than the women in Hemingway's work. (Or you may discover the reverse.) Working out your reasons for this preference can make for a fascinating essay.

But not every comparison is illuminating. Any two things can be compared, but you should use comparison only if the comparison tells you something significant. In comparing Pilar with other women in Hemingway's work, for example, you might notice some development in the author's sensibility. In comparing her with a strong woman in a Faulkner novel, you may show two different views of women written at about the same time by authors with different sensibilities. In comparing Pilar with women in Henry James, you might demonstrate a change in women in literature from early in the century to 1940.

I love reading papers written by those rare students who bring knowledge of other disciplines to papers they write for me—the woman who brings some knowledge of religious studies to her paper on *Hamlet* or the man who uses something he learned in an economics class to illuminate a point about Thomas Jefferson. My students don't do this sort of thing often. My colleagues in other disciplines encounter the same one-track thinking. The student in a history course doesn't think a reference to literature belongs in a history paper; the student in economics believes that history has no relevance to economics. Therefore when teachers like me find a paper that reaches across disciplines, we are likely to leap for joy and show the paper to every colleague we find in the hall.

Scanning your previous knowledge and experience to illuminate the topic at hand is a form of comparison. You compare when you study the changing reputation of a character, the place of a work of art in art history, or a social attitude. To live each day, we consciously or unconsciously interpret our present experience by comparing it with experiences from the past. The good writer brings that impulse consciously into his or her work.

Remember that our experience includes everything we read, study, and research. "Experience" doesn't happen only to the body; it happens to the mind. You have experience in reading, in reflection, in conversation. Your experience in writing is as intimate as any experience you have. It is your ceaseless effort to make sense of things and to communicate your understanding to others.

6. Look for contradictions in the evidence.

Most interesting topics if probed far enough reveal contradictions and paradoxes. Some things don't add up. Every good reporter learns to interview people with an ear open to contradiction. In a good press conference, reporters ask questions to get the speaker to consider contradictions: "Mr. President, how do you reconcile your statement that you support education with the budget cuts you have recommended for schools and student loans?"

Contradictions are not necessarily moral flaws. They are simply part of human character. Ralph Waldo Emerson said in his essay "Self-Reliance," "A foolish consistency is the hobgoblin of little minds, adored by little statesmen and philosophers and divines. With consistency a great soul has simply nothing to do." Good writers recognize inconsistencies and take them into account, recognizing that some are only part of the human comedy and others may be efforts to deceive.

Inconsistencies abound in texts, and the contradictions may be just the place where careful study may fuel a good paper. In *Utopia,* published in 1516, Thomas More had his mythical Utopians practice religious toleration. They had to believe that God exists, that He rewards and punishes men and women in an afterlife, and that He guides the world by His providence. Utopia is an imaginary island off the coast of the New World, and many readers through the centuries have assumed that in his little book about the place More expresses a plan for an ideal society. But when the Protestant Reformation burst on Europe and spread to England, More wrote hundreds and hundreds of fiery pages demanding that Protestants be burned at the stake. While he was Lord Chancellor of the realm, he ordered several Protestants to be put to death by fire. What do we do with the contradiction between what More wrote in *Utopia* and what he wrote and did when the Protestants started making converts in England?

Keep your eyes open for disagreements among authorities—another sort of contradiction. Some years ago, a student of mine named Simon Frankel, now a lawyer in California, did a fine paper comparing essays written through the years about *The Age of Jackson,* a book by Arthur Schlesinger, Jr. My student showed that when the book came out, in 1945, scholars all over America praised it. But after this first enthusiasm cooled, other scholars took a second look and began to argue that the work was badly flawed. Simon read about ten reviews of the book written over some twenty years and sketched his findings in an interesting and original paper. Most interesting topics create arguments; if you survey these various arguments and try to discover the reasoning behind them, you may make some important contribution to knowledge.

Never pretend that contradiction and inconsistency in your evidence do not exist. Knowledge of any subject is partly clear, partly obscure, and partly perverse. We don't know what some of it means. Too many writers are like bad mechanics: When something doesn't fit, they look for a bigger hammer. If you try to pound your evidence into a scheme where everything fits perfectly, you are certain to distort the truth. Be bold enough to face contradictions squarely when you meet them, and be honest enough to admit defeat when you cannot reconcile them.

7. Study results.

We love to know how things turn out. Good papers establish chains of cause and effect and sometimes try to point at the end to some enduring result of an act, a book, a battle, a treaty, a court case, a critical appointment, a presidential election, or whatever. Sometimes you may wish to speculate about what might happen if a certain course of action were adopted. As you will see in the chapter on argument, the connection between cause and effect is often more difficult than it may seem at first glance. The difficulties should not deter you from trying to sort out both cause and effect, for such speculations may enlighten us about the events we study.

In 1898, the United States fought a war with Spain. What were the consequences? We became more deeply involved in Asia. We took over the Philippine Islands and Puerto Rico. We made Cuba independent. We reunited our own country, which had been emotionally split by the Civil War. We created a crisis of conscience in our theory of democracy because a great part of the American tradition had been against imperialism, a crisis heightened when the Philippine people took up arms against the American soldiers who came to "liberate" them. So it goes. You can extend the consequences of any important event into a list and then convert the list into an essay.

Sometimes questions about cause and effect stir up "what if" papers. What if the British had won the American Revolution? What if the United States had not made the Louisiana Purchase from Napoleon? What if Shakespeare had died in 1600? What if Ernest Hemingway had been a woman? What if Martin Luther had been killed by the lightning storm in 1505 that frightened him into becoming a monk? We can never answer "what if" questions to anybody's complete satisfaction. But asking them may help us see more clearly what *did* happen.

Virginia Woolf wrote a great "what if" piece in her book *A Room of One's Own*. She poses the question, "What if Shakespeare had had a sister as gifted as he and as ambitious as he was to be a playwright?" The question allowed Woolf to make a vital critique of how badly women have been treated in Western society.

The "what if" question is a good, playful one to ask when you prepare to write a paper. The creative person frequently has a playful mind, the ability to ask questions that may at first seem nonsensical but then can open a serious inquiry. Never imagine that genius must be somber.

Use your notebook to play with ideas. Scribble notes to yourself that overcome your inhibitions, that ask unanswerable questions, that follow leads that you may think at first unpromising. As you write, even in play, your mind generates ideas, and some of these ideas may turn out to be worth writing about because the way you develop them is interesting and valuable to others.

Writing Drafts

Finally, the moment comes when you sit down and put your words on paper—or on the computer screen. It's always a good idea at the start to list the points you want to cover. A list is not as elaborate as a formal outline. In writing your first list, don't bother to set items down in the order of their importance. Simply list your main points and trust your mind to organize them. You will probably make one list, mark it up, rearrange things, write it again, study it some more, and perhaps make yet another. You can organize each list more completely than the last. This preliminary process may save your hours of starting and stopping.

It may help you also to write out a one-paragraph summary of what you intend to do in the paper—or the book. In a book I'm working on now, I found it liberating to sit down and write a long summary of what I thought the book ought to be. I have now rearranged that summary a couple of times. But it has been a great help in organizing what I am doing.

Once you start writing, stay at the task. Don't get up until you have written for an hour. Write your thoughts quickly, steadily if you can. Let one sentence give you an idea to develop in the next, and then go to it. Organization, grammar, spelling, and even sentence clarity are not nearly so important as getting the first draft together. No matter how desperate you feel, keep going.

Keep your mind open to new ideas that pop into your head as you work. Don't become a slave to your summary. Writers often do their research and start an essay with one topic in mind only to discover that another topic pushes the first one aside as they work. Ideas you had not even thought of before you began writing may pile onto your paper, and five or six pages into your first draft you may realize that you are writing about something you did not imagine when you started.

If such a revelation comes, be grateful and accept it. But don't tear up or erase your draft and start all over again. Make yourself keep writing, developing new ideas as they come. If you suddenly start all over again, you may break the train of thought that has given you a new topic. Let your thoughts follow your new organizing idea, or "thesis," sailing on that tack until the wind changes.

When you have said everything you have to say in this draft, print it out if you are working on a computer. Get up from your desk and go sit in a chair somewhere else to read it, without correcting anything. Put it aside overnight if you can. If possible, read your rough draft just before you go to bed. Many psychological tests have shown that our minds organize and create while we sleep if we pack them full before bedtime. Study a draft just before sleep, and you may discover new ideas in the morning.

Be willing to make radical changes in your second draft. If your organizing idea changed while you wrote your first draft, base your second draft on this new subject. Even if your major idea has not changed, you may want to move some paragraphs around, eliminate some sentences, or write in some connections to make your paper read more smoothly. Inexperienced writers often suppose that revising a paper means only changing a word or two or adding a sentence or two. This kind of editing is part of the writing process, but it is not the most important part. The most important part of rewriting is the willingness to turn a paper upside down, shake out of it the ideas that most interest you, and set them in a form that will interest the reader, too.

I mentioned earlier that some writers cut up their first drafts with scissors. They toss some paragraphs into the trash; others they paste up with rubber cement in the order that seems most logical and coherent. Afterward they type the whole thing through again, smoothing out the transitions, adding new material, getting new ideas as they work. The translation of the first draft into the second nearly always involves radical cutting and shifting around. Now and then you may firmly fix the order of your thoughts in your first draft, but I find that the order of my essays is seldom established until the second draft.

The computer has made the shifting around of parts easier. We can now cut and paste electronically with a few key strokes. We can also make back-up copies of our earlier drafts so that we can return to them if we wish. But as I said earlier, computers do not remove the necessity to think hard about revising.

Always be firm enough with yourself to cut out thoughts or stories that have nothing to do with your thesis, even if they are interesting. Cutting is the supreme test of a writer. You may create a smashing paragraph or sentence only to discover later that it does not help you make your point. You may develop six or seven examples to illustrate a point and discover you need only one.

Now and then you may digress. If you digress too often or too far, however, readers will not follow you unless your facts, your thoughts, and your style are so compelling that readers feel drawn along. Not many writers can pull such digressions off; most editors will cut out the digressions even when they are interesting. In our hurried and harried time, most readers get impatient with the rambling scenic route. They want to take the most direct way to their destination. To appeal to most of them, you have to cut things that do not apply to your main argument.

In your third draft you can sharpen sentences, add information here and there, cut some things, and attend to other details to heighten the force of your writing. In the third draft, writing becomes a lot of fun—at least for many of us. By then you have decided what you want to say. You can now play a bit, finding just the right word, choosing just the right sentence form, compressing here, expanding there.

I often find it helpful to put a printed draft down beside my keyboard and type the whole thing through again as a final draft, letting all the words run through my mind and fingers one more time rather than merely deleting and inserting on the computer screen. I wrote four drafts of the first edition of this book; I preserved the final draft of that edition on computer diskettes. But when I wrote the second edition, I propped the published first edition up beside my keyboard and typed it all through again.

With this, the third draft, I have propped the second edition up beside my keyboard and typed through more than half the book. I found myself making a great many stylistic changes and also rearranging much of the material. Then, about half or two-thirds of the way through, I began using the computer files for the second edition, working through them to make fewer changes than in this section and the chapters immediately to follow. Having worked my way all the way through the third edition, I have gone through it carefully several times, bringing up the various files onto my computer screen and working at every sentence. It would be easy enough for you to compare the three editions and see the changes I have made, most of them unforeseen until I sat down here to work.

I have outlined here my own writing process. It works for me. You must find the process that works for you. It may be different from mine. A friend tells me that his writing process consists of writing a sentence, agonizing over it, walking around the room, thinking, sitting down, writing the next sentence. He does not revise very much. I think it unnecessarily painful to bleed out prose that way, but he bleeds out enough to write what he needs to write. Several friends tell me they cannot compose at a typewriter. They must first write with a pencil on a yellow pad. These are the people most likely to cut up their drafts with scissors and paste them together in a different form. They also tend to be older. Most young writers learn to compose at a keyboard, and they cannot imagine another way to write. I have composed at the keyboard since I was 16 years old. But I often go back to my mechanical pencil, with a soft black lead, writing on a yellow pad or in notebooks for pages at a time. When I have produced a certain number of pages, I go back to my keyboard to put what I have written on the computer.

The main thing is to keep at it. B. F. Skinner used to point out that if you write only fifty words a night, you will produce a good-sized book every two or three years. That's not bad production for any writer. William Faulkner outlined the plot of his Nobel Prize-winning novel *A Fable* on the wall inside his house near Oxford, Mississippi. You can see it there to this day. Once he got the outline on the wall, he sat down with his typewriter and wrote, following the outline to the end. If writing an outline on a kitchen wall does the trick for you, do it. You can always repaint the wall if you must.

   Think of writing as a process on its way to a product—sometimes painfully. Don't imagine you must know everything you will say before you begin. Don't demean yourself and insult readers by letting your first draft be your final draft. Don't imagine that writing is easy or that you can do it without spending time on it. And don't let anything stand in the way of your doing it. Let your house get messy. Leave your magazines unread and your mail unanswered. Put off getting up for a drink of water or a cup of tea. Don't drink alcohol when you write; true, lots of writers were alcoholics, but their writing was not helped by booze. Don't make a telephone call. Don't straighten up your desk. Sit down and write. And write, and write, and write.

Three

Kinds of Writing

❖❖❖

I find it useful to classify writers as either reporters or essayists. Like most categories, these two overlap. But let's try to think of them as distinct for a moment.

A reporter collects information and presents it much as one does a news story on a big city newspaper. The reporter's point of view is in large measure limited to the choice of data, and we all know that that choice is important and can be dishonest. But on the surface, at least, the reporter is not personally wrestling with an idea that he or she wants readers to accept in opposition to the ideas of others. Newspaper readers do not read the reporter's story to see what the reporter thinks; they read to see what has happened. When the reporter writes an interpretation, it is usually a quotation or summary of the opinion of an authority. For example:

> Movies are less violent than they used to be, J. C. Flack of Hollywood Pictures, Inc., told a meeting of the National Council of Parents and Teachers last night. "In the last Clint Eastwood movie, Clint gunned down only eight men, and there were only six other violent murders in the film. The woman whose face was slashed by a cowboy did not die from her wounds. Yes, you saw a lot of blood," Flack admitted. "But, hey," he said, "we all have blood in us, and that's natural." Flack said that most of the people in a Clint Eastwood movie deserve to die anyway.

Here the reporter is quoting another authority; she is not giving an opinion of her own.

In an essay, the writer is the interpreter, thinker, explainer, the authority. The essay inevitably has about it the scent of argument. It may not present forensic argument against a sharply expressed point of view (although some essays do just that), but in one way or another the essay informs us that the writer has studied the issue or experienced it intimately enough to interpret it. The essay involves a line of reasoning, beginning with commonly accepted assumptions and proceeding to consequences that are not self-evident.

Some people mistakenly believe that the essay must be about the writer's experience, that essays have to be autobiographical. Some teachers now say that student writers should shape essays around some image out of the writer's personal experience. Then a woman's suffering with anorexia might give her a new insight into standards of beauty represented in nudes painted by male artists; a young man's recollections of an abusive father might help him interpret some of the stories in James Joyce's collection called *Dubliners*. I see such essays coming out of college writing programs now, and they make me uneasy. Many examples of such essays seem self-indulgent and narrow, and teachers who give assignments that call forth such essays seem often to think that young writers cannot think about anything other than their most intimate experiences.

In over thirty years of teaching in three schools—a small private college, a large Southern state university, and a large northeastern private university—my best papers have come from students who became excited about books, ideas, paintings, architecture, science, history, and a whole world of other topics that did not require them to make explicit reference to their own experiences.

Yes, writers like Richard Selzer, Annie Dillard, Loren Eiseley, Maxine Hong Kingston, and many others have written personal autobiographical essays popular among many readers. Mark Twain's autobiographical narratives *Innocents Abroad, Roughing It,* and *Life on the Mississippi* are classics of American literature. But the demand in most college courses and in life beyond college is for writing that makes sense of texts outside ourselves. And inexperienced writers writing personal essays seem easily to me to fall into misplaced passion, sentimentality, and even dishonesty in a mistaken effort to make themselves interesting by displaying their feelings rather than their knowledge or understanding.

Although we can never free ourselves entirely from the influences of our own experiences, part of becoming educated is learning how to stand off somewhat from ourselves and bring a certain detachment to the subjects we write about. Certainly it is no part of the definition of the *essay* that it be autobiographical or "familiar," as some writers now call the autobiographical essay. The essence of the essay is that it involves wrestling by the writer to resolve or clarify an issue. Essays are, in the current jargon, "think pieces." They involve efforts to think seriously about important matters.

The word *essay* was coined by a Frenchman, Michel de Montaigne, in the second half of the sixteenth century, to describe his written reflections on various subjects. His essays resembled public letters about his observations, his reading, and his ruminations. He rambled much more than essayists do now, letting his thoughts move from one idea to another. He was curious, as all good writers are, asking questions and seeking to answer them. He died in church in 1592, but his integrity and wit make disciples of his thought four centuries after his death.

Montaigne wrote with an independent mind, without accepting the prejudices of the crowd and without seeking favor from the powerful. His writing is natural, unaffected, simple. "I speak to the paper," he wrote, "just as I speak to someone I meet for the first time."[1] He never talked down to readers. Nor did he pander to their prejudices; he never feared to be in the minority. He tried to see things as they were, and his observations were surprising for their freshness. He proved that an honest observer always has something new to say.

He called his pieces *essays,* from the French word *essai,* meaning "attempts" or "trials." For him, an essay was just that—an attempt to think clearly. He was far too humble to claim that he had established truth beyond all doubt. "I freely give my opinions on all things," he wrote, "even those that may go beyond my competence and on which I by no means claim to be an authority. And so my thoughts about them are only to reveal the extent of my vision and not the limits of things themselves."[2] He supposed that he had made an "essay" toward truth—observing honestly, marshaling his evidence, reflecting on his experience, interpreting it as fairly as he could. When he could not answer a question, he admitted his ignorance. He never claimed to have found the truth about everything.

He knew his conclusions would not satisfy everyone. Still he advanced them tolerantly, serenely, without insulting his opponents, without heating his prose with passion except on the rare occasions when he condemned the religious wars burning across France in his time. He was confident without being arrogant. He did not believe he had to save the world. He believed that reason, clearly and gently set down on paper, would win its own battles. He did not try to crush his foes. He remained somewhat detached, like a man calmly taking us across a varied landscape, expertly pointing out features we otherwise might have missed. He claimed not to be an authority, but he was; his opinions demonstrate wide reading and deep thinking.

Most good essays are akin to Montaigne's—civilized efforts to arrive at truth without rancor, without destroying those who disagree. Good essays appeal to the best in readers, to their sense of fair play, to their best emotions, to their wish to do the right thing, to their ability to think.

Now and then you may be tempted to write passionately for a noble cause. Resist the temptation. A few writers manage great passion for great causes, but success is rare in passionate writers because few of them control passion well. Angry passion easily becomes bombast and self-righteousness. Sentimentality often becomes cloying. Most readers dislike prose dipped in syrup. Superheated prose is usually embarrassing.

One of the greatest essays of modern times is "Letter from a Birmingham Jail," written by the Reverend Martin Luther King, Jr., when he was arrested by a city government whose police chief had turned savage dogs on black citizens—including children—peacefully demonstrating for their rights. Young and old black Americans had been whipped, beaten, bitten, maimed, and killed, and King had every reason to be furious. But his essay does not project fury. Instead, it rises to a quiet eloquence and power just *because* it is calm and reasonable. King had such confidence in the righteousness of his cause and the fundamental fairness of his readers that he did not have to scream his convictions.

King's example teaches us that writers who rudely dismiss opinions with which they disagree do not have much effect on those opinions. You can't write, "That's stupid" or "It's all baloney" or "This is totally ignorant" and expect anybody to take you seriously. Readers usually scorn contemptuous language in writers. If you disagree with something, you have to work out the reasons for your disagreement and present these reasons in careful steps, maintaining the calm and the confidence of one who is unthreatened by dissent. Such careful responses can be crushing and memorable—as Dr. King's "Letter from a Birmingham Jail" proves.

The best prose is tolerant and cool. If you are temperate and measured and reasoned, and if you think of your reader as a friend to persuade rather than a foe to slay, you will have a far better chance of carrying your point than if you dip your pen in fire and write to burn.

Qualities of the Good Essay

Here are some qualities of good essays. Study them carefully.

1. Most essays are short enough to be read at a sitting.

Some books may be called *essays* since a serious nonfiction book involves a sustained argument meant to make us accept the writer's view. In the more common meaning of the word, an *essay* is a shorter nonfiction piece that can be read at one sitting. An essay is extended prose in that it is more than a sentence or a paragraph. Just how long you make an essay depends on your purposes and your audience, but all of us should recall the sound advice of Polonius in *Hamlet:* "Brevity is the soul of wit." Perhaps the Spanish writer Baltasar Gracian said it even better: "Good things, if short, are twice as good."

For new writers, an assignment to write a 2500-word essay may seem monstrous. Experienced writers find the *short* essay far more difficult. They cannot fit all they know into the space available. They must decide what is most important in what they know and how to present it in the most striking way possible. Every word must count; every sentence must be just right. Every unnecessary word must be chopped out.

2. A good essay gets to the point quickly.

Readers want to know right away why they should read your work. Nothing annoys a reader like delay. "What is this writer trying to say? Why am I reading this?" Remember "Little Red Riding Hood." In the first couple of sentences, we get to the tension that will be the subject of the story, and we read on. Let your readers know quickly where the tension in your essay lies, and get on with it. Don't keep them waiting. Some inexperienced writers love surprise endings. Such endings seldom work in essays. I have never received an effective surprise ending from a student in all my years in the classroom.

3. Write effective titles.

A good title is part of your beginning. Use it to sharpen your purpose so that the reader will know at once what you are writing about. Scholars are fond of titles with a colon in the middle: "Inventing Siberia: Visions of the Russian East in the Early Nineteenth Century." That was the title of a recent article by Mark Bassin in the *American Historical Review.* A title in PMLA (the Publication of the Modern Language Association) was "My Hideous Progeny: Mary Shelley and the Feminization of Romanticism." Such titles have the advantages of a catchy opening and an explanation immediately after the colon.

Titles in popular magazines often do not use colons, but they have subtitles that explain the article to come. The lead story in *Sports Illustrated* for December 21, 1992, had as its title, "The Eternal Example." The subtitle said, "Arthur Ashe epitomizes good works, devotion to family and unwavering grace under pressure."

HOW TO BEGIN

No book can tell you all the ways to begin an essay. Your best bet is to study beginnings written by professional writers and to imitate them. Here are some examples of common types of beginnings. Not that all of them develop a point of tension at the beginning. Something is out of balance or unfinished or in some way portends conflict or opposition.

Tell a story In the January 1993 *Atlantic,* Erik Larson begins like this:

> On December 16, 1988, Nicholas Elliot, barely sixteen, walked into the Atlantic Shores Christian School, in Virginia Beach, Virginia, with a semi-

automatic handgun hidden in his backpack. By midmorning a forty-one-year-old teacher had been shot dead, and another teacher, struck by two nine-millimeter bullets, was extraordinarily lucky to be alive. Two other teachers narrowly escaped Nicholas Elliot's bullets. One found herself running a zigzag pattern through the school yard as Nicholas fired round after round at her back. The other, a man who tackled Nicholas and in the process saved the lives of a roomful of crying and praying teenagers, felt a bullet breeze past his head.[3]

When we read a story like this, the tension is obvious. We want to know what happened next—and why all this happened in the first place. We love stories. They seem to be part of our natural inheritance as human beings.

Two cautions! Be sure the story truly introduces the essay that comes after it. Erik Larson's essay argues that we should regulate gun ownership at least as strictly as we regulate the right to drive a car. The story fits this essay exactly.

And don't represent a story as true when you have no evidence for the details. Don't make things up. For example, don't start a paper like this:

It was night in the royal palace in Greenwich, and a sleepy silence hung over the dark corridors and the rooms where servants lay snoring abed. Only Henry VIII was awake, and he walked the floor aimlessly before the great fire that blazed on the hearth in his room. He could not sleep because he could not purge his mind of the greatest problem of his reign: How could he have a son?

It's perfectly all right to imagine that Henry VIII had every reason for walking the floor at night, worrying about the succession to the throne of England. But no document gives any evidence that such a scene took place. If you are ever caught telling a lie when you write something you claim to be the truth, your reputation as a writer will be ruined forever.

Describe a scene   Akin to telling a story is giving a description that arouses curiosity. The reader wants to know, What exactly is happening here? Why is this significant? The scene being described must be interesting in itself. And it must point to the essay that follows. Here is the first paragraph of an essay on Appalachia from the *National Geographic:*

It's hard to know Appalachia. Plenty of people think they do. I thought I knew it before I left my home there, in Kingsport, Tennessee, for the Northeast ten years ago. I knew it as a place that was lush and moody in the summer. Mist clung to the green mountainsides, and the creek beds I waded in to search for salamanders were filled with the scent of honeysuckle. In autumn, slopes and ridges teemed with maples, dogwoods, and oaks—with color that set the land on fire. I remember hiking to Abrams Falls in Virginia with my girlfriends to swim in a chilly pool under the potent column of white water and sitting on a friend's farmhouse porch at dusk listening to rain fall on the roof.[4]

Notice that even this descriptive paragraph begins with a note of tension. "It's hard to know Appalachia." This writer seems to know it well; she describes it powerfully. But she is going to reveal what she finds are its difficulties and contradictions in the article to follow.

Use a provocative quotation   The quotation must say something provocative; we want to know what it means. The essay to follow can then explain it and reveal its significance.

> "Romance with commitment. That's what today's woman wants."
>
> These were the words of Calvin Klein, introducing a floral-scented fragrance named Eternity five years ago. That's when *commitment* was in, a word that has gone from connoting entrance into a mental institution to its modern meaning of "permanent relationship" or perhaps a mutual understanding to date steadily at least through New Year's Eve. If you want a word to stand for a long-range commitment, *eternity* cannot be topped. (*Forever* must have been considered, but the diamond people have a lock on that word; *forever* is expensive.)[5]

The quotation must also be significant enough to build your essay upon. A bland quotation will not interest readers, and it may not be enough for you to build an essay upon.

Begin with a simple, definite statement   Sometimes it's best to renounce all art and begin with a simple statement that will provoke agreement or curiosity.

> On two visits this year I walked, rode, and interviewed people all over Portland, Oregon, trying to figure out how this courteous, well-kept city of 453,000, and especially its downtown, has become a paragon of healthy urban development at a time when most American cities find themselves mired in seemingly intractable problems.[6]

Ask a question   Occasionally a question makes a good beginning. The writer may answer it and then proceed to the rest of the article. Or the writer may leave it there to be puzzled over until later in the essay. The question does not have to be the first sentence in the article, but it does have to come quickly.

> An African Eve is a seductive idea—dark-skinned, strongly built, the primeval woman, mother of us all. But did she actually exist? Was there actually an evolutionary Garden of Eden in Africa where we all originated more than 150,000 years ago?[7]

Use contrast   Very often good essays begin with a statement of common belief or practice and quickly declare a contrary view. You set up a position or a situation that will be recognized by your readers, and you declare after a paragraph or two that you are going to take an opposite, or at least a different, view.

> The three best-known buildings of Thomas Jefferson's own design deserve their fame. Monticello, his home, shaped over the years, breathes with his mind like the shell of a living thing, protecting and revealing it. The University of Virginia brings buildings into intimate conversation with one another on a high, ideal plane. The Virginia state capitol, in Richmond, is a frontier temple, democratically elite.
>
> But other buildings important in Jefferson's life are far less visited, though each reveals something about him. All of the five considered here were closed to the public until recently, and even now when they are open they are not heavily trafficked. Each offers a special angle of entry into Jefferson's world, an opening into his mind. Two are ruins (Rosewell and Barboursville), with enough remaining to suggest their former elegance. Two are presidential houses (Montpelier and Poplar Forest), held by private owners until this decade. The one that has remained least changed is the first building Jefferson ever knew.[8]

BEGINNINGS TO AVOID

Here are some beginnings to avoid. Some don't introduce the essay; some are just boring.

The dictionary definition   Never begin an essay like this: "Webster's dictionary defines *crisis* as 'a decisive or crucial time, stage, or event.'" Ugh!

We see beginnings like that all the time. That's what's wrong with them. They are the mark of a writer who won't take the time to think of something better.

Yes, the dictionary is an authority, and writers need authority. A dictionary definition contains an outline that an inexperienced writer may follow. Writing teachers see the tired old dictionary beginning hundreds of time—and groan every time.

You can write a good essay about a definition only if different people use the same important word in different ways. If people did not use the word in different ways, the essay would be unnecessary. What does *socialism* mean? You can't satisfy demanding readers if you begin an essay on socialism by referring to a dictionary. Almost every important thinker who has used this word has used it in a special way. Socialism in Sweden is one thing; socialism in the former Soviet Union was something utterly different. A member of the British Labour party will use the word with an entirely different sense from that of an official of the American Medical

Association. Your definition of an important word, derived from your own study, could make the substance of an excellent essay, but it will not be the bare-bones outline of a dictionary. It will be long enough to consider the important variations among the definitions of another.

A vague declaration about history   The appeal to history is another old standby that makes teachers and other readers groan.

> Throughout history, the family has been an important part of human life. Families were known to the ancient Israelites and to the Greeks and the Romans. They remain important to us today, but they are changing. What are the important challenges facing the family today?

Another ugh! Many subjects require historical background; for example, an essay defining *socialism* or *liberalism* or *humanism* would have to take history into account. But don't start with history unless the historical background of your topic is essential to what you want to say about it.

The justification of the topic   Many inexperienced writers begin essays with a kind of apology. Their first statement defends their choice of topic: "Why should we discuss the minor characters in Shakespeare's *Macbeth?*" or "The difference between the theology of Luther's sermons and his formal theological treatises has often been considered by scholars of the Reformation." They follow these opening statements with a survey of previous scholarship, leaving themselves a tiny window through which they can scramble with their own contribution. This is the typical beginning of dissertations. The implied comment seems to be something like this: "I know you think that nobody as young and inexperienced as I am can possibly have anything to say on this subject, but if you will just be patient and give me a break and don't hit me, I'll prove that I have a modest contribution to make."

You don't have to have the permission of previous scholars to make your point. If you think the minor characters in *Macbeth* are worth saying something about, get to work and prove your point. If you find Luther's theological treatises different from his sermons, show your readers what you mean. Don't unroll a long and tedious list of previous scholarship. You may use other scholarship along the way. Indeed you should if you are to have any authority. Refute it, modify it, or use it to confirm your case. But don't begin with an uninteresting summary of what others have done as if you had no right to consider a subject without starting with a recapitulation of the past.

Real writers want to tell readers something. They don't apologize for daring to have an idea. Begin with something strong, something to catch your readers' eyes and make them continue.

The blueprint beginning   I've already given an account of the blueprint beginning above in discussing "Little Red Riding Hood." Avoid it. Imagine how startled you would be to find the following beginning of an article in *Sports Illustrated:*

> In this article I am going to tell you about the World Series. I shall tell you what teams played in it, provide some background about the seasons and their victories, and describe their coaches. I will also tell you about the star players—their tantrums over their contracts, their run-ins with drugs, their infidelities, and their adorable children—and I shall make some remarks about their parents. I shall include a summary of each of the games and will conclude with the results and, at long last, tell you who won.

You know—almost unconsciously—that this kind of beginning is deadly dull and that reading the story to follow will be like wading knee-deep in mud to get to the end. Don't use it.

The "man from mars"   Variations on this beginning include the archaeologist from a future civilization or the person awakened from the dead of an earlier epoch to look on our own time. "If Thomas Edison were to come back from the dead, he would be astounded to see how far the motion picture has progressed since his primitive invention that set film turning through cameras." If Thomas Edison were to return from the dead, he would be on so many talk shows and would have so much to say that his impressions of film would be unimportant. These are tired old beginnings. If they once had verve, it withered long ago. Don't use them. Thousands of uninspired writers have worn them out.

4. A good essay stays with its subject.

A good essay explores a major theme, perhaps from several angles and perhaps with subthemes. It shows the writer thinking, thinking, thinking. It may develop some thoughts only to reject them. Even so, it is finally about one subject. When you are checking over your last drafts, make sure everything contributes to the matter at hand. Don't wander into interesting but inconsequential details. If, for example, you are writing about how the kings in Shakespeare's history plays claim the right to rule, don't wander off into a general plot summary of the plays that will dilute your main topic. Don't, for example, digress to tell us how poetic Richard II is or how much Shakespeare was influenced by Thomas More when he wrote about women. These ideas, interesting as they are, have nothing to do with your topic.

Digression in a rough draft may help you clarify a topic, for when you put words on paper, you may be the sort of writer who wanders all over the place, sniffing out a topic. But by the time you write your final draft, you should have decided what you want to say and be able to take your reader directly to it. Look at each sentence, each paragraph, to be sure it suits your purpose. If it doesn't, cut it out—no matter how much you may like it.

5. A good essay rests on solid evidence.

Not long ago I read an essay that compared the 1960s with the 1980s. It made some points that seemed more or less correct. The 1960s were much more sexually free than the 1980s when AIDS became a frightening possibility to those who had many sexual partners. The 1960s featured a great deal of protest on campus; the 1980s were calmer. So it went.

But not once in this essay did the writer quote a text from the 1960s or the 1980s. Not once did he compare films from the two decades. Nor had he tried to look at the art of both those periods. He cited no statistics of any kind. He wrote as if he had only to make a generalization and we would accept it because it was a truth everybody agreed on.

In fact, most generalizations we make about reality are flawed. When we look closely at the evidence, we find that all of it does not conform to received opinion. One of the most important parts of your education will be learn to question generalizations—to decide where they come from, why people make them, and who profits by them. If you keep your mind fixed on the specific, on evidence, you will have the authority to question those generalizations because you have some evidence to support your opinion.

Here is a generalization I have often heard: "Latin should be required of all students who want to write because people who know Latin write English better than people who do not." But how do we know that people who know Latin write English better than people who do not? Has somebody tested the writing ability of those who know Latin and those who do not? Are journals published by classics scholars better-written than journals published by English scholars? If we had such a test, and if somebody made a study of the scholarly writing in classics journals and in English journals, we might have some evidence. But without evidence, we have only sound and fury.

One of the best habits you can develop as a writer is to provide a specific example to support every generalization or opinion you put in an essay. My best students pour factual information into their writing. Reading their papers is a continual encounter with the real world—the world of people and places, objects and events.

But all of us who teach run into papers—sometimes on big topics like abortion, drugs, capital punishment, homosexuality, religion, or whatever—written by people who seem to think no one else has ever written on these topics. Most university libraries now have their catalogs on-line and available on computer monitors throughout the library buildings. In many libraries you can type a subject like "abortion" into the computer and find articles written about it for the past three or four years in both academic and popular journals. In this computer age, the first obligation of a writer considering a topic is to look into the library's computerized catalog to see what sources are available. (In checking my own library's on-line service, I discovered 2476 articles on the subject "abortion" published in the past four years.) When you write, remember that others have thought about the same subject, that their thoughts are out there in libraries, and that you can find them with just a little effort.

What is evidence? I discuss the matter at greater length in Chapter Four, "Making Arguments." But here are some rapid answers to the question.

Experience

Your experience counts as evidence if it relates to the topic at hand. If you write about violence in the public schools of America and you happen to have attended a school where kids brought knives and pistols to class, your experience is evidence. So is the experience of others that you may read about in newspapers or magazines. The epidemic of violence in the schools has been written about frequently in recent times.

Experience does not happen just with the body; it happens with the mind. Every book and article you have read is part of your experience. Some other course you have taken may provide evidence for any course where you have to write an essay. When I am teaching Shakespeare's history plays and a student brings in something he or she has read in a history course or a psychology course or a course in philosophy or economics or religion, I leap and dance for joy.

One reason for trying to find a topic to write about as soon as you get an assignment is that you will start viewing everything in your reading and in your personal experience as possible evidence for your essay. I happen to be writing a book about Martin Luther as I am writing this book. I can't go into an art museum now without thinking about the differences in religious art before Luther's time (in the sixteenth century) and afterward. I can't read *Hamlet* without thinking about Luther's views on predestination and without recalling that Hamlet presumably attended Luther's University of Wittenberg—and naturally I have to consider the inconvenient facts that given the supposed dating of the action of the play, Hamlet was at Wittenberg before Luther was born and centuries before the university was founded.

Samuel Johnson told James Boswell in the eighteenth century, "Depend on it, sir, when a man knows he is to be hanged in a fortnight, it concentrates his mind wonderfully." Most writers will not be hanged in two weeks, but the name "deadline" maintains its somewhat macabre connotation. Knowing that a deadline lies ahead should make us focus our thoughts from every source on the writing we will hand over to readers.

Statistics

Medical statistics show that cigarette smokers are much more likely to die of lung cancer and heart disease than are nonsmokers. Baseball statistics show that left-handed batters are more successful against right-handed pitchers than against left-handed pitchers. American students score much lower on average than their Asian counterparts when they take generalized tests in mathematics but much higher when they are tested for self-esteem.

Statistical data must be interpreted fairly and intelligently; someone has said that statistics don't lie but that liars use statistics. Even so, statistics represent evidence, and they can strengthen your essay. My student who compared the 1960s and the 1980s could have strengthened his paper immeasurably by comparing some statistics from the two periods.

Quotations

If you interpret a literary or historical or scientific text, you must quote from it, providing the exact words that will help us to hear a voice or catch a tone.

Vladimir Nabokov, teacher and author of many novels, including *Lolita,* used to tell his students to begin their study of a novel or story by noting *exactly what the writer said.* This close reading, this intense preoccupation with exactitude, should guide the careful writer in the search for evidence. Study the text, and see exactly what it says. Quote from it to prove your point.

But be careful. Nothing is quite as tedious as the long essay that is hardly more than a quotation. Long block quotations can be especially annoying. They break the rhythm of style in the essay where they are set. The writer who uses them may assume that they can stand by themselves without interpretation, but readers may find them obscure. Sometimes, of course, we must all use block quotations. An example is this book. Since it is a descriptive account of American writing, I could not make my points without giving block quotations of writing that has something to teach us.

But in other kinds of writing, block quotations should be used sparingly. And always provide an interpretation to fit them securely into the topic of your essay. Don't use them just to fill up space.

It is far better to quote a sentence or even a phrase that will give the precise flavor of a writer's work that you are trying to convey. Too often a block quotation contains much more than the essay writer wants to convey, and the reader gets lost. If you quote a sentence or a phrase, readers can get the point and follow you.

A caution: Never accept a quotation as the final authority for an argument merely because the speaker is a well-known figure. Suppose a noted male chauvinist declares, "Males are doomed to extinction unless they band together, go off to the woods, beat drums, and utter primal screams to recover the virility that feminist rhetoric has taken away from them." Nonsense is nonsense, and a quotation from a book of nonsense is no proof that men should buy drums and head for the woods. Quotations from well-known people should be put to the test of common sense and bolstered by evidence before being accepted as proof of anything.

Quote for one of the following reasons:

1. Your source has said something in a striking and memorable way that fits your argument. "Nothing but honey is sweeter than money," Ben Franklin wrote in *Poor Richard's Almanack*.

2. The quotation confirms a point you have argued or will argue in your essay.

> Political renegade Pat Buchanan raised his umbrella against the gray, damp sky last week as he surveyed the line of guests filing into the White House for the Ronald Reagan Presidential Medal of Freedom ceremony. "The last roll call," he said.
>
> He was right. There were 250 members of the power establishment of 12 years and earlier, and they flocked and laughed together, even as workers nearby hammered together the inaugural stands for the installation of Bill Clinton. An era ended with more than a tinge of sadness for its creators, yet cheer lingered from the exhilaration of such a journey.[9]

3. You wish to tell what the quotation means.

> "Is social work now a profession?" a didactic 1930 essay anxiously queried in the *Survey,* Paul Kellogg's journal of social service reform. "Yes," replied author Hazel Newton, a social worker who had become general manager of the Cooperative Workrooms in Boston. And, she added, through the medium of her fictionalized "Miss Case-Worker" named "Jane," professionalism meant they were "going scientific." Social workers like Jane were learning to beware of "putting too much of one's own prejudices, sentiments, loves and hates, into one's job." Against an old-fashioned, voluntary Lady Bountiful, Newton celebrated the "scientific" Miss Case-Worker, an "objective" social investigator. Because objectivity and rationality were conventionally associated with male professional culture, however, the scientific model created its own tensions for female social workers.[10]

In the above article, the writer considers the significance of the quotations at the time they were made.

Authorities

A renowned medical researcher is an authority on blood cholesterol. If he says cholesterol is not as dangerous to the heart as most medical scientists think, you can use his comment as evidence. But it not conclusive evidence. The opinion of an authority is only another opinion, respected because we assume that the authority has done something worthy of respect. Authorities can be wrong; they often are. It is best to mention an authority only after you have given other evidence that supports the position you and the authority take.

And remember that an authority in one field is not necessarily an authority in another. Not long ago I looked through a book by a prominent lawyer who argued against Charles Darwin's hypothesis of biological evolution. The lawyer was doubtless intelligent and a fine lawyer, but I was not at all convinced that he had any scientific competence to denounce Darwin. Every working biologist I know of accepts Darwin's fundamental tenet of evolution by natural selection. When a working scientist denounces Darwin, I will take the matter seriously.

6. A good essay considers evidence that may seem to contradict the writer's argument.

If you write on a controversial subject, you must consider contrary evidence and interpretations different from your own. Careless or dishonest writers ignore contrary evidence. They imagine they will weaken their case if they mention the arguments on the other side of the issue. The reader who discovers such a deceit quickly loses respect for the writer.

Every year thousands of writers in college courses argue important issues without considering contrary evidence and often without acknowledging that any contrary evidence exists. Important controversial issues seldom have all the good guys on one side and all the bad guys on the other. Papers that assume such a moral division convince only the naïve; they do not change the minds of those in the thoughtful audience who are looking for guidance, the very audience you should be trying to persuade. If you write as if every opponent is a knave or a fool, fair-minded readers will dismiss you and your work.

One of the greatest writing problems my students face is within themselves. They want to believe that knowledge is a seamless garment, that all its parts fit so closely together that there is no room for disagreement among honest people. They want to pretend that they know everything. But knowledge is seldom so tidy, and it is never complete. Knowledge comes in pieces with rough edges and holes, and some pieces are always missing. Honest writers admit the difficulties.

Even concession can be a powerful argument. Concede the truth of contrary evidence when you believe it is true. You may argue that it does not damage your case. Or you may argue that it has been misinterpreted by your foes.

Never be too proud or too frightened to make a concession. To concede a point gives the appearance of fair-mindedness and confidence—an appearance valuable in persuasive essays. Strategic concession has been recognized since the orators of ancient Greece as a major strength in both speaking and writing. A writer might include in an essay the following concession:

> Yes, I concede that the bottle bill will be a pain to all of us. We can't toss the bottles out anymore. We will have to pay more for Cokes and beer. We will have to haul bottles back to stores to collect our deposit. The bottle bill will cost all of us more time and money than we like if it is enacted into law.

Such a concession clears the way for the writer to come back with a stronger argument for the essay's position.

> But the bottle bill may save some money, too—money now spent in cleaning up the litter tossed along our streets and highways, money spent in repairing the damage done to tires and sometimes to bare feet by broken glass. The experience of other states with bottle laws is that litter is dramatically reduced when people have some financial incentive to return bottles to the store rather than toss them away when they are empty. Once people experience the cleaner environment, they may well decide that it is worth the little extra time and money the bottle bill costs them.

Those who argue vehemently and blindly for a cause sound like fanatics. Only fanatics listen to fanatics. Your aim should be to attract another kind of reader.

7. A good essay is written with its audience in mind.

Remember your audience, the readers you want to like your work. We have already posed some important questions about audience. What do your readers know? What do you share with them? What will interest them? How can you win their respect?

Share your writing with friends. Ask them to tell you what it said to them, what they think you are trying to say. Don't ask them, "What do you think about this?" Most of them will say, "I like it." Friends are like that; they sometimes lie to make you feel good. When you ask them to tell you what they think you have said, you put a different obligation on them, and you may learn much more about your prose. If they can't tell you what you've said, you need to revise some more.

Most professional writers share their work with somebody. An acquaintance of mine says he writes for about five women he knows—all of them critical but tolerant. I write for my editor, who has worked with me for more than twenty years. She is a woman of taste and intelligence, not afraid to ask questions, not afraid to tell me she doesn't know what I'm trying to say or that she doesn't know why I'm saying this or that. I believe that if I can interest her, others will be interested, too.

Writing for an audience does not mean a hypocritical effort to please at any price. You have your own opinions, your knowledge, your ambitions for your writing. Express them to please and persuade people you know. You can take pride in making someone you admire say, "I like this; you have convinced me."

My editor is a good human being who loves to read. She will not let me insult people or make sweeping generalizations. She will not let me be silly or vague or bad-tempered. Writers writing about things they care about may make all these errors in early drafts. My editor marks them with a strong blue pencil; I know what she is likely to mark, and I keep her in mind as I write, trying to avoid the flaws that irritate her. I do not always succeed. But she is my audience, the kind of person I want to read my work, and my sense of her as a person makes my writing better than it would be without her.

Respect your audience. Make your audience respect you. Wayne C. Booth, a noted authority on writing, has said that every piece of writing has an "implied author," someone your readers find standing behind the words on the page. Your implied author may not be the person you want to be. Some inexperienced writers think they are being bold and superior when they adopt a slangy style of writing only to discover that their readers find them arrogant and shallow. To reach the widest audience, your own implied author should be sincere, humane, convincing, tolerant, interested, fair-minded, and honest, showing confidence in the intelligence and fair-mindedness of the readers. A little humor always helps.

Don't be cute or silly, but be lively. Write naturally. Use simple words rather than complicated ones—unless your thoughts can be expressed only with complicated words. Don't qualify statements too much; don't sound wishy-washy. Write as if you like your readers and trust them to have good sense. Don't show off; don't condescend. Be honest and forthright, simple and direct.

8. A good essay makes internal connections.

A good essay will march step by step to its destination. Each step will be clearly marked; it will depend on what has gone before, and it will lead gracefully to what comes afterward. Good transitions are essential to good writing; your readers need to be able to follow the development of your subject, and transitions help them see the relation of the parts to the whole. As I said earlier in this book, good transitions are like the yellow arrows painted on the road to show a bicycling group where it needs to turn to stay on route to the goal.

The verbal signs of such transitions are words such as *because, furthermore, therefore, thus, but, and,* and *nevertheless.* You seldom write these words to make the transitions, but you may imply them in various ways. In a good piece of writing, a reader senses the connections and uses them to move easily from one part of the essay to the next.

Here again, a good essay resembles a good story. In telling a story, we construct a chain of cause and effect. We say, "This happened; and because of it, the next thing happened; and because of that next thing, another thing happened." Or else we say simply that one thing happened after another. Were we to leave out a step, the rest of the story would be confusing or incomprehensible or simply dull. Leave the wolf out of "Little Red Riding Hood," for example, and you're left with a little girl who goes through the woods, delivers some cakes to her grandmother, and comes home again. It's as dull as watching a pig sleep. Good fiction involves a connected series of tension-building episodes beginning with the first and going forward to resolution at the end.

A good essay proceeds in much the same way. The essayist may say something like this: "*A* is true. Because *A* is true, *B* is also true. Because *A* and *B* are true, *C* is also true." Sometimes the connections are more tentative. "*A* is true. If *A* is true, *B* may also be true. If *A* and *B* are true, *C* may also be true." Whether the connections are certain or tentative, they exist, and they hold the parts of the good essay together. One thought leads clearly to the next. Readers are not left wondering how the writer got here from there or why the writer is telling them this. Good writers read and reread their work carefully. When you read an essay you have written, look at every paragraph. Be sure that each paragraph flows smoothly out of the paragraph that comes before it. You do not have to have transitional words such as *therefore* or *furthermore*. But you should be able to see where they are implied so that one part of your essay clearly leads to the next.

9. A good essay is well-integrated; it does not drift without clear purpose from item to item.

It is not a plot summary. This point is related to the requirement that an essay have a single guiding purpose and that it be clear throughout. Find ways to subordinate your evidence to categories that allow you to unite your data under a major theme. Make a distinction between major points and minor ones.

Frequently, my students give me what I call the "museum-tour essay." They are the guides; I am the visitor. "Here is an impressionist painting by Renoir," they say. "And here is one by Manet. And look! Here is one by Monet. And look there—a painting by Pissaro."

The "museum tour" may a plot summary of a literary text. The summary may be loosely united by a broad and general idea. The idea may be so obvious that no one needs to write about it.

> *Macbeth* shows the dangers of ambition. Macbeth is ambitious until the witches tell him he will be king and that from his friend Banquo a long line of kings will come. Macbeth then resolves to kill Duncan, the lawful king, and he does, driven by his wife who is also ambitious. But he cannot stop with Duncan; he must also try to kill Banquo and Banquo's son

because having fulfilled one part of the prophecy, he is eager to keep the other part from coming true. His ambition drives him to try to destroy all his enemies, and so he has the family of Macduff also killed.

All of this is true, but anyone can read the play and see that it is true. To make an essay on *Macbeth* interesting, you must find some organizing principle that will help you integrate these various facts. You should not merely lead your readers from the beginning of the play to the end, pointing out interesting facts along the way. Remember that a good story—like a good essay—works toward a climax where everything we have been told comes together in some sort of resolution. It is not merely a collection of interesting facts; the facts are organized by the climax, the resolution, by the goal that makes you tell the story.

If you write about *Macbeth,* you may write about *conscience,* the human sense of right and wrong. And here you find something interesting: Macbeth starts with a tender conscience but becomes harder and harder as the play goes along. At first, Lady Macbeth seems the stronger of the two, but her bad conscience overwhelms her, and she is finally driven to madness and death by her guilty dreams. Here is a question worth a paper: What do these opposite reactions mean?

The question provides the possibility of real analysis. The word *analysis* means that something is broken down into its parts and put together in a different form. If we analyze water in a laboratory, we discover that it is composed of two parts hydrogen, one part oxygen, and, in its natural state, various other materials, such as microbes, earth, and various "impurities." When we analyze a text, we break it down into various ideas that will help us understand what makes it work; and once the work is broken down, we use it in a different form. So here is a tip to help you judge your own work to see if you are giving just a plot summary, or "museum tour." Beware if you find yourself following this pattern: The essay begins with the beginning of your story or document; the middle of the essay is about the middle of your document; the end of the essay is about the end of your document. It is not impossible to write a good essay following that pattern, but it is rare. I suggest that you try always to make the form of your essay different from the form of the document you are writing about.

10. A good essay is mechanically and grammatically correct and looks neat on the page.

Telling a writer to use correct grammar, punctuation, and spelling is like telling a pianist to hit the right notes. You can make lots of errors when you are writing drafts; we all do. But you must care enough about your work to proofread it before you turn it over to the audience for whom it is intended.

The mechanical conventions of writing have developed historically, sometimes without much logic. English spelling seems especially illogical, and whether you spell well or not has nothing to do with your basic intelligence. Some people are bad spellers, and all that means is that they are bad spellers.

Even so, the mechanical conventions are essential symbols of communication, and you must observe them. Otherwise readers will struggle with your prose. If you do not observe the conventions, most readers will suppose you are careless, illiterate, or even stupid. They may also suppose you don't care enough about them to want to give them your best effort.

Learn to use a keyboard and a computer. If you do not know how to type, learn. Learn to compose at the keyboard. Mark up your early drafts. But when your work goes out to your readers, it should be neat, clean, and correct. If you do not respect your own work, others will not respect it either.

Ask your friends to correct your work. I've been responsible for some strong friendships among my first-year students when they were paired off and had to proofread each other's work. Use the dictionary and the spelling checker on your computer's word-processing program. I keep by my keyboard the *Instant Spelling Dictionary* published by Career Publishing of Mundelein, Illinois. It contains 25,000 words without definitions. I can flip through it quickly to discover if I have spelled *dilettante* correctly. I also have a dictionary within reach at every desk and table where I work at home or in my office. Think of your readers. Misspelled words, bad punctuation, the odd use of quotation marks—all make reading hard. Observing the conventions is a form of courtesy.

11. A good essay concludes swiftly and gracefully.

Conclusions are difficult, and many writers have trouble with them. You can conclude in many ways, but almost always your final paragraphs should reflect some of the thoughts presented in your first paragraphs. An essay is like a snake biting its tail; at the end it always comes back to its beginning. Here is the first paragraph of an essay by Lewis Thomas called "To Err Is Human." Note that it does what a good beginning should do—it creates tension about the topic the writer is going to pursue.

> Everyone must have had at least one personal experience with a computer error by this time. Bank balances are suddenly reported to have jumped from $379 into the millions, appeals for charitable contributions are mailed over and over to people with crazy-sounding names at your address, department stores send the wrong bills, utility companies write that they're turning everything off, that sort of thing.[11]

Now, here is the end of Thomas's essay. Notice that the last paragraph picks up some of the thoughts from the first. We can read these two paragraphs and have a pretty good idea what the essay is about and about its general message.

> We should have this in mind as we become dependent on more complex computers for the arrangement of our affairs. Give the computers their heads, I say; let them go their way. If we can learn to do this, turning our heads to one side and wincing while the work proceeds, the possibilities for the future of mankind, and computerkind, are limitless. Your average good computer can make calculations in an instant which would take a lifetime of slide rules for any of us. Think of what we could gain from the near infinity of precise, machine-made miscomputation which is now so easily within our grasp. We could begin the solving of some of our hardest problems. How, for instance, should we go about organizing ourselves for social living on a planetary scale now that we have become, as a plain fact of life, a single community? We can assume, as a working hypothesis, that all the right ways of doing this are unworkable. What we need, then, for moving ahead, is a set of wrong alternatives much longer and more interesting than the short list of mistaken courses that any of us can think up right now. We need, in fact, an infinite list, and when it is printed out we need the computer to turn on itself and select, at random, the next way to go. If it is a big enough mistake, we could find ourselves on a new level, stunned, out in the clear, ready to move again.[12]

From this beginning and ending, we can tell that Thomas finds something positive in computer error. Mistakes with computers are common, and he finds that they open a way to progress. How? We have to read the rest of the essay—the part between the beginning and the end—to find out. Even so, we find the gist of his argument in the first and last paragraphs.

Like Thomas, you may end by drawing some conclusions suggested by the argument you have presented in the rest of your essay. The whole essay adds up to the conclusion you present at the end. The last paragraph is like the sum of a column of figures you might add. It is the total of all the points you have made so far.

Quotations make good conclusions, just as they make good beginnings. When a quotation stands at the start of an essay, it demands to be explained by what comes after it. When a quotation stands at the end of an essay, it reflects the conclusion the essay has made, sometimes summing it up.

It is not good to introduce important new ideas or information in a conclusion. Your readers will feel cheated when you do not develop these new thoughts. And you should always avoid the blueprint ending, just as you should avoid the blueprint beginning.

> I have shown that little girls who carry baskets of cakes into woods where lurk big, bad wolves are likely to come to a bad end.

Concluding Remarks on the Essay

We take for granted our amazing ability to recognize different forms of literature when we read them. We know a poem when we see one; we know we are reading fictional prose or a play when we read these texts. We may not know whether the fictional prose is a short story or a novel if we read one page at random from the whole. But we know we are reading fiction unless the author has made a deliberate attempt to deceive us into supposing that he or she is writing about truth. (George Orwell never shot an elephant, although he wrote a celebrated account of this supposed deed; and he never helped hang a condemned prisoner in Burma, although he also claimed to have done so.) Fiction usually tells us by its form that it is fiction.

We also know quickly when we are reading nonfiction, even if we pick up a piece and start in the middle without having any idea as to the title or the author. We may not know whether it is an essay or a book, but we know that the author intends to make us think we are reading something "real" or "true."

The essay belongs to the general family of nonfiction. But it relies on fictional techniques in that like a good story it begins with something out of order and attempts to explain or fix the problem. Readers begin essays with certain expectations. If they do not find these expectations fulfilled, they stop reading. I have tried to summarize these expectations in this chapter. Check your own essay against my list and see if they conform to it. If not, think your essay through again to be sure your deviation is worth the risk you run when you deny readers the fulfillment of their expectations.

The essay will be useful to you throughout life as you write memos, business letters, reports, and articles. Develop the habit of studying essays you find enjoyable. Check the advice in this chapter by studying any essay you like to see how it is put together. As you become more aware of the habits of good writers, you will develop these habits yourself. Your prose will reflect what you read. Be a good reader, and you will not need this or any textbook to help you write well.

Four

Making Arguments

*A*ll essays make arguments. A good term paper, an M.A. thesis, a dissertation, or a book does not merely report facts. The writer argues that the facts should be understood in a certain way. Good writers interpret the facts, and all interpretations are arguments. Some have said that all writing argues that we should do something or believe something.

Such a general definition of argument does not necessarily imply opposition. If you interpret a new author's work, one about whom little or nothing has been written, you do not have to take into account other interpretations, for none may exist. But usually when we write an argument, we write to disagree. The argument may have two goals—to prove an opponent wrong and to prove our own view right.

Some people dislike the word *argument* because it sounds pugnacious. But it is a civilized term; we make arguments instead of war. We persuade people rather than beat them into submission. Democracy depends on argument. Candidates argue that they are more qualified than their opponents; elected representatives argue that their policies are better than the alternatives. Lawyers and judges argue about what the laws mean. Citizens argue with each other about what's right or wrong with society. In tyrannies, people don't argue—at least not in public. Democracy is unending disputation.

Argument depends on some form of logic, based on evidence, to determine what is plausible given the premises or assumptions on which the argument is based. Persuasion is a larger category, involving all the means of getting people to take your side. A logical construction of existing evidence indicates that cigarette smoking is dangerous to one's health. Nevertheless, tobacco companies try to persuade young people to smoke by offering ads showing manly-looking cowboys or cartoon camels in sporty clothes puffing away at cigarettes apparently with no harmful effects.

Television, movies, advertising in the print media, roadside signs, and most other "texts" in our society offer subliminal means of persuasion that vary from age to age—vivid or quiet ways of presentation that we take for granted merely because they are repeated again and again. The first television generation was presented with the sappy family sitcom "Ozzie and Harriet," on the subliminal premise that television should set a good example. In "Ozzie and Harriet," the family was middle-class, looked on the father as the head of the household who worked while the mother stayed at home and enjoyed housework, owned its home, never had financial problems or real conflicts between parents and children, and never dreamed of divorce. It had little to do with the reality of the American family even at the time, but it seemed bent on persuading families to be more like the television family.

Many arguments are explicit. A lawyer making a case for a client accused of robbery argues either that the client is innocent or that mitigating circumstances require judge and jury to consider this no ordinary robbery.

If you think taxes should be raised to erase the deficit in America, you must make an argument for your position. If you want to persuade your friends that a movie they have enjoyed is lousy, you have to do more than say, "I thought the movie was *terrible.*" If you believe that gays and lesbians should serve in the armed forces, you must be prepared to argue against great numbers of people who passionately oppose your views.

You cannot argue well about issues that no one disputes. Few activities bore a college teacher more than reading papers that argue positions so safe that no one disagrees with them, positions such as "Economics is important to society," "Shakespeare wrote some interesting plays," "Dickens often treated poverty in his novels," or "Abortion is a much debated issue." Few things please readers (including teachers) more than papers that make original and unexpected arguments, such as "Some people may be allergic to exercise," or "King Lear got what he deserved."

But please, don't make arguments just to be cute. An argument without evidence is a bucket without a bottom. I once had a student argue that if the Roman Empire had had electricity, it would never have fallen. The argument was pointless. College teachers are paid to read anything students write. Teachers are usually kind and generous people. (At least they start out that way.) Sometimes they become so tired from grading dozens and dozens of papers that they let themselves be bullied into giving a paper a good grade even if it is absurd or trivial. The reality of writing is that once out of college, we find few readers as patient as our teachers. We gain a worthwhile audience only if we are interesting, challenging, disciplined, and coherent. We waste the time we put into writing and lose the reward for our work if we mistake being cute for being challenging.

Making a Good Argument Paper

Here are steps in writing a good argument. Read them carefully, and check your own arguments against them.

1. Begin on ground the writer and readers share.

This step might be called, "Begin with premises you share with your audience." Premises are the starting points of arguments, and you cannot argue without them. They are the assumptions that stand behind many statements in ordinary language, and we must identify them before we can even have an argument.

Suppose I walk into your room to go with you to lunch and say this: "It's raining hard; be sure to bring your umbrella." The premise of that statement is something like this: Rain is unpleasant. Since umbrellas protect us from rain, you can avoid this particular unpleasantness by carrying one. But if you happen to like rain, the premise for you, at least, is faulty.

The best arguments begin with premises the writer assumes are shared with a great many readers who must then be persuaded that those premises lead plausibly to the conclusions the writer wants to draw from them. In every worthwhile argument, some people have already made up their minds for or against the proposition being debated. The writer aims at the great undecided middle group and hopes to lead the people in it to the writer's side.

Never begin an argument by assuming either that everyone agrees with you or that everyone disagrees with you. Don't condescend, and don't scream in outrage. Don't treat your opponents like fools or criminals. The best arguments assume that writer and reader share some values, some information, some purposes—some premises.

I have already mentioned Dr. Martin Luther King's "Letter from a Birmingham Jail," written on April 16, 1963, when Dr. King had been arrested for leading nonviolent demonstrations against racial segregation in Alabama. A group of white ministers of religion had taken out an ad in a newspaper objecting to his tactics. They wanted to postpone racial integration of schools and other public places in the South, and in particular they opposed Dr. King's decision to make Birmingham a focus of the civil rights struggle.

Dr. King might have begun his response to those ministers with a withering denunciation of their hypocrisy. Could they believe in the loving God of Jews and Christians and support not only racial segregation but the violence and mockery that enforced it in the South? Dr. King could have made a head-on attack. He might have insulted these ministers with a sarcasm that raised blisters on their humiliated faces.

Instead, he chose to begin gently by calling attention to the religious heritage he shared with these ministers. They all accepted the God of Judaism and Christianity. From this common premise, he argued that they should also share his goal—equal justice for all God's people. His arguments and his gentle tone made this appeal a classic.

Now and then you can make a frontal assault on your opponents, displaying anger, contempt, and righteous indignation. But you can do so only if you are sure that the readers you want to reach are already emotionally aroused about the issue and if you are sure that your evidence overwhelmingly supports your side. You may then use a smashing attack to rally your side. Winston Churchill's contemptuous assaults on Adolf Hitler united the English people against Germany during the gloomiest days of World War II. He balanced his invective with eloquent depictions of the peaceful and just world that would come with victory over Germany and Germany's allies.

Few arguments can count on this emotional support from those who read them. When you try to persuade the undecided, look for common ground with your readers. Experience has shown that most readers hate shrill, discourteous, and angry arguments. Even when readers agree with you, most will feel uncomfortable with a diatribe. Remember that people want to believe that something in you, the writer, is akin to them, and not many of us want to believe that we are mean and ugly, ungenerous and spiteful. We like to think that we are reasonable, civil, and generous.

The tone of your beginning is as important as the premises you assume you share with your audience. Many speakers establish a common ground with their audience by beginning with a joke. Laughter unites audience and speaker and disposes the audience to listen to the rest of the speech. Writers seldom begin with jokes. But as we have seen, they may begin with stories, quotations, statements of fact, or interpretations of fact that will attract readers' attention and reveal common premises. The beginning says to a group of readers, "We share something; we are alike; go with me and give me a chance to prove that I'm right."

When you begin well, you dispose your audience to consider your position and your argument is half won. If at any time in your writing you break the bond between yourself and your readers by making unfair and offensive remarks, you will lose them unless your evidence and your arguments are so compelling that they must keep going.

I have spent so much time on this issue because, in my experience, incivility is the single greatest flaw in the arguments of inexperienced writers. You may discover an occasion when you want to argue by insult. But don't start out that way. I have discovered that people use insults when they are unsure of their own position and feel threatened by the truth. Confident people argue graciously.

2. Get to the point of your argument fast.

The rule that governs any essay also applies here. Define your point and get to it quickly. Make sure you know why you are writing and what you want to prove. Don't argue merely to make a fuss.

Always define your premises and major terms. Be clear on what you assume you share with your audience. A sharp definition helps put you and your readers on common ground. Arguments often go astray because various readers define words differently. When you define your terms, you help yourself and your readers stay on track.

Some definitions are simple. A dictionary definition classifies a word and sets it off from other members of the same class. The ninth edition of Merriam-Webster's *New Collegiate Dictionary* defines *lemon* as "an acid fruit that is botanically a many-seeded pale yellow oblong berry and is produced by a stout thorny tree." *Lemon* is shown to belong to a class of similar things called *fruits*. It differs from other members of that class by its acidity; its pale yellow coloration; its being produced by a stout, thorny bush; and its being botanically a berry.

But dictionary definitions in an argument are boring, shallow, and misleading. Words have histories, and essayists must consider the details of those histories much more fully than writers of dictionaries can cram into the small space alloted to a dictionary definition. Fair-minded writers know that words like *liberalism* or *reason* or *socialism* or *communism* or *fascism* or *romanticism* have historical connotations. To say that Johnson is *romantic* may mean to his girl friend that he loves to tell her that his love for her will be more enduring than the mountains. But Johnson's writing teacher may declare that Johnson is being *romantic* if he thinks he can write an essay on Hamlet without reading the play. In both examples, use of the word *romantic* implies something unreal, but the differences in the unreality are considerable.

Be cautious in using terms that cannot be precisely defined, even if the terms are common ones. Someone writes, "Machiavelli's little book *The Prince* was a typical product of the Italian Renaissance." But what does *typical* mean here? And what was the Italian Renaissance? So many people have given so many different definitions of "Renaissance" that it is impossibly vague to say that any book was "typical" of the period. Spell out the definition you mean, and say something like this: "Machiavelli's little book *The Prince* was typical of the theory and practice of secular rule during the Renaissance, when princes thought more about how to get and hold onto power than they thought about being good men." My point is that a brief, precise definition sets your argument better than a vague word.

Yes, we see and hear words used in broad, sweeping ways all the time.

The talk-show plague that seems to have infected American radio features fast-mouthed "personalities" who love enemies and who fling vague, hateful labels against them. We love to label things, believing, in an almost primitive way, that giving something a label somehow makes it manageable. Ancient religions held that when you named something, you controlled it. People like Rush Limbaugh speak and write as if they believe that superstition today.

A label may be misleading or simply dishonest, and when a label is likely to be misunderstood, the writer should be all the more careful to define it precisely. Often the best definition includes ambiguities and other difficulties, and writers have to take these slippery matters into account in the same way that Professor Gilbert Allardyce introduces his article "What Fascism Is Not: Thoughts on the Deflation of a Concept" with some of his ruminations about a definition. He explains why his article undertakes a much more precise definition of a much used word.

> "Perhaps the word fascism should be banned, at least temporarily, from our political vocabulary," S. J. Woolf wrote in 1968. Historians who have confronted the problem of defining this mulish concept may sympathize with this modest proposal. Unfortunately the word "fascism" is here to stay; only its meaning seems to be banned. Nevertheless, the German philosopher-historian Ernst Nolte is probably correct in stressing that historians do not have the responsibility to invent new terms simply because the existing ones are inadequate. But they do have the responsibility to confess how truly inadequate the term fascism has become; put simply, we have agreed to use the term without agreeing on how to define it. This article is concerned with the reason for this unfortunate state of affairs.[1]

Take care to define your use of broad and general terms as you are going to use them in an argument. General words originate to describe qualities shared by a class of things or people—works of art, essays, novels, political views, rulers of states, or whatever. Soon the general word assumes a life of its own, a phantom existence that provokes writers—and speakers—to suppose that they have said something important if they apply it to anything they choose.

Many of us recall the 1960s, when angry students hurled the term *fascist* at anyone they hated, whether a university dean, a scholar, a police officer, or a parent. Everybody was a *fascist* who believed in the exercise of authority, even when the authority was legitimate. Others, calling themselves *conservatives,* used the word *radical* to describe anyone who opposed American involvement in the Vietnam War, and some found themselves berated as "radical" merely because they exercised their First Amendment rights to oppose a government policy. In the 1950s, the words *red, communist, pinko, fellow traveler,* and *socialist* were used with devastating effect against people devoted to various humanitarian causes. In recent political campaigns and on many radio talk shows, words such as *liberal, feminist,* and *multiculturalist* are used almost as if they were obscenities. People fling them around like stones, having no idea how complex they are, how different, even contradictory, are the various people who may claim to espouse positions represented by these words.

Fiercely hateful people may stir up emotional storms by such imprecise language and thereby threaten democracy, which depends on the ability of its citizens to think carefully about issues and make reasonable decisions about them. We do care passionately about some issues; but our passion makes the need for precise definition all the greater. When words take on lives of their own, moral writers should put them under the microscope. Do enough individuals within a group share enough qualities to permit any general word to describe them? Before you start using vague terms like *socialism, democracy, romantic, liberal, conservative, humanistic,* and others, ask yourself what you mean by them, and write your definition into the argument.

Be fair. Take into account those who disagree with you, especially if their views are honest and well thought out. You do not have to discard your position merely because others honestly disagree with it. But you help yourself and your readers if you describe the disagreement and give your views precisely and forthrightly. If you define your words unfairly or in sharp opposition to their common usage, you lose your audience quickly. "Any American who opposes prayer in the public schools is opposed to religion." Come now! It's not that simple, and fair-minded readers know it.

Define your premises. I want to say again and again that all arguments begin with premises shared by writer and readers. "We all agree that *A* is true," we say or imply. "Because we agree that *A* is true, I will show that we should also believe that *B* is true." Before we can accept such a chain of reasoning, we must know what *A* is so we can decide if, indeed, we all agree that it is true. You must get to the premises before you can argue.

The late Allan Bloom, a once obscure professor at the University of Chicago, became famous all over America because, in his best-selling book *The Closing of the American Mind,* he condemned this generation of college students for being ignorant of the "great books," which he identified as works by Plato, Aristotle, Kant, Marx, and many others. Bloom mentioned only a handful of American writers with any praise, and most of these are male and safely dead. His critics rejected his premise that one is ignorant if unfamiliar with the works of Plato and the great books and yet knows nothing of modern writers, including living black American woman authors such as Toni Morrison, Maria Angelou, Alice Walker, and a host of others. Bloom's critics argue that education cannot be defined by a single reading list, and they claim that he has misconstrued the cultural situation he addresses. By defining his assumptions and attacking them, they reduce his book to absurdity. If you do not define your own assumptions, you may suffer the same fate.

❖

Your readers should understand both your premises and those of your opponents at the beginning. To define the premises you accept and reject, you must think hard and dig beneath the easy surface generalizations that may give the appearance of authority while having none.

3. Use evidence.

Here we return to a point I made earlier. Writers must know things. They must quote texts. They must tell stories about real people. They should use statistics. You cannot toss a good argument off the top of your head.

You must stuff your head with facts to be a good writer. Lawyers speak of "fact patterns" in the evidence for a trial. That is, at a given moment, the facts begin to point to a conclusion, to mean something. A lawyer points out to judge and jury that the facts tend in a direction.

Patterns, once discovered, reveal connections between data. Paul Fussell, in his remarkable book *The Great War and Modern Memory,* noticed that soldier-poets in World War I wrote continually of the sky—dawn, sunset, the stars. He realized that they wrote of the sky because they spent long months looking up at it from trenches stretched across Europe, where the opposing armies faced each other in a bloody stalemate that lasted four years. For soldiers, wars always involve more waiting than fighting. Often, soldiers in World War I had nothing to do but look at the sky. Fussell argues that the sky was the mirror in which they saw their own experience reflected. He notes that in World War II, British soldier-writers did not write lengthy descriptions of the sky. He reasons that this was so because World War II was a war of motion. Here is a pattern. Fussell saw it; we now say "of course." But he had to see it before we could agree with him.

Patterns exist in everything we read and in everything we observe. The trick is to see them. We see the facts, the basic data. (Somehow the word *fact* seems inadequate to what I'm trying to express.) We try to relate these facts to one another, to find some underlying pattern or principle that will explain or connect them. Our explanation should account for as many of these facts as possible. The failure to account for some facts indicates that some new explanation, or at least some further explanation, is necessary.

The discovery of the planet Pluto in our solar system is a model for the discovery of patterns and connections and meaning. Nineteenth-century astronomers discovered the planet Uranus and then the planet Neptune, both unknown to the ancient world. By the end of the century, it appeared that neither of these planets followed a regular orbit around the sun. Something seemed to be slowing them down at times, speeding them up at other times, making them wobble just a bit. Astronomer Percival Lowell became convinced that yet another planet out there revolved around the sun, causing these variations. In 1930, long after

Lowell's death, another astronomer discovered tiny and distant Pluto, confirming Lowell's theory.

Very often we discover some fact that does not fit our previous explanations, and so we must devise interpretation to account for the discrepancy. We have to know a lot to get to the point where we can question our own reasoning. In argument, as in every other kind of writing, knowledge is the writer's indispensable friend.

Arguments in Various Disciplines

I have always doubted that the requirements for writing across the disciplines were really different from one another. To my mind, the writer of a paper on English literature makes arguments in much the same way as does the scientific theorist. Each gathers information by careful study, and each tries to find some pattern as yet undiscovered by others. If the writer about English literature and the student of natural science study the data carefully, they come to a creative moment, an instant of illumination, when they see a pattern of connections and everything suddenly makes sense. And as I say time and again, much of the study involves writing down observations in a notebook.

Charles Darwin kept notebooks all his life. In his youth, on his voyage around the world in the ship *Beagle,* he noted—sometimes with the aid of drawings he made—small differences between the beaks of birds on the Galapagos Islands and their cousins on the distant mainland of South America. He wondered what caused those variations. The birds' beaks were by no means the only biological problem he found on those blackened volcanic chunks of land sticking out of the blue Pacific. But they loomed large in his mind. He decided that at some earlier time the birds on the islands had been identical to birds on the mainland. But through generations of isolation in a different environment, a new species had evolved, similar to the species on the mainland but differing from them in many features, including their beaks. Species were not fixed eternally; all living things were in continual, random change through generations because of the way they reacted to their environments.

Darwin knew that changes from generation to generation were a normal part of life. Children resemble their fathers and their mothers, but no child is an exact copy of either parent. Darwin's next step was to assume that some of these changes aid organisms—plants and animals— in their struggle for survival. And the organisms that survive have progeny that may likewise have a slight advantage in the battle for life. These were the building blocks he finally put together in *The Origin of Species,* one of the most revolutionary books of all time. It is also a readable book, in which Darwin presents a staggering quantity of data in a style that allows readers with little scientific knowledge to understand his theory. Inspiration comes out of knowledge. Our most creative moments come from wrestling with what we know, trying to fit the pieces of our knowledge together.

How does insight come? What makes information suddenly come together to form a pattern in the writer's mind? No one can give a precise answer. "The light dawned" is a common cliché to describe the process. Always the light dawns after hard work—observing, assembling data, thinking, worrying, proposing various patterns to see what seems to embrace most of the data and what theory provides the most plausible explanation for what we observe.

The creative process depends on asking questions. The investigative reporters who wrote about the Watergate burglary of June 17, 1972, put together details until they had a theory that accounted for most of them. They had some evidence that the burglary had been planned by White House staff members. But did Richard Nixon know about it beforehand or soon afterward? Did he try to cover up for his associates?

Their case for Nixon's involvement was plausible and so they kept working at it. *Plausible* is the key word here. Their case was believable because it fitted the facts they had uncovered, even if no "smoking gun," no conclusive proof, could be found. No one else could come up with another case that was equally plausible. Had these reporters spun out their theory without the long, difficult, and sometimes dangerous work of gathering data—evidence—no one would have paid any attention to them.

The great literary scholars follow much the same process in studying and writing about poets, playwrights, and other writers. They first read the texts—not once but again and again and again. Then they make notes. They ask questions. They make comparisons. How does this work of this writer compare with her other works? How does this writer compare with other writers in her own time? How does this writer compare with writers before her? After her? How have opinions about this writer changed from her own time until now?

Critic Cleanth Brooks, studying William Faulkner's novel *Absalom, Absalom!* early in the 1960s, realized that Faulkner does not tell us exactly what brought about the doom of his mysterious character, Thomas Sutpen. Two college boys, Quentin and Shreve, sitting in a cold dormitory room hundreds of miles from Mississippi, go over the fragments of an old story about the mysterious Sutpen and try to make sense of them. They spin out hours of speculations. But Brooks pointed out that we do not know, finally, if their solution to the mystery is correct.

Most of us reading *Absalom, Absalom!* for the first time overlook the significance of how the story is told—how much of it is "fact" and how much speculation about those facts. Brooks remembered the detective stories most of us read at one time or another in our lives. He said that

Absalom, Absalom! was this kind of story. But in the detective stories written by writers such as Agatha Christie, all the clues are wrapped up in the end; everything fits together. Brooks realized that Shreve and Quentin have a lot of clues, but we never know whether their "solution" to the mystery in *Absalom, Absalom!* is the right one. Brooks brought together his experience of reading detective stories and his experience of reading Faulkner and wrote a brilliant critical essay published in the Spring 1962 issue of the *Sewanee Review.*

I have said that one of the saddest recognitions of a college teacher is that students seldom bring together the various disciplines they study. They write as if all their experiences can be put into watertight compartments, like a catalog of distinct courses. If they write a paper in English, they do not imagine that they can enrich that paper by citing evidence from sociology or economics. If they write a paper in history, they do not think of comparing an important historical character with a character in a novel written about the same time. Good writers scan all their experience—what they have done themselves, what they have read, what they have heard from others—to see if they can find something to illuminate the topic they are writing about.

Effective arguments rest on evidence. In this book, most of my evidence is made of quotations from other writers. The quotations support my analysis of what writers do. You must present evidence to support your arguments; otherwise, you will be reduced to making naked assertions. If you have a reputation as a great authority in the field, your assertions may be worth something. Most of us lack the authority to carry an argument by the weight of assertion alone. We convince readers only when we present evidence.

The Rhetoric of Argument

Evidence is a collection of facts that support an argument. What we do with evidence may be called the *rhetoric of argument*—how we present the evidence in a persuasive way. The rhetoric of argument is based on inference. (I discussed inference at length in Chapter Two.) We argue only when a conclusion is not obvious, and inference is our major tool in understanding things we cannot confirm by direct observation.

We may use different modes of inference when we argue, and these modes are the subjects of the following sections of this chapter.

THE *A FORTIORI* ARGUMENT

A fortiori is a Latin term that means "to the stronger." Stripped down, the *a fortiori* argument reads like this: "If we know that *A* is true, it is all the more likely that *B* is true." In Chaucer's *Canterbury Tales,* the "poor parson of the town," explaining his longing to be virtuous, used this metaphor: "If the gold rust, what shall iron do?" He counted the priests as gold in English society, the ordinary folk as iron. If priests become corrupt, how much more likely it is that the people to whom priests minister should also be evil!

We use the *a fortiori* argument often in daily life. If cigarette smokers run a much higher risk of cancer of the mouth than do nonsmokers, cigar smokers run an even higher risk of the same cancer because cigar smoke is so much stronger.

Lawyers frequently use the *a fortiori* argument in court. If a lawyer can prove that a witness has lied once, in a less important matter, it is much easier to make the jury believe that the witness is lying about a more important issue. "We have proved that the accused lied when he said he was not having an affair with the victim's wife; isn't it likely that he also lied when he testified that he shot the victim by accident?"

The *a fortiori* argument turns up in advertising with monotonous regularity. A computer software company advertises that its update of a word-processing program includes 500 new features. The implied argument is this: If the program was good before, it should be much better now. And how many times have you seen on a box of soap powder, "New and Improved"?

The *a fortiori* argument influenced the course of the Vietnam War. Some U.S. Air Force generals argued that American air power could bomb the North Vietnamese into submission. Foes of bombing pointed to the failure of heavy British and American bombing to break the will of the Germans in World War II or even to slow German war production. Many studies concluded that bombing German cities only increased the German will to resist. Therefore, they argued, it was unlikely that bombing could reduce the will of the North Vietnamese. The *a fortiori* argument was this: If heavy bombing failed to break the will of a concentrated urban population in World War II, it is even more unlikely to break the will of a rural population living in widely scattered hamlets. The effect of bombing such a country will only be to make a lot of holes in the ground.

The *a fortiori* argument is essential to the inferences necessary in writing history. The evidence historians rely on is always fragmented and incomplete, and history itself is a process of assembling a puzzle made up of broken and missing pieces. Historians fill in the blanks by making intelligent speculations drawn from inferences. They can know some things with a fair degree of certainty; for example, that South Carolinians subdued Fort Sumter with artillery in April 1861 in the first combat of the Civil War. Other things remain forever uncertain. Did Lincoln deliberately provoke the South Carolinians into becoming aggressors? Did he move quickly to trigger war because he feared that the British might recognize South Carolina's "independence"? Did he think that faced with armed conflict, the South Carolinians might draw back from war?

Historians assemble all the evidence they can collect and try to frame it into a plausible, coherent picture—just as we try to find meaning in our experiences in the present. Historian Barbara Tuchman describes this process of inference from her own research.

> If the historian will submit himself *to* his material instead of trying to impose himself *on* his material, then the material will ultimately speak to him and supply the answers. It has happened to me more than once. In somebody's memoirs I found that the Grand Duke Nicholas wept when he was named Russian Commander-in-Chief in 1914, because, said the memoirist, he felt inadequate to the job. That sounded to me like one of those bits of malice one has to watch out for in contemporary observers; it did not ring true. The Grand Duke was said to be the only "man" in the royal family; he was known for his exceedingly tough manners, was admired by the common soldier, and feared at court. I did not believe he felt inadequate, but then why should he weep? I could have left out this bit of information, but I did not want to. I wanted to find the explanation that would make it fit. (Leaving things out because they do not fit is writing fiction, not history.) I carried the note about the Grand Duke around with me for days, worrying about it. Then I remembered other tears. I went through my notes and found an account of Churchill's weeping and also Messimy, the French War Minister. All at once I understood that it was not the individuals but the *times* that were the stuff for tears. My next sentence almost wrote itself: "There was an aura about 1914 that caused those who sensed it to shiver for mankind." Afterward I realized that this sentence expressed why I had wanted to write the book in the first place. The "why," you see, had emerged all by itself.[2]

Aside from being a splendid account of the role of inference in writing history, this paragraph provides an *a fortiori* argument: If so many brave men wept in 1914, may we not all the more assume that the Grand Duke wept out of a sense of impending doom and not out of a fear that he was inadequate?

The *a fortiori* argument can be falsified—as all good arguments can. No baseball fan would make this statement: Since Roger Clemens struck out twenty batters when he pitched against the Seattle Mariners in a meaningless game, isn't it likely that he would strike out even more batters when he faced Oakland in the American League playoffs? And in rape cases today, courts generally rule out the *a fortiori* argument: Since this woman willingly had sexual intercourse with several men before the alleged rape, isn't it likely that she consented on this occasion, too?

A *non sequitur* (Latin for "it does not follow") is involved in both these instances. That is, the conclusion does not follow from the first statement. Clemens does not control his pitching by his will alone; and no matter what a woman has done in the past, it is still possible that in this instance, she was raped.

THE ARGUMENT FROM SIMILITUDE

The argument from similitude holds that because people or events or things are alike in some ways, they must be alike in others. Because this argument allows predictions to be made about groups, pollsters use it regularly. It is indispensable for research in the social sciences, but it can lead to dangerous inaccuracies.

A study a few years ago revealed that Volkswagen owners were likely to be further to the left politically than were owners of Fords and Chevrolets. The same study showed that owners of Swedish-made SAABs and Volvos were likely to be even further to the left on the American political spectrum. The study did not claim that every Volvo owner was a political radical; it made its statements about groups rather than about individuals. No one argued that *because* a woman bought a Volvo she would move further to the left in politics; that argument would be absurd. If the study had any validity, it was only to show that a willingness to break with long-established American tradition might express itself in both car buying *and* in politics.

Some life insurance companies offer lower rates to nonsmokers. Most nonsmokers live longer than most smokers. But no one would argue that *every* nonsmoker lives longer than every smoker. A few nonsmokers die every year from lung cancer, and perhaps one's great-grandfather smoked two packs of Camel straights every day and died at age 85 when run over by a truck while jogging home from visiting his fiancée. Comparisons that classify people by groups offer only probability to individuals within the groups.

The argument from similitude can be used fraudulently when someone claims that because the people or things being compared are alike in some ways, they are alike in all. When Richard Nixon ran his first campaign for the U.S. Senate in 1950 in California, he faced Helen Gahagan Douglas, a member of the U.S. House of Representatives from California. Nixon thought he could win against the popular Douglas if he could make voters think she sympathized with Communists at home and abroad. At the time, Senator Joseph McCarthy of Wisconsin was claiming, in one emotional speech after another that hordes of Communists had infiltrated the United States government. The United States had just gone to war to repel a Communist invasion of Korea, and the terror of Stalinism in the Soviet Union made Americans think Communism was a cancer that was about to overcome the world.

Nixon made the argument from similitude. He compared the voting record of Douglas in the House with that of one Vito Marcantonio, a radical congressman from New York. Marcantonio had supported the Soviet Union's foreign policy through every slippery twist, and he was soon to disappear from the American political scene. In domestic policy, he had supported price controls, public housing, civil rights, and health insurance—positions taken by many Democrats and Republicans in the Congress. But most people knew him only for his hysterical speeches in support of the Soviet Union.

Nixon's staff members isolated 353 issues in which Douglas and Marcantonio had voted on the same side. These issues had nothing to do with the Soviet Union or Communism. But Nixon went doggedly from the indisputable fact of these 353 votes to a fallacious conclusion: If Helen Gahagan Douglas had voted with Marcantonio on so many occasions, she must agree with him in everything else. It was very much like saying that because Marcantonio liked milk and Douglas liked milk, Douglas also agreed with Marcantonio about the Soviet Union.

Frank Mankiewicz, a Douglas campaign worker, pointed out that Nixon himself had voted with Marcantonio 112 times in four years. Even the most hysterical anti-Communist might, on reflection, doubt Nixon's implication that 353 bills submitted to the House of Representatives of the United States were Communist-inspired. But it was a crazy time, and few people paused to reflect on the issues. They voted their fears, and Nixon won the election—and a reputation for deceit that got him the nickname "Tricky Dick" and dogged him until he resigned from the presidency in 1974 to avoid being impeached.

People do not forget dishonest arguments. Remember that before you make one.

THE ARGUMENT FROM CAUSE TO EFFECT

The argument from cause to effect or from effect back to cause is one of the most common in human discourse, one of the most necessary, and one of the most dangerous. We want to know why things happened—why war was declared, why cancer struck, why the economic recovery came, why a novel was popular, why crime increased, why the President was elected, why Hamlet called death the "bourne from which no traveler returns" when the ghost of his father had very obviously returned to set the play in motion.

On the surface, the argument from cause to effect appears simple, but this supposed simplicity can be misleading. Why do black players dominate professional basketball? One school of thought holds that blacks have a muscle mass that enables them to jump higher and with greater agility than most whites. The argument—which to some seems racist—is supported by some respectable researchers and the fact that most great players in the National Basketball Association are black. But another school of thought holds that basketball is the only sport open to the poor urban child. It requires little space and only simple equipment. Black children start playing it early and play it often while white suburban children do other things. With more black children devoting much more time to basketball, more of them grow up to be professionals. On which side does the truth lie? As yet, we really do not know.

This debate illustrates the difficulty of cause-and-effect reasoning: The causal relation between two events may be impossible to establish beyond any doubt. When the argument is emotionally charged—as any argument about race may be—the difficulties are all the greater.

Some causes produce more than one effect; it is misleading to isolate only one cause and pin all the effects on it. No reputable historian would dare argue that World War I was caused solely by the assassination of the heir to the throne of the Austro-Hungarian Empire in 1914 when he visited Sarajevo or that the Civil War was caused only by the election of Abraham Lincoln in 1860. Good historians know that the great crises in history build up like gas escaping slowly from a leaking pipe in a basement. Suddenly a spark causes an explosion. But without the accumulated gas, the spark would remain only a spark.

The scientific model of cause and effect often leads us astray. In the last century, Louis Pasteur discovered that heating milk to a temperature slightly less than the boiling point would kill harmful germs without ruining the taste of the milk itself. Here is a clear relation between cause and effect; pasteurization caused safer milk.

We wish for that kind of certainty in all our arguments; but it seldom exists, especially in the humanities and social studies, and only the dishonest pretend that that mythical assurance is there. Informed readers become impatient and annoyed when they see a writer making absurdly simplistic claims about cause and effect.

At the other extreme are those who find elaborate conspiratorial explanations for everything. Many people are unable to believe that President John F. Kennedy was murdered in 1963 by a lone gunman. On no good evidence, they argue that the Mafia did it or the Cubans did it. In 1991, movie director Oliver Stone produced a film called *JFK* in which he argued that the Central Intelligence Agency of the federal government did it. No matter that the motion picture is a tissue of distortions and outright lies, easily refuted by anyone with any knowledge of the evidence in the case; in our time, movies have become the new opiate of the people, and millions believe Stone's "argument." They saw it on the screen and can't tell the difference between movies and reality.

If you make Stone's kind of argument, you may feel smug because *you* have not been deceived. *You* stand above the gullible masses. *You* have seen everything clearly—whether you have any evidence or not. It seems that your argument *ought* to be true. Such explanations appeal because they seem to make the great mysteries of human existence more manageable and less subject to chance. But they are almost always false; readers recognize them to be false, and fair readers scorn the writers who make them.

It is all right to suggest plausible causes and effects for which you do not have final proof—so long as you are careful to let readers know how tentative your arguments are. Many great scientific theories have been developed by careful observers who supposed that the facts could be accounted for if they assumed something unproven or even unprovable. The notion of black holes—stars that have collapsed into tiny points of matter so dense that their gravity prevents even light from escaping from their surfaces—fits the theory that physicist Albert Einstein developed to explain many forces in the universe. But no one has ever seen a black hole with a telescope, for by definition a black hole *cannot* be seen.

Historians often suggest cause-and-effect relations between events, although they cannot finally prove them to the satisfaction of everyone. In his *The Rise and Fall of the Great Powers,* Yale historian Paul Kennedy argued that the cause of the decline of the great powers in modern times has been excessive military spending. Both the United States and the Soviet Union, Kennedy wrote, fell into the trap of spending more for the military than their economies could afford. Kennedy provided a great deal of data to support his argument, and his conclusions seemed all the more plausible when the Soviet Union collapsed and broke up not long after his book appeared. But he knew that he could not prove his case beyond any doubt, and he vigorously attacks those who interpret his book to mean that the United States is in an *inevitable* decline. He wants to avoid the accusation that he has proved too much.

Always be cautious in what you claim to know about cause and effect. But you have every right to suggest daring hypotheses that explain cause and effect *so long as you do not allow your reader to suppose that you have proved your case beyond the shadow of a doubt.* You must have some evidence for your hypothesis; you can't construct it out of thin air. But you can think of the evidence in daring ways.

Many arguments that began as daring hypotheses have been increasingly substantiated by further research. The argument for the existence of black holes is one example. Darwin's theory of evolution by natural selection is another. So be daring. But be sure you have a foundation of evidence on which to build your daring ideas.

Cause-and-effect reasoning abounds in fallacies. One of the most common is called *post hoc; ergo propter hoc,* a Latin phrase meaning that because one thing happens after another, the first is the cause of the second. A few years ago, I read in a Tennessee newspaper a passionate letter to the editor arguing that sex education in the public schools has caused an increase in violent sex crimes. The writer argued that before sex education came to the classroom, sex crimes were much less frequent;

therefore, sex education caused these crimes. Another letter writer quickly replied that the demise of the television program "Leave It to Beaver" was the real culprit. It could be demonstrated, this writer said, that sex crimes dramatically increased after that program went off the air.

It is easy to spot fallacies like these because the relation between cause and effect is so nebulous. But many fallacious arguments are more complicated and subtle, and many people—including the writers who use them—may be deceived. Honest writers examine the evidence critically. If it does not support their case, good writers will say so; if it may be interpreted in different ways, honest writers will say that, too, even while they argue that their interpretation is the best one. We may yearn for simple answers, but truth is always best served when we recognize how complicated some events are, how difficult they are to explain, and how mysterious they may remain even when we have done our best to understand them.

Despite its obvious dangers, the argument from cause to effect or from effect back to cause is indispensable in every field of thought. Strange indeed would be an essay without at least one paragraph devoted to it.

THE ARGUMENT FROM NECESSITY

The argument from necessity holds that no choice exists in a matter requiring action. The writer or speaker says, in effect, "Things are as I say they are, and you must do what I say you must do." It is an argument intended to make people do something without second thoughts. It is almost always the argument of those who call nations to war, for if we had a real choice, most of us would prefer to remain at peace.

On Monday morning, December 8, 1941, President Franklin D. Roosevelt made a great speech to Congress asking for a declaration of war against Japan. He began by presenting an undeniable fact in an unforgettable way.

> Yesterday, December 7, 1941—a date which will live in infamy—the United States of America was suddenly and deliberately attacked by naval and air forces of the empire of Japan.

Roosevelt moved from this statement of fact to the argument that the United States now had no choice but to declare war on Japan. The Congress and the American people believed him.

A more modern version of the argument from necessity arises from various ecological issues. Many ecologists argue that the greenhouse effect requires us to reduce the pollutants we are pouring into the atmosphere. These pollutants increase concentrations of carbon dioxide, which holds in heat and turns the air around us into a vast greenhouse that warms the earth, melts the polar ice cap, raises the level of the oceans, and threatens to drown the coastal cities of the earth. Concerned people argue that we must take dramatic measures to cut down atmospheric pollution or we will face catastrophe.

The argument from necessity is always vulnerable from two angles. An opponent can always say, "But the facts are not as you present them" or "Even if your facts are true, your conclusions about what is to be done are false."

During the Vietnam War, President Lyndon Johnson argued that if South Vietnam fell to communism, all Asia would then go communist in a so-called domino effect, as if these countries were a row of upright dominoes that would all fall if one was toppled. Therefore, he said in speech after speech, the United States had to win the war. Opponents countered that the domino effect was a myth and that even if other Asian countries should become communist, they could not act in concert to harm any vital interest of the United States. In effect, Johnson's opponents countered his argument from necessity by saying there was no necessity.

The argument from necessity embraces a contradiction. It assumes a choice; yet the argument is that no choice exists. I am asked to choose war and am told at the same time that I have no choice but war; I am asked to vote for a candidate who promises a balanced federal budget, and I am told that if I do not want the country to fall into ruin, I have no choice but to vote for such a candidate. The argument works only if the audience believes the necessity exists and assumes that people will do willingly what they are compelled to do anyway. This argument can backfire and damage the reputations of those who use it carelessly.

THE ARGUMENT FROM AUTHORITY

Aristotle called the argument from authority the "ethical" argument. He meant *ethical* in the Greek sense, meaning character. The ethical argument depends on our opinion of the person making the argument.

We believe some people because they exude authority. We believe them not merely for the logic of their discourse but because they seem to know what they are talking or writing about. We may believe them because they tell us about their experiences. We trust them. So the argument from authority may be the least logical of all arguments; but it may also be the most believable. Certain religious groups that depend on testimony demonstrate great vitality. At their services, people arise and tell—often with great emotion—stories of what God has done for them or shown them. Their hearers believe them, and the religion makes converts.

Strange as it may seem, the argument from testimony may be the decisive argument in historical writing. Historians sometimes assume a kind of logical explanation for past events that, on examination of the testimony of participants, proves to be untrue. Sir Thomas More, the "Man for All Seasons," died heroically for his Catholic faith during the rule of King Henry VIII of England in 1535. More was witty, courageous, and affectionate to his family. He also passionately believed that Protestants in England should be burned at the stake.

In 1935, a worshipful biographer of More wrote that More hated Protestantism not out of "religious bigotry" but because he thought Protestants would bring civil disorder to England. The writer's logic went something like this: A witty, courageous, and affectionate man cannot oppose the religious convictions of others merely on the grounds of religion alone. Therefore More's hatred of the Protestants could not have been for religious reasons. The biographer's "logic" breaks down, however, before the thousands of acid pages More wrote against the Protestants and his incessant demands that they be burned alive.

The argument from authority or testimony is the best witness against perversions of history. A recent poll showed that about one-fourth of Americans do not believe that Hitler deliberately tried to exterminate Jews in Europe during World War II. The testimony of thousands of survivors from death camps should be enough to prove to any honest person that yes, there was a Holocaust, and that yes, Hitler and the Germans did try to destroy European Jews.

Authority also arises from careful study. When you have the facts and present them carefully, readers believe you. Try to be an authority yourself when you can. Study the subjects you write about. Learn the pros and the cons of every issue. Be able to defend your position with the facts. Nothing is so tedious as prose whose author has been so unsure of himself that he cannot take a position and argue it cogently.

You should also use the authority of recognized experts. Lawyers call on experts in trials. The authority of scholars is great in academic essays. You can quote books, articles, interviews, and other sources. When you write a literary essay about a novel, you can help your case by finding an article by a well-known critic who agrees with you.

The opportunities for using testimony are limitless. Good testimony supporting your side can help you persuade readers. But be sure your witnesses are fair and truthful, and quote them accurately.

Arrangement of Arguments

I have chosen to call *arrangement* what others call *deductive and inductive reasoning*. I find it valuable to think of deductive and inductive reasoning as ways of arranging the evidence. Some evidence and some forms of argument fit naturally into deductive reasoning. Some fit better into induction. Your choice of which to use at a given moment depends on your evidence and how you decide to use it. You will use both deduction and induction in almost every good argument.

DEDUCTIVE REASONING

The path of deduction is from something we know to be a fact to a conclusion about something else. It involves inference. Deductive reasoning goes on in a form traditionally called the syllogism. And here again we meet our necessary friend, the premise—the assumption on which an argument is based. Syllogisms have three parts—a major premise, a minor premise, and a conclusion. The major and minor premises are statements of fact. The conclusion involves comparing or reading those two statements so that an additional statement of fact may be made about the minor premise. The following syllogism has been used for centuries to illustrate the syllogistic form:

Major premise: All men are mortal.

Minor premise: Socrates is a man.

Conclusion: Socrates is mortal.

Such an example makes deductive reasoning seem neat and easy. In practice, however, such reasoning may be more complicated. Yet a little study will often reveal a syllogism in an argument, and it is good practice to look for such syllogisms when you read. Astronomers in search of the planet Pluto made this argument:

Major premise: The gravitational pull of a nearby planet may cause variations in the orbits of other planets.

Minor premise: Uranus and Neptune show variations in their orbits.

Conclusion: Another planet may be out there, one we have not yet discovered.

Yet another syllogism might run like this:

Major premise: People write about those topics that most concern them personally.

Minor premise: Ernest Hemingway wrote many novels and short stories about men who sought to prove their manhood and courage.

Conclusion: Hemingway felt a great need to prove his own manhood and courage.

Even such cautious syllogisms may seem awkward when they are arranged in the bare-bones way that I have used here. Yet writers must be able to find such syllogisms in their own thought and in the thoughts of others. Once we have reduced a line of deductive argument to a syllogism, we should check the terms to see if the conclusion is valid.

In most deductive arguments, the major premise is not stated; it is only implied. A presidential candidate attacks his opponent for being inexperienced in foreign policy. The implied major premise is that no one should become president without having made decisions about foreign policy. A scholar may object to another scholar's use of Freudian psychology to interpret someone's life in the past. The implied major premise may be that Freudian psychology is invalid or that it cannot be used to psychoanalyze the dead.

Deductive reasoning offers some obvious problems. The major premise may be wrong or at least disputable. For example, the presidential candidate with vast experience in foreign policy may have had no influence on events. Or, if he did, he may have bungled and blundered on five continents. A look into history may cast doubts on syllogisms used in the present. Harry S Truman had virtually no experience in foreign policy when he took office after Franklin Roosevelt's sudden death in 1945. But by general consensus, modern historians rate him high on achievements such as the Marshall Plan that aided European economic recovery and his quick response to counteract the Soviet blockade of Berlin by creating an airlift to ferry in supplies across Soviet lines to the isolated city. Is the premise valid, then, that a presidential candidate experienced in foreign policy is necessarily superior to an inexperienced candidate? Perhaps not. A British wit has said that the major premise of some politicians is that nothing should be done the first time.

Deductive reasoning must take observation into account. Deduction is crippled when it ignores observation and works only off principles someone thinks are logical when, in fact, they do not fit the facts. The ancient Greeks are often credited with the discovery of modern science. But, in fact, they were more apt at working out logical systems than they were at observing nature, and some of their conclusions were contrary to the facts. In the seventeenth century, the prestige of Greek philosophy was a wall against the progress of a true modern science based on observation. When Galileo argued that the earth moved, he ran into the Greek logic of his adversaries. Among other propositions, they put forward the following:

Major premise: People feel motion when they are moving.
Minor premise: We do not feel the earth move.
Conclusion: Therefore the earth stands still.

Those lacking Galileo's mathematical ability and his experience with the telescope were reduced to a Greek "logic" that has long since been proved wrong.

Yet many people continue to uphold ideas that fit false premises that they refuse to correct by observation. "Liberals are unpatriotic; Jones is a liberal; therefore Jones is unpatriotic." "The Marlboro Man smokes cigarettes and looks handsome and tough; I want to look handsome and tough; therefore I will smoke Marlboros." "No sensible person can be religious; Smith is religious; therefore she cannot be sensible."

Many false syllogisms come from not observing enough. It's foolish to imagine that all French people are rude because a French post-office clerk was angry with you when you could not speak French.

Despite its abuses, deductive reasoning is essential in argument, and we encounter and use it every day. "Computers are sensitive to slight changes in electrical voltage; surge protectors block voltage changes from the computer; computer owners should use a surge protector." "College graduates usually get better-paying jobs than do non-college graduates; Jones wants a job that pays well; Jones should get a college education." "Democracy depends on the free flow of information; reading is an important means of acquiring information; therefore democracy depends on a free press." All these arguments represent deductions from facts most of us can accept.

INDUCTION

We have encountered induction in our discussion of fact patterns. *Induction* is the process of observing facts until we perceive a relation between them. Induction has been at the heart of modern medical research. Pasteur observed that certain bacteria were present in milk and that people who drank such milk were often afflicted with disease. He concluded that the bacteria caused the disease—and his conclusion changed modern medicine for all time.

By the same sort of induction, researchers in this century noted that lung cancer afflicted cigarette smokers at ten times the rate that the disease afflicted nonsmokers. They concluded that cigarettes caused lung cancer, although as yet they are not sure just how the cancer starts.

In literary studies, you may notice that certain themes come up again and again in a writer's work. You may be justified in drawing conclusions from this recurrence. Many critics have noted that the women in John Updike novels appear to exist chiefly as sexual objects for Updike's male characters. Feminist critics have attacked him for this limited view he takes of women in his work.

Archaeologists have discovered identical Greek pottery pieces in southern England, Spain, southern France, Egypt, and Palestine. They conclude that Greek trade extended all over the Mediterranean and as far north as England at the time the pottery was manufactured.

In using inductive logic, we assemble clues that add up to the solution of a mystery. For the writer, induction requires the careful collection of facts and careful thought about how these facts hold together—if indeed they do.

Induction and deduction go hand in hand. By induction, researchers determined that nonsmokers living with cigarette smokers ran a much greater risk of heart disease and cancer than did nonsmokers living in smoke-free houses. Lawmakers in some cities deduced from this research that nonsmokers had the right to a smoke-free workplace and smoke-free areas in restaurants and other public places. Once induction leads us to a conclusion, we deduce other conclusions from it.

Logical Fallacies

No discussion about argument can be complete without a few words about logical fallacies. An honest writer avoids fallacious reasoning; careful readers recognize bad logic when they see it and immediately lose faith in writers who use it.

FALLACIES OF DEDUCTION AND INDUCTION

We have already noted fallacies of deduction. A fallacious deduction may arise either when the major premise is wrong or when the connection between the major premise and the minor premise is faulty. We will look at more examples of faulty deduction below.

Fallacies of induction most commonly occur when we try to draw conclusions from too few instances. An American fortune-teller included the assassination of John F. Kennedy in her list of predictions for 1963. For a few years, editors of many newspapers paid her big money at the New Year to predict events in the next twelve months. She became a joke, her predictions about as accurate as darts thrown at a target in a dark room, and she fell into obscurity. Among her thousands of predictions came one lucky guess about a national calamity, and the gullible rushed to believe she could see into the future.

In much the same way, people may generalize from one or even several experiences or incidents and be wrong. The baby-boomer generation of the 1960s is often said to have been high on drugs, promiscuous in sexual matters, and rebellious against society. But anybody who was teaching in a university during that period knows that those qualities fitted only a minority—albeit a very loud and aggressive minority—of students in that decade.

Sweeping generalizations about people in any group or time are likely to be wildly inaccurate. Often writers make such generalizations because they are too lazy to check out the evidence. The evidence is usually much more complicated than the sweeping generalization allows and therefore requires the writer to do more work to get it right. Any time you are tempted to say, "Everybody during the Renaissance was creative," or, "The 1960s generation thought nothing of going to class in the morning and to the riots in the afternoon," you had better ask yourself if you are too lazy to do the investigation that your writing project requires.

STRAW MEN

A *straw man* is an argument one claims one's opponents are making when in fact they are not making that argument at all. One attacks this imaginary argument rather than face the real issue. The setting up of straw men that can be easily burned or pushed aside is a curse of our times. Someone opposes prayer in public schools, and advocates of school prayer accuse him of being against religion. Someone objects to the decision of a school board to ban *Huckleberry Finn* from the school library, and someone accuses her of racism. Someone opposes abortion, and someone accuses him of wanting to enslave women. Someone favors a woman's right to choose abortion, and someone accuses her of being a murderer. A presidential candidate supports the U.S. Supreme Court decision that children may refuse to pledge allegiance to the flag, and his opponent claims he is unpatriotic—though the children may be following a religious conviction.

In serious writing, setting up straw men is an immoral act, and readers with their wits about them disdain this cowardly practice. Writers who set up straw men fear to face the arguments of their opponents at their strongest points. Examples of straw men have been almost endlessly multiplied in this society. Presidential debates happily burn straw men before national TV audiences every four years, thus contributing to the dumbing of American politics. Notice the practice in others, and avoid it in your own writing.

THE *AD HOMINEM* ARGUMENT

The words *ad hominem* are Latin for "directed toward the man," and the fallacy called by this name is an attack on a person rather than a serious effort to deal with that person's arguments. Like the straw-man fallacy, the *ad hominem* argument is all too common in politics. It has now become rare for candidates facing one another in an election to treat each other as honorable human beings. Once again, the presidential debates, which are supposed to help us choose someone for our highest national office, have become examples of the lowest forms of rhetoric. The candidates fling labels at each other and call the exercise *politics*. How sad it is!

The *ad hominem* argument usually resembles a faulty deduction.

> My opponent is a homosexual; therefore nothing he says about national politics can be trusted. I consort only with members of the opposite sex; therefore my sentiments about national affairs are infallible.

Most people would recognize the obvious faulty reasoning in the example above. But what about this one?

> My opponent was expelled for cheating when he was in college thirty years ago. Therefore you cannot trust him to be President.

This argument assumes that because the speaker's opponent did something dishonest thirty years ago, he is still dishonest and that dishonesty taints everything he says on any subject, including foreign affairs. It does not consider the opponent's life since the act of dishonesty, and it ignores his present views on foreign policy, views that may be sensible and farsighted. It assumes a syllogism like this:

> Anyone who cheats once in school will always be dishonest.
>
> My opponent cheated thirty years ago.
>
> My opponent is dishonest now.

At times, a person's character is a genuine issue. We don't want to elect to high political office someone practicing sexual harassment, child abuse, or flagrant dishonesty. We don't want a racist President or a bigoted secretary of state. But too often in our political campaigns, *ad hominem* attacks are used to divert attention from the real issues. When that happens, the *ad hominem* argument is the rhetorical refuge of a scoundrel.

THE BANDWAGON ARGUMENT

According to the bandwagon argument, since everybody is doing something, we should do it, too. In fact, everybody may *not* be doing "it," whatever "it" is. But people who want us to follow them tell us that we should go along with this proclaimed majority.

The strength of the bandwagon argument stems from our desire to seek the company of our own kind and to be accepted. Most of us hate to speak out against strong public opinion. The bandwagon mentality makes some people hesitate to express an opinion until they know what others are thinking. A group of college students discussing a movie will often wait cautiously for someone to express an opinion; then they may all agree. Likewise, their professors may hesitate to express dislike for a great literary classic because they fear being thrown off the bandwagon of academe. I greatly admired the courage of one of my English department colleagues for admitting to me one day that he found *Moby Dick* one of the most boring books he had ever read.

The bandwagon argument is often fallacious. Although public opinion supports a war or a political candidate or a social program or a piece of legislation relating to some moral issue, public opinion may be wrong. Remember, public opinion supported Hitler. Some brave writer or speaker may have to get off the bandwagon to try to stop it before it rolls over a cliff. The strength of the United States Constitution and our democracy rests on the freedom to stand alone. The mere statement of near unanimity of views does not mean that those views are correct. When

I was a child growing up in the rural South, the bandwagon mentality said racial segregation was moral and desirable and that the "outsiders" or "Yankees" who wanted integration deserved to be condemned and even killed. That bandwagon for decades kept the region in economic and moral ruin.

BEGGING THE QUESTION

Another common fallacy is *begging the question,* which is setting up an argument so that its terms can lead to only one conclusion. The argument often affirms certain things to be true that on examination, prove to be much less certain.

As I am writing this chapter, the United States is engaged in debating the question of what we ought to do about Serbian atrocities in Bosnia, in what is called "the former Yugoslavia." On television and in newspapers, we see terrifying photographs of civilians, including children, killed by Serbian artillery pounding the city of Sarajevo. The question is this: Should the United States send troops and warplanes to stop the fighting?

The argument for military intervention is expressed in many newspapers like this: If we want to consider ourselves a moral nation, we must send our armed forces to stop the killing in Bosnia. This argument affirms both that morality calls on us to send in our troops and that sending in our troops will stop the killing in Bosnia. Opponents to military intervention point out that it is not at all certain that sending in our troops will stop the killing in Bosnia, that indeed the country there is so mountainous that an occupying army would be easy prey to guerrilla fighters and that rather than stopping the killing, it might well increase it. They say that it is begging the question simply to say that to be moral, we must intervene to stop the fighting. The question is more complicated than that.

ARGUMENT BY FALSE ANALOGY

The fallacy of argument by false analogy often corrupts political thinking and newspaper columnists. American leaders who wanted to continue fighting the Vietnam War kept going back to the Munich agreements of 1938. There, France and England agreed to give Hitler those parts of Czechoslovakia he wanted rather than fight a war with him. But within a year, Hitler had not only taken all of Czechoslovakia but had gone to war with England and France anyway. The analogy seemed plain. The democracies should have resisted Hitler before he became strong enough to threaten all of Europe; the democracies should resist communism before it became strong enough to threaten all of Asia.

The flaw in the argument is that two events in history are never exactly alike. A great many things in Vietnam in the 1960s were different from the situation in Europe in the 1930s. Most arguments from analogy are similarly superficial.

Concluding Remarks on Argument

Argument is essential to democracy, to public discourse, to scholarship, to daily life. From the smallest meetings in our communities to the greatest debates in Congress, argument helps us see our way. It is a high mark of civilization. When people lose the ability to argue well or to follow the arguments of others, or when they cannot discern fallacies when they see them, all our democratic institutions are threatened. Never be afraid to argue; but always be prepared to argue well.

To argue well you must command information. You cannot create an argument out of nothing. You must also be honorable. Admit it when all the evidence does not stack up in your favor. Concede points where the evidence requires concession. Treat your opponents with respect. Marshal your evidence. Remember that the solution to many arguments is neither this nor that but some of both.

Here it is worthwhile to repeat something I have said in various ways already: Knowledge seldom has neat edges that all fit together like the parts in a good jigsaw puzzle. It comes with ragged corners, with missing pieces, and with uneven sides. We make our best arguments in an attitude of confident humility.

Five

Paragraphs

*P*aragraphs are a modern invention. Greek and Latin writers did not use them. Until the nineteenth century, written English scarcely noticed them. The word *paragraph* originally meant a pi mark like this π placed at the head of a section of prose to announce that the subject of the discourse was changing slightly. After the mark, the section might go on for several pages. Eventually, the paragraph mark was replaced by an indented line. Even then, the indentation might introduce a long section of unbroken prose. The paragraphs of John Stuart Mill and Charles Darwin, both great prose writers in the nineteenth century, often went on for several pages. Only gradually did the paragraph assume its modern form—a fairly short block of prose introduced by an indentation, organized so that every sentence in it contributes to a limited subject.

Paragraphs help both writers and readers. They order our thoughts and make writing easier to follow. They break down our ideas into manageable units. They let us arrange an essay one step at a time. They allow readers to follow our thoughts along a stairway of prose that we build for them.

Paragraphs give readers a sense of pace; from paragraph to paragraph, we see that the prose is going somewhere. They also provide relief for our eyes. The long gray columns of unindented type in early nineteenth-century newspapers look dark and forbidding today. (Indeed, the most probable cause of the paragraph's popularity was the expansion of literacy fed by the penny press. Ordinary people—sometimes not well educated—wanted their newspapers to be more readable, and editors wanted their stories to be more flexible for inserts and deletions that let a piece slip neatly into the space available.) We hesitate to start reading unparagraphed material because we subconsciously think we can't get through it. By showing a piece of writing in small blocks, paragraphs give us confidence that we can absorb the piece one block at a time.

The Structure of Paragraphs

A lot of nonsense has been written about paragraphs, much of it not only wrong but harmful. Much of the nonsense arises from the false notion that every paragraph should be a short essay and that the thesis for the essay should be expressed in a topic sentence. Some books teach that a topic sentence may be at the beginning, in the middle, or at the end of a paragraph. Many teachers command their students to underline the topic sentence, and the students dutifully underline a sentence whether the paragraph contains a topic sentence or not.

A *topic sentence* is said to be a general statement supported by evidence contained in the rest of the paragraph. A good topic sentence is supposed to develop paragraph unity.

Paragraph unity is important. When we read, we don't like to be jerked from thought to thought without seeing any connection between them. Paragraphs let us see connections. Sometimes a paragraph includes a general statement that fits the standard textbook definition of the topic sentence. The other sentences in the paragraph support the generalization. Such paragraphs usually explain things. But in most other paragraphs, no textbook topic sentence can be found.

Let's consider the textbook topic sentence first. Here is a paragraph that explains why olives grown in California are tasteless compared to olives grown in Europe—at least by the time they get to us.

> Americans are used to tasteless olives because that's what industrial processes yield. California olives are treated with lye to remove a very bitter substance called oleuropein (from *Olea europea,* the olive's botanical name). The lye also removes most of what gives the olives flavor, and leaves them bland and hard without being crunchy. Lye-treated olives need help to taste like anything: spices and herbs in the prime, a stuffing with mushrooms or almonds or anchovies or pimentos.[1]

This paragraph begins with a general statement—which we may call a *topic sentence*—that the rest of the paragraph explains. The writer expands on the topic and provides details that make us believe it.

But many paragraphs, especially paragraphs in narration or description, are not introduced by general statements. Here, for example, is a paragraph from the late James Baldwin's "Notes of a Native Son":

> On the 29th of July in 1943, my father died. On the same day, a few hours later, his last child was born. Over a month before this, while all our energies were concentrated in waiting for these events, there had been, in Detroit, one of the bloodiest race riots of the century. A few hours after my father's funeral, while he lay in state in the undertaker's chapel, a race riot broke out in Harlem. On the morning of the 3rd of August, we drove my father to the graveyard through a wilderness of smashed plate glass.[2]

We could summarize the paragraph above in a general topic sentence such as this: "Several interesting things happened on the day my father died." Such a sentence would be tedious and unnecessary. As Baldwin tells us what happened, we easily follow along. We see the unity of the paragraph as we read it.

But how do paragraphs work? What do paragraphs with general topic sentences have in common with paragraphs that lack such sentences? How do paragraphs attain unity?

I believe that we write anticipating when we are going to make a slight shift in the subject we are treating. When we move onto another point, another idea, another incident, we indent and write a sentence. The first sentence of the paragraph contains ideas we wish to expand on in the next sentence. We pick up one of those ideas and use it in the next sentence. We connect the two sentences by a repetition—a word, a pronoun, or a synonym for an idea in the first sentence. The sentences are thus woven together like a net with threads reaching from place to place in the fabric.

Let's examine that process in the paragraph from James Baldwin.

On the 29th of July, in 1943, my father died.

Think for a moment of all the possibilities in this sentence. We have several key thoughts—"29th of July," "1943," "my father," and "died."

Baldwin picks up the thoughts of the date and of the father. The important topic here is "when." He develops this thought in the next sentence:

On the same day, a few hours later, his last child was born.

"On the same day," is a synonym for "On the 29th of July, in 1943," and "his" refers to "my father." Baldwin develops a thought of what happens on July 29, 1943. Now he develops a further thought, also related to the question "when."

Over a month before this, while all our energies were concentrated in waiting for these events, there had been, in Detroit, one of the bloodiest race riots of the century.

Two thoughts are picked up here: "Over a month before this" develops the thought begun in "On the 29th of July, in 1943," and "on the same day." "While all our energies were concentrated in waiting for these events" relates to the ideas of the death of Baldwin's father and the birth of the father's last child.

Baldwin continues in the next sentence to develop the idea of "when," also referring to his father's death by mentioning the funeral.

A few hours after my father's funeral, while he lay in state in the undertaker's chapel, a race riot broke out in Harlem.

Again referring to his father's funeral, and also referring to the race riot mentioned in this sentence, he develops the next sentence.

> On the morning of the 3rd of August, we drove my father to the graveyard through a wilderness of smashed plate glass.

This sentence concludes the paragraph. We see in these sentences a network of interlocking thoughts that begin with the first sentence. The first sentence is not a general topic sentence; it is a simple statement of fact. The other sentences are similar statements, all tied to the first sentence by words that develop ideas contained in that first sentence. Every sentence picks up some words or ideas from the previous sentence and adds something new.

These are the qualities of all paragraphs, whether they have a general topic sentence or not. They reflect the writer's mind. If the writer had other interests, the paragraph would have gone off in another direction, but it still would have been carefully laced together by this network of connections. Suppose someone else had written this:

> On the 29th of July, in 1943, my father died. I scarcely had come to notice the event because on that day, I was ordered to fly yet another raid against Hamburg; and we had to take off within an hour after I received the telegram from home. I was the navigator on our B-24 "Liberator" bomber and had to fly the mission because there was no one to replace me. It was our second raid on Hamburg in four days, and I was so tired I did not have the energy to grieve for a loss so far away.

Again we have the familiar connections we expect between sentences: Each sentence after the first one reaches back to pick up a previous word or idea and extends the thoughts, adding new information. What makes the two paragraphs different? The different purposes of the writers. But the structure in each is the same—a looking backward and a moving forward in each sentence.

Always remember that the first sentence is all-important to any paragraph. The writer, setting down that first sentence, makes a commitment to develop some word or phrase in it as he or she proceeds to the second sentence, to the third, and to the fourth. You will begin many paragraphs with a general statement that must be supported and explained in the rest of the paragraph. You will begin others by telling of an event followed by another event and another, all without having one general sentence that ties them all together. But however you begin, connect the first sentence to the sentences that come after it by this network of repetition and development.

In every paragraph, the first sentence presents several thoughts. The second picks up the thought the author wishes to develop and goes on. Sometimes inexperienced writers forget to carry that development from the first sentence through the others in the paragraph. They skip from thought to thought, writing a kind of shorthand that leaves out necessary information. Readers are left to leap from sentence to sentence like agile children jumping from stepping-stone to stepping-stone over a brook. Readers want a smooth bridge to carry them to their destination without unnecessary strain. Always review your sentences to see that each sentence in your paragraphs picks up and develops an idea mentioned in a previous sentence.

The first sentence is key to the rest. Sometimes paragraphs begin with a broad, general statement as a first sentence, then follow it with a second sentence that limits the general statement. The rest of the paragraph builds on the second, limiting sentence. Here is such a paragraph by historian Barbara Tuchman. She describes the Anarchist movement in America in the late nineteenth century.

> Men who were Anarchists without knowing it stood on every street corner. Jacob Riis, the New York police reporter who described in 1890 *How the Other Half Lives,* saw one on the corner of Fifth Avenue and Fourteenth Street. The man suddenly leaped at a carriage carrying two fashionable ladies on an afternoon's shopping and slashed at the sleek and shining horses with a knife. When arrested and locked up, he said, "They don't have to think of tomorrow. They spend in an hour what would keep me and my little ones for a year." He was the kind from which Anarchists of the Deed were made.[3]

The first sentence makes a general statement about the violent movement known as Anarchism; the second limits this general idea to a particular incident; and the rest of the paragraph provides details of that incident. This kind of paragraph occurs often in professional writing. The first sentence provides a general introduction; the second focuses on something more specific; the following sentences develop the specific incident. But even here, the second, limiting sentence depends on some idea expressed in the first sentence. *The first sentence is always the sentence that gives direction to any paragraph.*

Unity and Disunity in the Paragraph and the Essay

I have described how a paragraph *tracks,* that is, how it moves from thought to thought smoothly, keeping the later parts in harmony with the earlier parts. An essay tracks on the same principle. Every sentence after the first sentence in an essay looks back to something that has gone before and looks ahead to something that will come after.

Disunity in paragraphs often leads to disunity in the essay, for if one paragraph jumps the track, it may derail those that follow. Such disunity usually occurs because the later sentences in a paragraph do not flow naturally from the first sentence.

Writers stumble into disunity when they are not sure what they want to say. Sometimes they write a first sentence, wait a long time to write the second, and, in the interval, forget what they said in the first. If you have trouble with paragraph unity, check your first sentence carefully. See what ideas it contains. Then see if your next sentence takes up one of those ideas and develops it. Read your work aloud; I repeat this advice again and again to my students. Your ear helps you edit when your eyes fail you.

You may check the unity of some paragraphs by trying to leave a sentence out. This is not true of all paragraphs, but it is usually true for paragraphs that argue, explain, or narrate. Such paragraphs build sentences into a chain, each sentence a link depending on the link behind it. Leave a sentence out, and the chain breaks. The paragraph comes apart.

Below is a narrative paragraph from Loren Eiseley in which he tells of the voyage Darwin made as naturalist on His Majesty's Ship *Beagle.* That voyage made Darwin start asking himself what accounted for the differences among various species of plant and animal life that seemed remarkably similar to one another—questions that led him to develop his theory of biological evolution by natural selection. See how these sentences are chained together by their subject matter. Ask yourself if you can leave a sentence out or put it somewhere else in the paragraph.

> They sailed from Devonport December 27, 1831, in H.M.S. *Beagle,* a ten-gun brig. Their plan was to survey the South American coastline and to carry a string of chronometrical measurements around the world. The voyage almost ended before it began, for they at once encountered a violent storm. "The sea ran very high," young Darwin recorded in his diary, "and the vessel pitched bows under and suffered most dreadfully; such a night I never passed, on every side nothing but misery, such a whistling of the wind and roar of the sea, the hoarse screams of the officers and shouts of the men, made a concert that I shall not soon forget." Captain Fitzroy and his officers held the ship on the sea by the grace of God and the cat-o'-nine-tails. With an almost irrational stubbornness Darwin decided, in spite of his uncomfortable discovery of his susceptibility to seasickness, that "I did right to accept the offer." When the *Beagle* was buffeted back into Plymouth Harbor, Darwin did not resign. His mind was made up. "If it is desirable to see the world," he wrote in his journal, "what a rare and excellent opportunity this is. Perhaps I may have the same opportunity of drilling my mind that I threw away at Cambridge."[4]

Take a few minutes to trace the linkages in this paragraph. The first sentence looks back to a previous paragraph with the opening pronoun *they.* "They sailed from Devonport December 27, 1831...." The possessive pronoun *their* that begins the next sentence extends the reference made by *they* in the first sentence. "The voyage" that begins the third sentence looks back to the action expressed in the first sentence by the words "They sailed..." So it goes through the paragraph, one sentence looking back to the last, and all of them falling into a chainlike order, thought building on thought. We could leave out this sentence: "Captain Fitzroy and his officers held the ship on the sea by the grace of God and the cat-o'-nine-tails," although it adds vigor to the whole. Otherwise, if we leave out a sentence, the meaning of the next one becomes obscure. The paragraph carries us along, repeating nothing unnecessarily but including enough backward glances to help us see easily the relation of each sentence to the previous sentence and to the next one.

You cannot always test paragraph unity by leaving out a sentence. Some paragraphs make a general statement in the first sentence and follow it with a list of detailed statements that support the generalization. You can change the list around or even leave part of it out, and the paragraph will still hold together. Descriptive paragraphs often have this quality. Let's take a look at a couple of descriptive paragraphs Eiseley wrote in an essay called "The Judgment of the Birds."

> It was a late hour on a cold, wind-bitten autumn day when I climbed a great hill spined like a dinosaur's back and tried to take my bearings. The tumbled waste fell away in waves in all directions. Blue air was darkening into purple along the bases of the hills. I shifted my knapsack, heavy with the petrified bones of long-vanished creatures, and studied my compass. I wanted to be out of there by nightfall, and already the sun was going sullenly down in the west.
>
> It was then that I saw the flight coming on. It was moving like a little close-knit body of black specks that danced and darted and closed again. It was pouring from the north and heading toward me with the undeviating relentlessness of a compass needle. It streamed through the shadows rising out of monstrous gorges. It rushed over towering pinnacles in the red light of the sun or momentarily sank from sight within the shade. Across that desert of eroding clay and wind-worn stone they came with a faint wild twittering that filled all the air about me as those tiny living bullets hurtled past into the night.[5]

As in all paragraphs, the first sentence in each of these sets the stage for what comes later. But the sentences after the first sentence could be rearranged in almost any order, and the paragraph would maintain its sense. Every sentence reaches back to the first sentence of the paragraph to amplify the thought expressed there.

Some paragraphs organize material in clumps of sentences that follow the first sentence. The sentences in each clump are closely related to each other, but the clumps themselves could be rearranged or even eliminated without disturbing the harmony of the whole. (In a well-written paragraph, the elimination of a clump of sentences would reduce the richness and dilute the thought.)

Here is a paragraph organized in clumps of sentences broken down in a schematic way. The paragraph comes from William Manchester's survey of American history from 1932 to 1972, *The Glory and the Dream*. It describes the journey of John Glenn, the first American astronaut to orbit the earth in a space capsule.

> The temperature in the capsule had risen to 108 degrees, he noted, but the air-conditioning in his suit kept him cool.
>
> He had been instructed to explain his every sensation—the audience, after all, was paying for the trip—and he began by reporting that he had no feeling of speed. It was "about the same as flying in an airliner at, say, 30,000 feet, and looking down at clouds from 10,000 feet."
>
> Over the Atlantic he spotted the Gulf Stream, a river of blue in the gray sea.
>
> Over the West Coast he made out California's Salton Sea and the Imperial Valley, and he could pick out the irrigation canals near El Centro, where he had once lived.
>
> His first twilight was awesome: "As the sun goes down it's very white, brilliant light, and as it goes below the horizon you get a very bright orange color. Down close to the surface it pales out into a sort of blue, a darker blue, and then off into black." The stars were spectacular. "If you've been out on the desert on a very clear, brilliant night when there's no moon and the stars just seem to jump out at you, that's just about the way they look."
>
> Approaching Australia he radioed, "Just to my right I can see a big pattern of light, apparently right on the coast." From a tracking station below, Astronaut Gordon Cooper explained to him that this was the Australian city of Perth. Its 82,000 inhabitants had turned on all their light switches, to welcome him and test his night vision." Glenn replied, "Thank everybody for turning on, will you?"[6]

The clumps of sentences in the preceding paragraphs are arranged chronologically. You could leave any clump out without substantially damaging the unity of what is left. You could even rearrange some of the clumps without making readers feel that they had lost anything.

We can summarize paragraphs with a couple of diagrams:

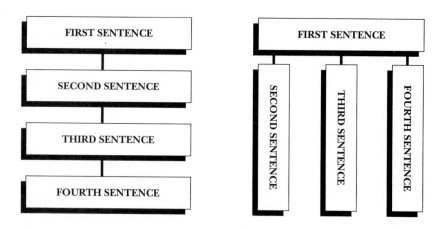

Transitions between Paragraphs

Paragraphs should not only hold together within; they should also allow smooth passage from one paragraph to the next. To ensure this smooth flow, pay attention to your transitions. *Transitions* are words or phrases that look backward, tying the paragraph to what has come before, and look forward, binding the first sentence of the paragraph to what comes afterward. Good transitions make life easier on readers; they also help writers with their own thinking, for they set up relations within prose that are essential to its shape and unity.

You will use two kinds of transitions. The more obvious of the two consists of words that tell your reader that you are moving from one idea in your paper to another. Words like *therefore, however, moreover, furthermore, nevertheless,* and others say to your reader, "I'm going this way; come along with me."

At times we all use these unambiguous transitions. But before we write one, we should pause. Must we use it? These are cautious, plodding words, words that leap quickly to mind when we are stuck. When we use them too frequently, they leave the rivets showing in our essays.

The best transitions rarely call attention to themselves. Here, as always, study the work of your favorite writers to check my advice. You can go for pages and pages without seeing a *thus* or a *therefore* in the pages of *The New Yorker, Popular Mechanics, Sports Illustrated,* or *The Atlantic.* In a good, lively book on a serious topic, you will rarely find such words. You don't see the rivets. You see paragraphs smoothly welded together so that you don't feel the bumps and the cracks. How do good writers achieve these effects?

A good device in making transitions is to use a word in the last sentence of one paragraph that you repeat in the first sentence of the next. Look at the following example, from John McPhee's essay called "The Swiss at War." Here are the first two paragraphs of the essay:

> It seems likely that the two most widely circulated remarks ever made about Switzerland's military prowess were made by Napoleon Bonaparte and Orson Welles.
>
> Welles said, "In Italy for thirty years under the Borgias, they had welfare, terror, murder, bloodshed—but they produced Michelangelo, Leonardo da Vinci, and the Renaissance. In Switzerland, they have brotherly love, five hundred years of democracy and peace, and what did that produce? The cuckoo clock."[7]

We have two transitions here. The primary transition is the word "Welles." It appears at the end of the one-sentence opening paragraph of McPhee's essay. It begins the next sentence, the first sentence in a two-sentence paragraph. (McPhee's essay originally appeared as an article in *The New Yorker,* a magazine that prizes the short paragraph.) The second transition is the word "Switzerland." It appears in the first paragraph and reappears in the second sentence of the second paragraph. These repetitions of nouns weave the paragraphs together and provide us with an unbroken tapestry of thought.

You can make these transitions between paragraphs not only by the repetition of words in the last sentence of one paragraph and the first sentence of the next. You can also use a pronoun in one sentence as a link to the other. Here is Lewis Thomas writing about "Late Night Thoughts on Listening to Mahler's Ninth Symphony":

> I took this music as a metaphor for reassurance, confirming my own strong hunch that the dying of every living creature, the most natural of all experiences, has to be a peaceful experience. I rely on nature. The long passages on all the strings at the end, as close as music can come to expressing silence itself, I used to hear as Mahler's idea of leave-taking at its best. But always, I have heard this music as a solitary, private listener, thinking about death.
>
> Now I hear it differently. I cannot listen to the last movement of the Mahler Ninth without the door-smashing intrusion of a huge new thought: death everywhere, the dying of everything, the end of humanity.[8]

Three transitional ideas are repeated in the short first sentence of the second paragraph from the last sentence of the first paragraph—the pronoun "I," the verb "hear," and the pronoun "it." But the pronoun "it" seems to carry most of the weight, for it refers to the word "music" and to the general topic of the paragraph that begins with a reference to Mahler's Ninth.

No book can show all the possible transitions in good writing. But the principle is obvious. Transitions work by looking backward and reaching forward, by repeating words or ideas. The repetition should not simply tell readers what you have already told them. The first mention should, rather, be a base from which you spring off to tell them something new.

From what you have learned so far in this chapter, you should be able to analyze the paragraphs in any book or magazine you enjoy. Test your own skill by locating transitions that bind paragraphs together in some enjoyable piece of prose. You will note that good writers seldom use the mechanical transitional words such as *thus, therefore, moreover, furthermore,* and *however.* Well-constructed paragraphs rarely require them; learn to connect your paragraphs without them.

Length of Paragraphs

How long should a paragraph be? Journalists break their paragraphs every two or three sentences. Most newspapers and many magazines are printed in narrow columns; copy editors indent frequently to break up multiple lines of type. In academic writing, paragraphs may run on for a page or more. One rule of thumb based on visual effect holds that the length of a paragraph should not exceed its width. In student papers, I like to see about two indentations on each page of typewritten copy. Experience tells me that when inexperienced writers run on and on without an indentation, their thoughts may be rambling or fuzzy.

No sure rule can guide us. Some long paragraphs are just right; some short ones are incoherent. The flow of one sentence into another makes a better measure of the unity of a paper than does the length of its paragraphs. If you weave your sentences together by the patterns of repetition and extension that I have shown, you may indent almost at will. I sometimes look at a page in my own writing and decide that I want to divide a paragraph that has become too long for my taste. I can always find a place where the flow changes just enough to justify a new indentation.

Whatever the length of your paragraphs, observe the first-sentence rule. Make your first sentence the introduction. Take a thought from it, and develop that thought in the next sentence. Then choose whether you want to make the third sentence develop a thought from the second sentence or whether you want to leap back over the second sentence and pick up something from the first. Always remember that an essay develops thoughts. Sentences repeat something mentioned earlier and push forward into something new.

Concluding Remarks on Paragraphs

Your first efforts to build paragraph unity may be hard. But as you get the hang of analyzing your own sentences, the going gets easier. Writing is like dancing: learning the first new steps requires concentration, and you may well step on your partner's feet or—in more modern dancing—collide with somebody on the floor. But suddenly, with practice, the knack comes; and you keep time to the music with your feet as if you were born to it. When you write, pay attention to the development of your thoughts. Look at the relation of your sentences to one another, and the paragraphs will take care of themselves.

Six

Fundamental Principles of Sentences

Sentences make statements or ask questions. We make sentences naturally when we talk. Otherwise we would not be understood. Some people say that we seldom communicate in complete sentences, but they are mistaken. In any conversation, we speak in complete sentences unless we are answering a question or adding information to something we said or something somebody else said. To say that a sentence is complete is only to say that it makes sense. Most sentences make sense by naming a subject and making a statement about it.

> My son is asleep upstairs.

Here the writer names a subject, "My son," and makes a statement about it: "is asleep upstairs." The completed statement is called a *predicate* to the subject; a predicate is any statement we can make about something else. Once you form a basic statement, clauses, phrases, and other modifiers may amplify it, just as harmonies amplify the theme of a melody. The statement itself is primary. Sentences may go wrong because the writers lose track of the statement they want to make. To reduce the confusion, name your subject, and make a statement about it. Once arrived at your basic statement, you can weave clauses, phrases, and other modifiers around it. Sentences like this one turn up in the first drafts of most writers:

> Since the Japanese, a people whose artistic care for the common things of the daily life has always excited Americans, live crowded together on their small islands, they have been forced to construct social customs to help them endure living so close together, which are the basis for much of their art, including their love of miniaturization.

The sentence loses us. Here is a revision, built on a main statement.

> The Japanese have made art from the necessity of living close together on their crowded islands.

Once arrived at the basic statement, we can do several things with it. We can add some elements.

> The Japanese have made art out of the necessity of living close together on their crowded islands—an art that includes social customs and miniaturization.

We can break our thoughts into several sentences, expanding some of them.

> The Japanese have made art out of the necessity of living close together on their crowded islands. Part of that art has been their social customs that provide careful ritual forms for daily life. Another has been their fondness for miniaturization. Americans have always been fascinated by Japanese art—probably because its dedication to the small is opposite to their own taste for the grandeur of the huge.

In writing each sentence, try to keep the core statement in mind before you start. Take a breath, form the main idea in your head, and, only then, start to write. As you write, add elements. Adding will be no problem if you know what the main statement of the sentence will be. Too many of my students appear to start sentences in the mood of a motorcycle rider who leaps onto his machine at night and, without turning on the lights, roars off into the dark, hoping that the gods of the road will help him get somewhere. They start writing without any idea of where they are going.

Think for a moment about what you want to say. What is happening? Who is acting? Who or what receives the action? Don't confuse readers by packing too many important details in a single sentence. But don't condense things so much that you leave out information required to complete your thought.

Kinds of Sentences

English sentences make three kinds of statements.

1. A sentence may tell us that the subject does (or did, or will do) something.

> Jones rode the alligator.

In this sentence the subject is Jones, and Jones did something: He rode the alligator.

2. A sentence may describe a condition, telling the state of the subject's existence.

> Jones was proud for five minutes.

In what condition was Jones? He was proud. Sentences describing conditions use a linking verb to tell what that condition is. The most common linking verb is some form of the verb *to be.* If we say, "She is tall," we describe her condition or some quality of her existence, and we link the subject *she* with the adjective *tall* by using the linking verb *is,* a form of the verb *to be.* But other verbs can also be linking verbs. "Jones *seemed* brave." "The alligator *looked* annoyed." "The spectators *felt* uneasy." All these verbs tell something about the condition of the subject. They link the subject to an adjective that describes it.

3. A sentence may describe an action done to the subject.

Jones was eaten by the alligator.

When action is done to the subject, we say that the verb in the sentence is in the *passive* voice. The subject does not act through the verb; the subject is acted upon.

With these fundamental principles in mind, let's turn to some more general principles of sentence style.

Writing Good Sentences

1. Use the active voice.

In the strongest sentences, the subject does something. The verb tells what the subject does. Although the passive voice is a good and necessary part of the English language, it will deaden your style if you use it too much.

We seldom use the passive when we speak. We don't say, "Jack's car was driven into the reservoir Saturday night." We say, "Jack drove his car into the reservoir Saturday night." We want to know agents. Who did it? The passive does not answer that question. Bureaucratic publications often use the passive to evade responsibility.

> "Mistakes have been made in my office," Congressman Jack S. Swindler told reporters. "Somehow a great deal of money contributed to my campaign was transferred to my personal bank account, and it was used to send me and some of my family members on a cruise in the Carribean."

Congressman Swindler really means that he took the money out of his campaign funds and used it to take a vacation with his family to the Carribean. But the passive voice lets him escape responsibility; it makes the whole affair sound like a computer error. Inexperienced writers may use the passive because they think it sounds impressive. But the passive often sounds impersonal, voiceless—or dishonest. Consider the following:

> Minor characters in Shakespeare's plays have often been studied.
>
> The book was highly recommended.

Who studied the minor characters? Who recommended the book? We want to know. Yes, you can add a prepositional phrase to provide the agent ("The book was recommended by the author's mother"), but it is better to be simple and direct. "The author's mother recommended the book, but most reviewers said the only reason for reading it would be if the penalty for not reading it were a good beating."

Use the passive when the recipient of the action is more important than the actor.

> Hoover was elected in 1928.
>
> My Uncle Mike was hit by a bicycle as he left the saloon on Saturday night.
>
> The *Mona Lisa* was once stolen from the Louvre.

Use the passive in paragraphs that make a series of statements about a subject. The writer wishes to keep attention fixed on one spot. To do so, he may use the passive as Robert Caro does in this paragraph from his biography of Lyndon Johnson. Caro describes Johnson's first congressional campaign in Texas.

> The speeches *were* generally *delivered* on Saturday: traditionally, rural campaigning in Texas *was* largely *restricted* to Saturdays, the day on which farmers and their wives came into town to shop, and *could be addressed* in groups. On Saturdays two automobiles, Johnson's brown Pontiac and Bill Deason's wired-for-sound gray Chevy, would head out of Austin for a swing through several large towns. On the outskirts of each town, Johnson would get out of the Pontiac ("He thought it looked a little too elaborate for a man running for Congress," Keach says) and walk into the town, while the Chevy would pull into the square, and Deason or some other aide would use the loudspeaker to urge voters to "Come see Lyndon Johnson, your next Congressman," and to "Come hear Lyndon Johnson speak at the square"; to drum up enthusiasm, records *would be played* over the loudspeaker.[1]

The passive verb phrases—italicized in this paragraph—allow Caro to keep his focus. Now and then, as in the first sentence, he might have changed to the active: "Johnson generally delivered these speeches on Saturdays," but Caro probably supposed he was repeating Johnson's name too often in his large book and shifted here to the passive to give readers some relief. Use the active whenever you can. When you do use the passive, have a reason for doing so.

2. Make most of your verbs assert action rather than tell a condition.

You can say this:

> It would seem that voters in Massachusetts are in favor of capital punishment, at least for convicted murderers, given the results of yesterday's referendum on the subject.

Or you can say this:

> In yesterday's referendum, Massachusetts voters approved capital
> punishment for convicted murderers by almost two to one.

Stating the action gives you a more vivid sentence. It also usually helps
you make a statement in fewer words.

Don't use too many "to be" verbs. Change them to more active verbs.
You can say this:

> Most Americans *are* believers in capital punishment.

But it is more vivid to say this:

> Most Americans believe in capital punishment.

You can say this:

> Many Americans *are* of the opinion that foreign cars *are* more durable
> than American cars.

But it is more vivid to say this:

> Many Americans *think* foreign cars *last* longer than American cars.

Occasionally check your use of the "to be" verbs—*is, am, are, was, and
were*—by circling them on a page. When you see too many of them, revise.
Don't be a fanatic about changing them, however. "To be" verbs are part
of the language, and you must use them sometimes, but too many will dull
your prose.

3. Don't digress in a sentence; support your basic statement.

Everything in your sentence should support your basic statement. Sometimes inexperienced writers throw needless information into a sentence
to show how much they know or simply because the information is
interesting.

> Napoleon Bonaparte, who some people now think may have been
> poisoned when he was in exile on St. Helena Island, invaded Russia on
> June 21, 1812.

Your basic statement is this: "Napoleon Bonaparte invaded Russia on June
21, 1812." What does a story about his death much later on have to do
with the invasion? Nothing. Cut it out.

4. Combine thoughts to eliminate choppy sentences.

We usually apply the term *choppy* to a string of short sentences, but
choppiness does not reside in the shortness alone. Choppiness occurs
when a writer is unable to subordinate minor thoughts to major thoughts
and needlessly and monotonously repeats the same sentence forms.

Choppiness may also result from a lack of connection between sentences. We read a paragraph like this with increasing annoyance:

> We biked steadily uphill. We biked along the river. We were silent now. We were too tired to talk. The ridges above us were covered with trees. Most of them were conifers. They were dark green. They gave a tinge of melancholy to the day. A wind blew. It was soft. It whispered in the trees. Below us the river splashed over the rocks. It was in the valley floor. We heard the two sounds distinctly. The wind in the trees. The river splashing over the rocks. And our own breathing. It was ragged and hard. That was a third sound. A fourth sound was the whisper of the bike tires on the road. The road was asphalt. That sound was scarcely audible.

Writing such a sentence in a first draft may not be a bad idea. Setting down these impressions in order helps you pull your memories together. But in revising, you should combine and subordinate some thoughts to others.

> We biked steadily uphill along the river. We were silent now, too tired to talk. Above us the ridges were covered with conifers, dark green, giving a tinge of melancholy to the day; and a wind blew, whispering in the trees. Below us the river splashed over the rocks in the valley floor, and we heard the two sounds and a third sound—the sound of our own breathing, ragged and hard. A fourth sound, scarcely audible, was the whisper of the bike tires on the asphalt road.

I have written of bonding sentences by repetition from one sentence to the next. But avoid *unnecessary* repetition that slows the pace of your prose. Don't make readers ask themselves why you are telling them something you have told them before. Repeat only enough to make transitions from your earlier thoughts in the essay.

5. Avoid a proliferation of dependent clauses in a single sentence.

Dependent clauses help us write with a mature style. All good writers use them to amplify thoughts in a sentence.

> *After he had done all his Christmas shopping for the many people who expected presents from him,* he bought a large gift for himself, wrapped it up in gaudy paper with a bright holiday ribbon, put it under the tree, and told visitors *that it was from his best friend.*

The italicized words represent three dependent clauses. The first, beginning with *After,* is an adverbial clause modifying the verbs *bought, wrapped, put,* and *told* in the independent clause. That adverbial clause includes an adjectival clause, *who expected presents from him,* which modifies the noun *people.* The final dependent clause, *that it was from his best friend,* is a noun clause, the direct object of the verb *told.* This sentence has one example each of the three general classes of dependent clauses—adverbial, adjectival, and noun. Every dependent clause serves as an adverb, an adjective, or a noun in another clause. An independent clause can usually stand by itself as a sentence.

Too many dependent clauses will clutter your thoughts, weakening the force of your basic statements. Be aware of them, and avoid the temptation to stuff too many into a single sentence. The lean style now popular in American writing keeps dependent clauses to a minimum. One dependent clause in a sentence rarely makes trouble, but don't put one in every sentence. When you put two dependent clauses in a sentence, a warning flag should go up in your mind. When you have three, the flag should start waving back and forth, and you should reexamine the sentence to try to simplify it. Now and then, three dependent clauses will be just right in a sentence. But don't write too many such sentences. The cumulative effect will be devastating. This sentence gives no trouble:

> Americans eagerly collect pennies, although the value of the penny is sometimes less than the copper that goes into making it.

This one begins to lose its focus:

> Americans, who sometimes show a mania for collecting, eagerly collect pennies, although the value of the penny is sometimes less than the copper that goes into making it.

This one gets out of hand:

> Americans, who sometimes show a mania for collecting, a hobby which may be part of our materialistic culture, eagerly collect pennies, although the value of the penny, which is used largely as an advertising gimmick as in the price $4.99 instead of $5.00, is sometimes less than the copper that goes into it.

In a first draft, you may write overcrowded sentences. When you revise, pull out distracting dependent clauses. Make them into sentences of their own, or eliminate them altogether. Like the other principles in this book, this one is observed with wide variations among writers. Weekly newsmagazines use dependent clauses sparingly, substituting for them modifying phrases. Such writing is sharp and clear. We can analyze this style by looking at two paragraphs from a *Time* story about television. In them we see only one dependent clause!

> It was reality-check time in network television last week. After a blizzard of press attention and network hype, ABC finally brought forth *Wild Palms*, Oliver Stone's dazzling, challenging, future-shocked mini-series. It fizzled in the ratings. After years of twisting and turning in an effort to adapt to a new TV landscape, the networks unveiled their fall schedules. It looked like 1973 again.

What a difference a year makes. Last May change seemed to be in the wind at the Big Three networks. Faced with steadily growing competition from cable and other video choices, the networks were groping for a way to stay relevant and healthy. Critically praised shows like *I'll Fly Away* and *Brooklyn Bridge* were renewed despite low ratings. The fall lineup included a batch of hip relationship comedies tailored to the thirtysomething audience *(Love and War, Mad About You)*, as well as a flock of *Beverly Hills, 90210,* clones aimed at an even younger crowd. The network mantra was demographics; these shows might not draw a huge audience, but they would, it was hoped, draw the right audience.[2]

Where is the one dependent clause? The "it was hoped" in the last sentence is the only one in these paragraphs. The result is an extremely readable style—a reason for *Time's* success. Readers know what every sentence means. They can also easily track meaning from sentence to sentence. They don't have to backtrack and read again to find the thread.

You can often revise a dependent clause into a modifying phrase. Clauses beginning with *who, which, that,* and *what* can often be reduced to phrases.

Don't write this:

The island, which had appeared as a spot on the horizon earlier, now broadened into a large land mass which had palm trees waving over a long, white beach.

Write this instead:

The island, only a spot on the horizon earlier, now broadened into a large land mass with palm trees waving over a long, white beach.

Don't write this:

Our captain, who was an arrogant young man who spoke to us as if he had been an old sea dog and we had been ignorant children, pointed at the shadowy blue rocks which lay beneath the surface of the sea.

Write this instead:

Our captain, an arrogant young man, spoke to us like an old sea dog instructing ignorant children and pointed out the shadowy blue rocks lying beneath the surface of the sea.

Don't write this:

What is important about the test is its measurement of how quickly students can respond to the questions it asks.

Write this instead:

The importance of the test is its measurement of the quickness of student response.

6. Begin most sentences with the subject.

The normal pattern for sentences is *subject + predicate*. Experienced writers follow this pattern. Look through a copy of almost any book or magazine, and you will discover about four-fifths of the sentences begin with the subject.

In this paragraph, in which Barbara Tuchman recalls how she wrote her book *The Guns of August,* which is about the first month of World War I in 1914:

> I do not invent anything, even the weather. One of my readers told me he particularly liked a passage in *The Guns* which tells how the British Army landed in France and how on that afternoon there was a sound of summer thunder in the air and the sun went down in a blood-red glow. He thought it an artistic touch of doom, but the fact was it was true. I found it in the memoirs of a British officer who landed on that day and heard the thunder and saw the blood-red sunset. The art, if any, consisted only in selecting it and ultimately using it in the right place.[3]

Every sentence begins with the subject. That is the most natural way to write. A writer does not begin *every* sentence with the subject. But if not the subject, what?

7. When you do not begin with the subject, begin with some form of adverb—a word, a phrase, or a clause.

About a fifth of published sentences begin with some form of adverb—a single word, a phrase, or a clause. Sentence-opening adverbs almost always modify the verb in the main clause. Adverbs answer the questions *where* and *when* and sometimes *how, how often,* and *how much.*

Here is a sentence that begins with an adverbial clause:

> When we recover the etymology of September, October, November, and December (seventh, eighth, ninth, and tenth), we know that the year once started in March, or that two additional months must have been added to an original calendar of ten months.[4]

Here is a sentence that begins with an adverbial phrase:

> When mounted knights attacked them in open country, the Swiss formed squares—ten thousand soldiers in a square, bristling with twenty-one-foot pikes: the Porcupine Principle[5]

Here is a sentence that begins with a simple adverb:

> Perhaps she had encountered him in the fields or on the mountain where the daughters-in-law collected fuel.[6]

Here is an inverted sentence, beginning with an adverb, followed then by a verb and then by the subject of the first clause:

There *are* lessons, of course, and when people speak of learning from them, they have in mind, I think, two ways of applying past experience.[7]

8. Avoid beginning sentences with *there.*

Now and then, all of us begin a sentence with *there is, there are, there were,* or *there was.* (In the example above from Barbara Tuchman, we find such a sentence.) We should not do so, however, without giving it a second thought. I have combed the third edition of *Modern American Prose,* the companion volume to this book, to find examples to illustrate my points, and I can discover only a sprinkling of sentences that begin with *there. There* can sometimes cause us to substitute vague description for action.

Don't say this:

> There were several reasons he refused to smoke.

Rather, say this:

> He refused to smoke because he feared cancer, his wife and children hated the smell, and he once set fire to his bed with a cigar.

Avoid the indefinite *it is* for the same reason that you avoid *there.* We can say this:

> It is common for people who tan every summer to get skin cancer.

But this is stronger:

> Skin cancer is common among people who tan every summer.

Now and then, we all use *It is,* just as we all use *there,* but minimizing its usage will make your prose more vigorous.

9. Avoid participial sentence openers.

A participial opener uses a participle as an adjective to modify the subject of the sentence. Professional writers sometimes use participial openers to compress information, especially in newsmagazines, where space is always short.

> Lining up for water at a Des Moines parking lot, Donna Bailey was upbeat in describing her family's coping strategy.[8]

A participial opener may let a writer invert a sentence, putting the subject after the verb, to obtain a pleasing variety.

> *Standing uninvolved for the moment but nevertheless carefully observing these practices* was the young Providence pitcher Monte Ward, who, before his time was out, would do much to revolutionize the whole player-owner relationship.[9]

But any study of professional writing will reveal that participial openers are rare. They violate the general rule that a readable written sentence follows the common patterns of speech. We rarely use participial openers in spoken sentences. We don't say, "Having been out in the cold wind all day, I'm nearly dead." We say something like this: "I've been out in the cold wind all day, and I'm nearly dead."

Participial openers must modify the grammatical subject; otherwise we get confusing sentences like this one:

> Buried under a pile of dust for forty years, he found all the records intact.

Was he buried under a pile of dust for forty years?

Or this one, immortalized in a collection of newspaper gaffs collected from the nation's press by the *Columbia Journalism Review:*

> Bound, gagged and trussed up nude in a denim bag, with plugs in her ears and tape over her eyes, Cleveland teacher Linda L. Sharpe told yesterday how she was kidnapped to Florida, not knowing where she was going or why.

We wonder if she was in this miserable condition while she was telling of being kidnapped to Florida.

A participle may dangle, seeming to modify nothing, as in this sentence:

> Flying every week between Boston and New York, it was hard for her to fear airplanes.

Was a mysterious *it* flying between Boston and New York every week?

The rule is this: Use participial openings sparingly. If you do use them, be sure they modify a concrete grammatical subject.

10. Be economical with adjectives.

Adjectives add qualities to nouns and pronouns. Use them only when they are necessary. Too many adjectives clog prose and weaken sentences. Here are paragraphs from two writers. See how few adjectives they use. See how the basic statements stand out sharply and clearly.

> In October 1347, *two* months after the fall of Calais, *Genoese trading* ships put into the harbor of Messina in Sicily with *dead* and *dying* men at the oars. The ships had come from the Black Sea port of Caffa (now Feodosiya) in the Crimea, where the Genoese maintained a *trading* post. The *diseased* sailors showed *strange black* swellings about the size of an egg or an apple in the armpits and groin. The swellings oozed blood and pus and were followed by *spreading* boils and *black* blotches on the skin from *internal* bleeding. The sick suffered *severe* pain and died quickly within *five* days of the *first* symptoms. As the disease spread, other symptoms of *continuous* fever and spitting of blood appeared instead of the swellings or buboes. These victims coughed and sweated heavily and died even more quickly, within *three* days or *less*, sometimes in *24* hours. In *both* types everything that issued from the body—breath, sweat, blood from the buboes and lungs, bloody urine, and blood-blackened excrement—smelled *foul*. Depression and despair accompanied the *physical* symptoms, and before the end "death is seen seated on the face."[10]

My computer tells me there are 191 words in this passage from Barbara Tuchman's chapter on the plague called the *black death* in her book of medieval history, *A Distant Mirror*. I count twenty-five adjectives, or a ratio of roughly one adjective to every nine words. But note that four of those adjectives are numbers and that the adjective "trading," used twice, has almost the quality of a noun in that it is used to define "trading ships" and "trading posts." She does not flood her work with adjectives. We find the power of this passage in its nouns and verbs.

Here is Philip Caputo, writing about the Vietnam War:

> They had been together for years and assumed they would remain together until the end of their enlistments. Sergeant Sullivan's death shattered that assumption. It upset the sense of unity and stability that had pervaded life in the battalion. One-Three was a corps in the *old* sense of the word, a body, and Sullivan's death represented the amputation of a *small* part of it. The corps would go on living and functioning without him, but it was *aware* of having lost something *irreplaceable*. Later in the war, that sort of feeling became *rarer* in *infantry* battalions. Men were killed, evacuated with wounds, or rotated home at a *constant* rate, then replaced by *other* men who were killed, evacuated, or rotated in their turn. By that time, a loss only meant a gap in the line that needed filling.[11]

In this passage of 140 words, we have only 8 adjectives, or a proportion of about 1 adjective to every 17.5 words. If any single quality marks the style of those counted as good writers in America today, it is probably stinginess in the use of adjectives. Weigh every adjective you are tempted to use; if it is not necessary, throw it out.

11. Don't use nouns as adjectives.

Much official language from bureaucracies groans under the tyranny of nouns pretending to be adjectives. Proper nouns can sometimes serve as adjectives. You can talk about the *Gettysburg* Address, the *Marshall* Plan, or the *Bowery* Bank. Some words have the same form whether they are nouns or adjectives—*volunteer, deputy, savage, poor,* and many others. But most common nouns—especially those ending in *-tion, -sion, -ism,* and *-ness*—do not work well as adjectives. A careful writer will avoid constructions like the following:

> They worked hard in skills acquisitions.
> She was expert in writing-improvement practices.
> He was a jaded-secretary retraining expert.
> The reporters learned scrutiny thoroughness.

A careful writer would revise:

> They worked hard to acquire skills.
> She was an expert at improving writing.

He helped retrain secretaries who had become jaded at their work.

The reporters learned to be thorough.

Some writers use nouns as adjectives in a mistaken effort to make their writing seem more important. Instead, such usage makes prose stiff and ugly. Here again, normal speech patterns offer a standard. We don't say, "We want to implement these quality-control procedures in automobile manufacturing." That's a mouthful. We say something like this: "We want to set up some procedures to control quality in making cars." We should follow the natural inclinations of the spoken language.

12. For sentence variety, occasionally use free modifiers and absolutes.

A *free modifier* is a participial phrase placed at the end of a sentence but modifying the subject. Free modifiers may replace dependent clauses. The free modifiers in these sentences are in italics:

> She sprinted up the street, *racing for the bus.*
> The house collapsed, *shattered by the earthquake.*

Several free modifiers at the end of a sentence, all of them modifying the subject, can provide a sense of vigorous action. Here is a paragraph from Bruce Catton's book *The Coming Fury.* Catton describes the preparations to defend Fort Sumter in Charleston's harbor at the start of the Civil War.

> The soldiers had not yet been called into action, but they were busy, and the materials to force a decision were piling up—in Fort Sumter, and on the mud flats that surrounded it in Charleston harbor. Major Anderson was doing what he could to perfect his defenses, *mounting additional guns on the barbette, making his walls more solid by bricking up embrasures that could not be manned, removing stone flagging from the parade ground so that shells that might be thrown into the fort would bury themselves in the sand before exploding.*[12]

The participles *mounting, making,* and *removing* introduce free modifiers, all modifying the subject *Major Anderson.* The three phrases—a couple containing clauses embedded within them—provide a sense of simultaneous action, showing a busy commander protecting his post.

Free modifiers may also carry a sense of progression, showing one thing happening after another, leading to a climax.

> She inched her way up the face of the cliff, *feeling* for holds in the rock, *moving* with infinite care, *balancing* herself delicately step after step, not *daring* to look down, *breathing* hard, *fearing* exhaustion, *going* on, *wallowing* at last onto a shelf of rock and safety at the top.

You can extend a series of free modifiers almost indefinitely because each modifies the same thing—in the preceding example the pronoun *she.*

Memorize the form—participle followed by a phrase, all modifying the subject. Some free modifying phrases imply the participle *being.*

He looked around, uncertain, frightened, and lonely.

You understand in this sentence that *he* was uncertain, frightened, and lonely, and your mind fills in a participle.

He looked around, [being] uncertain, frightened, and lonely.

Absolutes share some qualities and stylistic advantages with free modifiers. Whereas a free modifier is a participle introducing a phrase modifying the subject, an *absolute* is a noun followed by a phrase that modifies the whole clause in which the absolute appears.

Robinson made a miracle stop behind third, *his throw beating Mays to first by a step.*

The absolute compresses action. Another writer might have done this:

Robinson made a miracle stop behind third. His throw beat Mays to first by a step.

The use of the absolute turns two choppy sentences into a vigorous one. Absolutes express action well, making them useful in both nonfiction and fiction.

Then she fled beneath his fist, and he too fled backward as the others fell upon him, swarming, grappling, fumbling, *he striking back, his breath hissing with rage and despair.*[13]

In this example, William Faulkner uses both absolutes and free modifiers, providing a sense of swift, violent action.

13. Use compound verb phrases for variety.

Compound verbs compress action and quicken the pace of prose. The triple compound verb, where a single subject controls three verbs, has become common in modern English and American.

From 1600 on, when modern warfare developed in Europe, the German states (even with the rise of Prussia) *spent* fewer years at war than any other nations except Denmark and Sweden, *engaged* in fewer battles, and *suffered* fewer casualties.[14]

To signify his right to punish, the Prince twice rejected a good price offered by towns to buy immunity from sack. His letters express only a sense of satisfied accomplishment. His raid *had enriched* his company, *reduced* French revenues, and *proved* to any wavering Gascons that service under his banner was rewarding.[15]

The attack on the Fascist redoubt which had been called off on the previous occasion was to be carried out tonight. I *oiled* my ten Mexican cartridges, *dirtied* my bayonet (the things give your position away if they flash too much), and *packed* up a hunk of bread, three inches of red sausage, and a cigar which my wife had sent from Barcelona and which I had been hoarding for a long time.[16]

The third example, from English writer George Orwell, points to another quality in modern English style—the fondness for *triads,* or groups of three. Note that he not only uses a triple compound verb but also a triple direct object at the end—*hunk of bread, three inches of red sausage, and a cigar.* Triads are everywhere in modern style.

> So Allen Ginsberg was speaking now to them. The police looking through the plexiglass face shields they had flipped down from their helmets were then obliged to watch the poet with *his bald head, soft eyes* magnified by horn-rimmed eyeglasses, *and massive dark beard,* utter his words in a croaking speech.[17]

Our fondness for triads is so great that sometimes we make them when they are not there. When Winston Churchill became prime minister of Great Britain in May 1940, when Germany seemed about to win World War II, he told his people, "I have nothing to offer but blood, toil, tears and sweat." But in popular memory his noble phrase has been translated to "blood, sweat, and tears." Triads are a vital part of our style now; use them to enliven your prose, and, like Churchill, sometimes surprise by using four elements instead of three. Tom Wolfe, writing here about Las Vegas, pulls off a foursome in a compound verb:

> But most of these old babes are part of the permanent landscape of Las Vegas. In they go to the Golden Nugget or the Mint, with their Social Security check or their pension check from the Ohio telephone company, *cash* it at the casino cashier's, *pull* out the Dixie Cup and the Iron Boy work glove, *disappear* down a row of slots and *get* on with it.[18]

14. Use appositives to speed the pace of your sentences.

An *appositive* is a word or phrase written after a noun to rename or otherwise define the noun. The simplest appositives are single nouns or adjectives.

> His car, a Buick, was less expensive than mine, a Volvo.
>
> Senator Joseph McCarthy, an alcoholic, terrorized American colleges and universities in the 1950s.

Sometimes an appositive may be a long phrase.

> An age of faith is almost certain to become an age of quarrels among the faithful. They divided into bitterly hostile sects, *each with his own leader and each hoping for support from one group or another among the infidels.*[19]

Or it may be a clause set off by dashes.

Napoleon said, "The best troops—*those in whom you can have the most confidence*—are the Swiss.[20]

You can often revise dependent clauses into appositives and so speed up the pace of your prose. Look carefully at clauses that begin with *who, that,* or *which.*

Abraham Lincoln, *who was born in 1809,* moved around as a boy and never developed a great attachment to any one state.

Revised to an appositive, this becomes:

Abraham Lincoln, *born in 1809,* moved around as a boy and never developed a great attachment to any one state.

15. When you must write long sentences, balance them with short sentences to give readers some relief.

Readers search for the basic statement in every sentence. The longer the sentence, the more difficult it is to find the basic statement. We can all understand this sentence, although it is fairly long:

Although the rain fell hard enough to strip the leaves from the trees, leaving the air thick with the smell of shattered foliage, the drought had been so severe that we still needed water after the storm had passed on up the valley and the rain had stopped.

But several sentences of such length running together on a page would force us to slow down in order to absorb them. Since readers read at a constant pace, they generally keep their eyes moving whether they understand the sentences or not. They tend to skip over what they don't understand, and so they lose your point. After a long sentence like the one above, therefore, a short one is in order.

An inch below the surface, the ground was dry.

No one can make an ironclad rule about the length of sentences. Short sentences are more readable than long ones, but no one wants to write like the old Dick-and-Jane readers. Our language is an almost infinitely complex pattern of different sounds that make sense because we give meanings to the differences. A cat is not the same as a bat or a hat or even a gnat. For reasons beyond the power of a mere writer to explain, we take pleasure in the differences between words, finding satisfaction in creating or hearing variety in language. This quality seems to be built into the human mind. Not only do we seek variety in our words, but we look for it in sentences, both in their structure and their length. We do not want all sentences to be alike. We don't want them the same length; we don't want them the same structure.

Good writers aim at clarity, but they aim at more than clarity: They try to give pleasure. Part of that pleasure comes from constructing sentences of different lengths that fit together "naturally." At least we think such sentences are natural when we read or hear them; we absorb them with ease and sometimes with delight. All this is to say that a steady progression of short, clear sentences might convey the writer's meaning but crush readers with boredom because such sentences do not satisfy the craving of the mind for variety in language. Somehow as writers we must find the golden mean between a clarity that sounds childish and a complexity that is beyond comprehension.

Concluding Remarks on Sentences

When you read something you enjoy, study the sentences. Look at the structure as well as the words. Try to incorporate into your own writing some of the stylistic devices you see in things you like to read. Remember that the main job of the sentence is to make a comprehensible statement. You can write foggy sentences in your first draft; let the light shine in your later drafts. Ask yourself this question: What is the most important thing I have to say in this sentence? Be sure you answer that question clearly in one statement. That statement should form the core of the sentence.

Seven

Avoiding Wordiness

*M*odern writing is efficient. Good writers use only enough words to express the meaning they wish to convey. Readers do not have time for wordiness; besides, wordiness confuses them. Long, convoluted sentences, senseless repetition, tortuous dependent clauses and phrases all work together to make readers despair. Despairing readers can be cruel. Writing about a biography of the Southern writer James Branch Cabell, a reviewer in *The New York Times* condemns the "stodgy, stilted prose that reeks of the classroom" and quotes an example: "The appearance of the new novel was anticipated by reviewers nationwide, owing to its predecessor's continued suppression. The extent and depth of its critical notice in the press was exceptional."[1]

Brevity does not mean mindless simplicity. You must use enough words to say what you want. If you do not give readers enough information, they cannot understand what you write. Nor does brevity mean that you write without drama, richness, and variety. It does mean that you cut every word that does not add essential information or create the effect you want. As you write and revise, rethink your purposes. Make your style conform to those purposes. Achieve them as efficiently as possible.

Not long ago I faced the task of cutting a 2000-page book manuscript down to a publishable 1100 pages. After ruthlessly slashing away chunks of my prose, I came down to 1400 pages. Then I played a game with the rest. I looked at every sentence, seeing how I could trim a word here, a word there, a phrase or a clause. How could I say what I wanted to say and yet be more economical? Did I truly need this paragraph? This page? I suppose the book that came out of all this labor is still too big: It printed out at 622 pages. But people read it and write me about it, and every letter makes me realize that the toil was worth the pain. When you revise, play the same game. Cut the fat. Make every sentence as lean as you can. When you develop the habit of revising, you will review sentences like this one, typical of a first draft:

> It may be concluded from his many angry interviews with representatives of the media that Red Sox pitching ace young Roger Clemens showed himself to be an unhappy millionaire.

You can turn the sentence into something like this:

> In angry interviews, Red Sox pitcher Roger Clemens showed he was an unhappy millionaire.

You don't have to say, "It may be concluded." Nor do you have to say that the angry interviews were with representatives of the media. Most baseball pitchers are young; we shouldn't state the obvious. Think through your sentences. Avoid the temptation to provide needless information ("young") or use clumsy phrases ("It may be concluded that . . ."). Simplify. Turn clauses into phrases when you can, especially clauses beginning with *who, whom, which,* and *that.* Sometimes you can turn a clause into an adjective. Don't say this: "The pharaoh who ruled Egypt at the time of the exodus was almost certainly Ramses II." Say this instead: "The Egyptian pharaoh at the time of the exodus was almost certainly Ramses II." The passive voice creates wordiness. Don't say, "It must be recognized . . ." Say instead, "We must recognize . . ." Don't say, "It is not to be thought . . ." Say, "We should not think . . ." Don't say, "The car was repaired by my neighbor." Say, "My neighbor repaired the car." Don't say, "You will be reminded by this letter that your bill is three months overdue." Say, "Your bill is three months overdue." Be natural. People who strain for effects may become wordy.

We find an unnatural style in many institutional publications. Professor Richard Lanham of U.C.L.A. calls this wordy jargon "the official style." It seems to be everywhere. The main problem of the official style is that its authors have contradictory motives. They want to communicate, but they want to seem impressive, too. Here is an example taken from a university job listing:

> Network Engineer. Office for Information Technology. Responsible for the planning, design, and implementation of communications networks carrying data, video and voice signals throughout the university. Evaluates the relative technical merits of alternative technologies and design approaches. Prepares initial system specifications and designs for proposed networks or subnetworks.

The author of this document intended to avoid ambiguity about the job. Unfortunately, the consequence is the "official style." Note words like *implementation* and *alternative* and nouns like *information* and *design* used as adjectives. Professional writers don't *implement* things; they *do* them. They don't talk about *alternative* technologies; they speak of *various* technologies or simply technologies, assuming that the plural form of the noun includes variety. Neither do they use *relative* unless they are talking about kin. Could the listing be translated into something like this?

> Network engineer wanted to design and install communications lines throughout the university. Should know modern technology and design.

We may eliminate the last line. Must a network engineer be told that she should be qualified to design and install various systems of communication? Such abilities should go with the profession. We would not think of advertising for a dentist by saying that he should be able to fill various kinds of teeth. But suppose we keep all the elaborate qualifications of the original. We could still write a simpler, less wordy announcement.

> Network engineer. Responsible for designing and installing communications networks for data, video, and voice signals throughout the university. Evaluates the merits of various technologies and designs. Prepares specifications for systems and designs for networks.

The official style arises from fear. Writers are afraid someone may blame them for something. Or they fear that readers will not take them seriously. So they become like trapeze artists afraid of falling and thinking only of their feet.

Many writers may fear that what they have to say is not worth saying but that if they put it in complicated language, others may think it profound. Here are a few sentences from a carefully researched article in a recent *American Sociological Review,* a professional journal aimed at sociologists. The authors investigated the "streaking" craze rampant on college campuses in the early 1970s. Students ran naked through the streets and sometimes across football fields during games. Why did people "streak"? The question could be of general interest, and the article is an intelligent work by two intelligent men. But it is hard to imagine that many people could read prose written like this:

> The greater the complexity and heterogeneity of previous streaking events, the greater the probability that schools will adopt the fad. The innovation is more likely to be adopted when the complexity of the previous incidents of the fad in neighboring schools is greater. The complexity of streaking incidents is a stimulus for potential adopters. For example, if many males and females, students and non-students, streaked repeatedly day and night, on and off campus, then many categories of persons in other nearby schools could identify with the faddish behavior. As a result, the events are no longer performed by the rowdy but become acceptable to many potential adopters.[2]

I don't think an ordinary reader can easily understand this text. After reading the whole article—a task somewhat akin to walking barefoot on briers—I believe the paragraph means something like this:

> The more people streaked, the more others were likely to streak—especially if streaking incidents were elaborate and highly publicized. If multitudes of students and nonstudents streaked day and night at a given school, the behavior would not be limited to the rowdy; many different kinds of students would streak in a neighboring school.

Why do the authors of articles in this journal write like this? The question deserves thoughtful reflection. The *New England Journal of Medicine* treats complicated medical issues in readable prose; so does *Scientific American*. Why must the *American Sociological Review* be unreadable? A major reason is that the journal itself (like streaking) feeds on habits created by the discipline. Several graduate students in sociology have told me they must write like this to be respected in the field. One can riffle through the pages of any copy of the journal and find articles written in this well-nigh incomprehensible jargon. Any budding sociologist may be forgiven if she supposes that she must make her writing as turgid as possible before it will be accepted by the editors of the review.

Such a style is a mark of fear. Fearful writers try to avoid any hint of ambiguity—an almost impossible burden for prose to bear. No writing except the thickest legal prose is entirely without ambiguity. Take this sentence as an example: "The greater the complexity and heterogeneity of previous streaking events, the greater the probability that schools will adopt the fad." Why both "complexity" and "heterogeneity"? Evidently the authors feared that we might suppose that complex events were not heterogeneous events. Some process like this must have gone on in their minds: "If we say, 'the more people streak, the more others are likely to streak,' we might not convey our feeling that the more *diverse* people streak, the more others are likely to follow their example." Taking this fear of misunderstanding into account, they spell out some of the diversity—males and females, students and nonstudents, streaking on and off campus. Later they speak of "many categories of persons" because they seem to think that if they said "many people," we might not understand that they meant many *different* people. The authorial mind at work here is like a lawyer's, resolved to write a will that no one can break. The authors do not trust their readers. In seeking to avoid every ambiguity, they write prose that is a misery to read.

Perhaps, too, they feel insecure about their own discipline. Sociologists yearn to be considered as "scientific" as physicists or mathematicians, and they suppose that no true scientist writes clearly. They believe that pedantic language indicates profound thought. As a consequence, their audience is limited to members of a closed circle of sociologists, all of whom are writing to impress one another and not trying to reach a more general audience. The discipline of sociology might seem to betray in such prose a gnawing lack of self-confidence, and that is a loss to those of us who might find their scholarship interesting and influential—as, for example, the great sociological work of David Riesman, Nathan Glazer, and Ruel Denney proved to be in *The Lonely Crowd* and Norbert Elias in *Power and Civility.*

Remember that good writing arises out of confidence. If you are confident that you have something to say, you can say it simply. Or at least you can say it as simply as possible given your purposes. If you study an issue, think about it, and resolve to make sense of your ideas by writing about them, you can be confident in yourself and your readers. Confidence helps build a sound style—one that uses no more words than necessary, one that uses the simplest words possible to express the meaning intended.

No one idea about brevity suits everyone, and no easy shortcuts create a brief style. You can pick up the habit of brevity only if you go over your drafts again and again. Read everything you write two or three times before you let it go. Read slowly but steadily. Give yourself time enough to think through every sentence, every word. Cut out vague words, verbose phrases, unnecessary modifiers. Combine sentences when you can, unless the combination makes a long and clumsy sentence.

Examine stock phrases to see if you can shorten them. Stock phrases can often be eliminated. In a first draft, you might write this:

> In the final analysis, the Japanese victory at Pearl Harbor may be regarded as a disaster for Japan.

Here are the stock phrases in the above: *In the final analysis* and *may be regarded as.* You can eliminate both.

> The Japanese victory at Pearl Harbor was a disaster for Japan.

You might write this in a first draft:

> What was most important was Hamlet's decision to accept his fate.

In a revision, this might become:

> Most important was Hamlet's decision to accept his fate.

Don't be afraid to be wordy in your first draft, when you are forming your thoughts. But afterward, slash and burn. Cut out the unnecessary.

Common Problems

No chapter in a small book can solve all the problems of wordiness. But here I will address a few common problems. As you study them, you may become sensitive to your own style. Cutting the fat out of prose is a habit—like bodily exercise. Cultivate the habit; let it control your writing. Nobody is going to hang you if you use one of the expressions I have listed below, and many of them spring to the fingers of most of us sometimes when we write. Now and then you can indulge yourself in a "perfectly good word" or a "final analysis." But prose fat with redundancies and wordiness becomes difficult or vaguely unpleasant for readers. The writer's job is to make the reader's task as easy as possible. (The writer's job may also be to make readers as uncomfortable as possible when thinking about the issue being addressed, but that's another matter.)

When you eliminate or abbreviate writing, you must sometimes rearrange the whole sentence. You cannot always be content merely to cut out an unnecessary word or two. Study the following examples.

Area/Region

Don't say, "The weather in the area of the southwest is hot and dry." Say this: "The weather in the southwest is hot and dry."

Aspect

Don't say, "Another aspect of the problem that should be considered is the feasibility of the project." Say this: "We should consider whether the project can be done."

At the present time/At this point in time/At that point in time

Cut these expressions. Use *now* or *then* instead, or let the present or past tense give the time you want.

Case/Cases

Try to cut these words. Don't say, "In this case we see Faulkner's use of an old woman as oracle." Say this instead: "Faulkner here uses an old woman as oracle." Don't say, "In some cases exercise can kill." Say this: "Sometimes exercise kills people."

Certainly/Assuredly/Surely/Obviously

Try to cut these words. Paradoxically enough, we use them only when we realize that a statement may not be obvious or certain to someone else. Someone may write this: "He refused to let the police enter his house without a search warrant; obviously he had something to hide." The writer cannot prove that the person had something to hide; the writer tags an inference with the word *obviously*. But it is not obvious at all.

Character/Manner/Nature/Color/Stature

Try to cut these words. Don't say, "Their love affair was of a complex nature." Say instead, "Their love affair was complex." Don't say, "Mr. Dawson had an ingratiating manner." Say this instead: "Mr. Dawson was ingratiating."

Close proximity

Use *near* instead. Don't say, "The barn was in close proximity to the house." Say, "The barn was near the house."

Completely destroyed/Totally demolished

If something is destroyed, it is destroyed. If it is not completely destroyed, it is damaged. *Demolish* has an even stronger connotation than *destroyed;* so to say something is "totally demolished" is to commit linguistic overkill.

Consensus of opinion

The word *consensus* implies opinion. Don't say, "The consensus of opinion in the group was that boxing was barbaric." Say this instead: "The consensus in the group was that boxing is barbaric."

Considering the fact that

Use *although* or *because* instead. Don't say, "Considering the fact that she had been sick, she ran the marathon in good time." Say this instead: "Although she had been sick, she ran the marathon in good time."

Different

Often used unnecessarily. Don't write, "He had taught in seven different states and knew five different languages with two different methods." No one could imagine that the states, the languages, and the methods were *not* different, so you do not need to use the word.

Doubled phrases

English has a special liking for doubled phrases such as *null and void, cease and desist,* and *advise and consent.* They come from the English legal tradition, and they sound like judges making their opinions stern but unremarkable. In ordinary writing, such doubling is usually unnecessary. Don't say "pick and choose." Say "choose" instead. Don't say "each and every one." Say "each." Don't say "first and foremost." Say either "first" or "foremost" or, if you want to praise someone, do it without clichés. Don't say, "For all intents and purposes, the Red Sox were out of the pennant race by May 1." Say, "The Red Sox folded in April this year."

Due to the fact that

Replace with *because.*

Each individual

Don't use these two as adjectives to modify a noun. Don't say, "Each individual member of the team has her own talents." Say, "Each member of the team has her own talents."

End result
Say "result" instead.

Final outcome
Eliminate *final*.

Free gift
Eliminate *free*. If we pay for a gift, it is not a gift.

Full and complete
This is a doubled phrase. Say "full" or "complete" but not both.

Future plans
Plans are always for the future. When you talk about "future plans," you sound like a flight attendant. Don't say, "If your future plans call for travel to Knoxville, we hope you'll choose Delta Airlines." Say, "If you come to Knoxville again, we hope you'll choose Delta Airlines."

If and when
This is a doubled phrase. Use either *if* or *when,* but not both.

In a sense
Often unnecessary. "In a sense, you could say he died of alcoholism." In what sense? Spell out your meaning. "He died of a heart attack brought on by heavy drinking."

Incumbent
In the "official style," many people write this: "It is incumbent upon us to write more readable memos." Most of the time I don't think they know exactly what the word *incumbent* means. It's much better to say this: "We must write more readable memos."

In effect
Usually omit.

In other words
This is a stutter in writing. Omit it.

Instrumental
This is often wordy. Don't say, "She was instrumental in establishing the poetry group." Say instead, "She helped form the poetry group."

Intensifiers
In informal speech we often intensify the effect of some adjectives by tacking on an intensifying adverb, usually spoken emphatically. "She was

really intelligent." These intensifiers clog up writing, and you should usually omit them. Now and then you may find a use for them—but only now and then. Your prose will be leaner if you shun *absolutely, basically, certainly, definitely, fabulously, incredibly, immensely, intensely, perfectly, positively, utterly, really, quite, rather, simply,* and *very*.

Really may be useful when you respond to a negative idea by making an affirmative statement. "The Red Sox *really* have a chance this year." This *really* responds emphatically to the commonsense assumption that the Red Sox never have a chance in any year, and it is acceptable in informal writing, though, as in this sentence, *really* often expresses more of a yearning than any realistic possibility.

In terms of

This is almost always wordy. Don't say, "Antigua, in terms of weather, was dry." Say instead, "Antigua is dry."

In the event that

Replace with *if.*

In the final analysis

Either say "finally" or make your final point without announcing that it is final. Your readers can see that for themselves.

In the realm of

Omit or use a shorter word. Don't say, "It is in the realm of possibility that he may come." Say instead, "He may come."

In a position to

Say "can" instead. Don't say, "She is in a position to help him." Say, "She can help him."

It is possible that

Say "can" or "may" instead. Don't say, "It is possible that some cholesterol is good for us." Say, "Some cholesterol may be good for us."

Located

This is a common word in *journalese*—the language of unthinking reporters. Don't say, "The house was located at 35 Oak Street." Say, "The house was at 35 Oak Street."

Observable fact

Usually omit. People who use this locution want to impress us with their powers of perception. They know that we can observe some facts and that we can't observe others. But we don't need to be told such a thing;

we know it already. Get to the point. Don't say, "It is an observable fact that people read magazines faster than they read their income tax returns." Say, "People read magazines faster than they read their income tax returns."

One of the things that

Usually omit. Don't say, "One of the things you need to do is practice revision." Say this: "Revise your work."

On the occasion of

Usually cumbersome. Don't say this: "On the occasion of her coming, we shall all proceed into the open to offer our greetings." Say this instead: "We will all go out to meet her when she comes."

Owing to

Use *because* instead. Don't say, "Coach Dixie was unable to win the Southeastern Conference football championship owing to the fact that boosters could not buy him enough good players." Say, "Coach Dixie was unable to win the Southeastern Conference football championship because boosters could not buy him enough good players."

Period of time

Don't use both *period* and *time* in the same phrase. Say either, "at that time" or "in that period."

Positive effects

This is usually pompous and vague. Don't say, "The rehabilitation program has had some positive effects." Say this: "The rehabilitation program has done some good."

Prior to

Replace with *before*. Don't say, "Prior to the game we had a picnic." Say, "Before the game we had a picnic."

Prove conclusively

Something is either proved or not proved. Omit *conclusively*. (See *Different* above.) The principle is similar. Do not use words to express supposedly subtle distinctions that actually no person of ordinary intelligence would miss.

Situation

A good word that often leads to wordiness and confusion. A bright Boston sportswriter once produced this almost incomprehensible sentence:

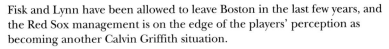

> Fisk and Lynn have been allowed to leave Boston in the last few years, and the Red Sox management is on the edge of the players' perception as becoming another Calvin Griffith situation.

He meant something like this:

> The Red Sox lost catcher Carlton Fisk and outfielder Fred Lynn because the owners would not pay them enough. The remaining players are on the verge of seeing the Red Sox as the Boston version of the Minnesota Twins, where owner Calvin Griffith gladly sells off good players rather than pay them high salaries.

I have lengthened this version for readers who are not baseball fans. For fans, the writer could have said this:

> The Red Sox lost Fisk and Lynn, and the remaining players are beginning to think that Boston's management is as stingy and unconcerned with winning as is Calvin Griffith.

Situation is a killer word. It is so vague that both writers and readers lose track of what it means.

Take into account

Use *consider* instead. Don't say, "We must take the weather into account when we make our plans." Say this instead: "We must consider the weather in our plans."

The question of whether

This is common padding phrase. You can trim it. Don't say, "We must consider the question of whether subways are efficient means of mass transport." Say this instead: "We must ask if subways are efficient means of mass transport."

To some extent

This is often redundant. Don't say, "To some extent, living in the suburbs has some advantages." Say, "Living in the suburbs has some advantages."

Veritable

This is almost always unnecessary and a little pompous. Don't say, "Charles was a veritable wonder." Say, "Charles was a wonder."

Voiced the opinion
Use *said.*

What was/What is

This is usually a wordy construction when it is used as the start of a dependent clause.

> What was essential for Russia was peace.
> What he wanted in life was not clear.

You can shorten by revising away the *what*.

> Peace was essential for Russia.
> His purpose in life was not clear.

With a view toward

Revise to eliminate. Don't say, "She bought the boat with a view toward fishing." Say, "She bought the boat so she could fish."

With regard to

Revise to eliminate. Don't say, "With regard to letter writing, she was slow." Say this instead: "She was slow to write letters."

These recommendations do not exhaust all of the possibilities for making your style more economical. But studying constructions like these will teach you how to trim and revise your work to make it more readable.

Eight

Good Diction

*D*iction is the choice of words we make when we write or speak. Good diction helps intelligent readers understand us, respect us, and believe us. Words are mysterious, puzzling, beautiful things, and although we use them every day, we never quite master them. They have histories, connotations, shades of meaning, associations with a long tradition of writing and speaking. If we call somebody an *opponent*, we mean one thing; if we call her an *enemy*, we mean another. If we say a man is *charming*, we usually mean to compliment him; if we say he is *smooth*, we imply a slight insult; if we call him *oily*, we mean a stronger insult, and perhaps we mean to warn off people who may meet him.

Finding the right word is one of the joys of language, defining our experience to ourselves, helping to convey it to others. Mark Twain said that the difference between the right word and the wrong word was the difference between lightning and a lightning bug. What word best describes the sun? Hot? Incandescent? Vengeful? Mild? Weak? Benign? Pale? White? Red? Each one of those words conveys a slightly different impression, useful under different circumstances.

English may be the most marvelously varied language. People sometimes ask me what one book I would take to a desert island. I always respond, "a good dictionary." No other book offers so many outlets to human sensibility or makes us better aware of the seemingly infinite shadings of human experience. At times we may feel a somewhat vague but powerful sensibility built up inside us like a reservoir of water, but how do we tap it and make it more specific? Finding the right word may help us discover a quality of meaning that is new to us, one that the word will make vivid to our readers. We look at a face; it inspires feelings within us, but how do we express those feelings? When we find the right word to express them, we understand the feelings better; the word may help us define our own attitude.

Principles of Good Diction

Words are always used with other words; they take meaning from one another. Because English is so gloriously flexible, diction has no rules, only principles. These principles are firm enough to enumerate; careful writers observe them and use them to interpret specific choices in language. As you review the following list, you will see that the various items overlap. I mentioned some of them earlier in this book.

1. Use words efficiently.

We should not pad our thought or inflate our utterances in an effort to be impressive. Some speak of *preplanning* because they think that word is more impressive than *planning*. Almost every bureaucrat nowadays speaks of *preconditions* for agreement when *conditions* would do as well. The use of *prior to* instead of *before* seems to have become a linguistic virus, calling forth awkward sentences such as the following: "Prior to the implementation of the recently recommended policies by your office, certain preconditions require to be satisfied." Such writers find it almost insulting if someone suggests that this highfalutin language be reduced to this: "Before we do what you ask, we [or you] need to meet certain conditions."

Many writers seem to struggle to make their sentences verbose and incomprehensible. Here is a medical example sent to me by a reader who is a doctor:

> The cancer burden and its financial ramifications have escalated to enormous proportions on the community level. Early diagnosis with open communication to the patient and cost containment are dominant in the perspective of community medicine.

By deciphering the article in which these sentences appear, I think they mean this:

> The personal and financial burden of cancer represents a crisis to community hospitals. They must contain costs while they seek early diagnosis of the disease and try to communicate frankly with patients.

The most efficient language is simple and natural. It creates its effects by the information it conveys and by the grace of the writing rather than by a pretense of erudition.

2. Use words in keeping with the written traditions of English.

Avoid words that might lead educated readers to suppose that you are ignorant of the traditions of the written language. Writing once enjoyed a supreme authority that carried over easily from handwritten copies of books to the revolution created by printing. What could be printed was severely restricted in all countries until very recently. Even in the United

States, with its constitutional freedoms, editors and censors regulated printing, giving an aura of almost holiness to the written language, reining it up before the limits of the unprintable.

Just about anything is printable now; "acceptable usage" is much broader than it once was because we hear words on radio and television and in the movies that once would have been considered inappropriate in polite society, and many writers use those words freely in their work. The speech patterns of talk-show hosts and guests and television commentators of various sorts have inserted themselves into written English. At times, this results in a loss of clarity. The television commentator can use tone of voice and even body language to convey meanings not conveyed by his or her atrocious vocabulary or garbled syntax. Students exposed to such language from their youth often fail to see that the written language must stand by itself, without a commentator to whisper the true meaning into the ear of the reader.

Standards for written English are probably more informal than they have been since the end of the seventeenth century. Even so, some words are still considered ignorant by many readers. *Irregardless* is one. *Regardless* is the accepted word. *Irregardless* is a double negative in a single word, for both the prefix *ir-* and the suffix *-less* convey negation. You will never find the word in a published essay unless it occurs in a direct quotation. Despite its popularity with high school and college students, *funner* is still not an acceptable synonym for *more fun.* And although many people now say, "Myself and Cleo are giving a party Saturday night," writers who wish to be taken seriously must say, "Cleo and I are giving a party."

Nor will you find the word *ain't* in normal literate discourse, although it occurs in quotations because all sorts of people use it in speech. For some reason, *ain't*—a cockney English word that originated in the eighteenth century—never caught on. Educated people consider it illiterate—perhaps because of its social origins. The cockneys were lower-class. Perhaps it should have made the grade, for we do not have a contraction for *I am not* or *am I not.* It would seem efficient to write, "I ain't" or "ain't I"? But we do not.

3. Avoid fads in usage that impoverish the language.

Fads in language come and go with mysterious speed, almost like epidemics. Someone calls a financial consequence "the bottom line," and suddenly millions are using the "bottom line" as a synonym for the most important consequence in any action or condition. "The bottom line of our love affair is trust." At the Watergate hearings, televised for the world in 1973, one witness after another stalled for time by saying—usually with great deliberation—"At that point in time," and suddenly *time* ceased to stand by itself. It had to have a *point* attached.

Commentator Edwin Newman has pointed out the sudden proliferation of -*ize* tacked on the end of nouns to make them verbs. He says, "The -*ize* have it," and so they do. People now "verbalize" instead of talk; they "concertize" instead of give concerts. A newspaper I saw some time ago urged readers to "accessorize your garden." When the radiators went dead in my office a few winters ago, dropping the temperature to just above freezing, a technician came in, felt the chill, knocked on some pipes, and left, telling me his crew would certainly "priortize" my office. I wanted him instead to thermalize it, before the cold finalized my health and traumatized my fingers and face.

We have many acceptable -*ize* words in English. I think it's fine to *summarize,* and I don't complain when people *utilize* things, although I have never thought that *utilize* says much that *use* does not. *Victimize* seems to be solidly lodged in our vocabulary now, and it's all right to be *scandalized* or to *theorize* or *fraternize.*

Still, we need to curb the promiscuous -*ize* lest we turn English into some species of pig Latin, where every word ends with the same sound. To use faddish new forms where perfectly acceptable forms already exist in the language betokens a poverty of mind. Experienced readers recognize the poverty when they see it and can seldom be persuaded to spend their time on writing that exhibits it.

4. Use language idiomatically.

Idiom is an unfamiliar word to most students. Yet it is as important as any word applied to English usage. It refers to habitual usages in language that have no clear logic. No language is entirely rational, and English seems more irrational than most. Its irrationality is perhaps a sign of the vitality of the people who use it, people who refuse to be squeezed into the bondage of excessive rules. Idioms are language at its most irrational. Foreign speakers learning English have trouble with idioms—and English speakers have similar troubles when they learn foreign languages. When someone says, "Why is such an expression wrong?" our only answer is, "That's not the way we speak English."

For example, to speak and write idiomatically, we have to know how prepositions are used. We recognize that if we make *up* with someone, we become reconciled. But to make *out* with that person implies something else, and to make *off* with something indicates some sort of dishonest flight. To pass *out* means one thing, to pass *off* means another, and to pass *on* means something else still.

We are more likely to encounter ill-used idioms in less obvious contexts. For some reason we do not guess *on* the answer, we guess *at* the answer—though logic tells us that we might merely *guess* the answer. Habit makes us speculate *on* the outcome of next week's game rather than speculate *in* it, though bankers speculate *in* stocks and bonds. We may say that the game is *up* and mean that someone has been found out, but when we say the game is *over* we mean only that the contest has ended.

Not all idioms involve prepositions. When we say that a carpenter *cut corners* on the job, we mean that his work was shoddy rather than that he used a saw on the wood. When we say that the speaker *took the floor,* we do not mean that she ran off with it and used it in her house. And I can *twist your arm* to get you to eat dinner with me and yet never touch you. We both may be *up in arms* because of the poor food without ever having drawn our swords on the servers. And even a bald boss can *let down his hair* at the office party.

Idioms change. In nineteenth-century prose, the idiom *to make love* meant to propose marriage, and Anthony Trollope in his hilarious novel *Barchester Towers* has the odious and slightly intoxicated Obadiah Slope "make love" to beautiful Eleanor Bold in a carriage. Both the gentle Trollope and his Victorian peers in England would have been outraged by modern confusions among students reading his work.

Idiom involves a subtle feel for language, a sense of what is appropriate to the context and the purpose. A student of mine writing a few years ago on the battles of Lexington and Concord in 1775 announced that the patriots gathered on hilltops and *affronted* the British as they came by. I had a vision of lines of patriots mooning the British troops and of puritanical British officers saying, "Don't pay any attention to them, men! What can you expect from these Americans!"

5. Accept change conservatively.

From what I have said so far and from your own experience, you know that language is always changing. Now it seems to be changing more rapidly than ever before.

New words come into English with amazing frequency. Some innovations show vitality. One of my favorite books is entitled *9,000 Words: A Supplement to Webster's Third New International Dictionary*—a collection of words introduced to English within the past fifteen years. In it I find modern coinages such as *software, dunk shot, monokini, printout,* and *life-support system,* all of them signs of the nearly miraculous talent human beings have for finding names to describe and control experience. (Only a few years ago, the ancestor to that book was called *6,000 Words.*)

I like some new words in appropriate contexts. When a baseball writer tells me that a shortstop is *showboating,* I find the word stronger than the older term *showing off. Ditsy* describes some of my students who seem too happy with the world to pay much attention to their work or much of anything else that requires prolonged concentration. I don't think I would like to read that John Paul Jones was one of the great *hot dogs* of the American Revolution or that Mussolini was one of the most *ditsy* politicians of the twentieth century. But I don't mind reading a lighthearted sports story that tells me that a former pitcher for the St. Louis Cardinals was a *hot dog* or that an outfielder for the Boston Red Sox was *ditsy.* Some new words fit into formal contexts; some do not.

In the summer of 1993, *Time* reported that some Bible merchants were selling scripture written in black "street language." In the *Black Bible Chronicles,* the Serpent in Genesis tempts Eve to eat the fruit God has forbidden to her and Adam, and Eve replies, "Yeah, snake, I can eat of these trees, just not the tree of knowledge or the Almighty said I'd be knocked off." The Serpent replies, "Nah, sister, he's feeding you a line of bull. You won't die. The Almighty just knows that if you eat from the tree you'll be hipped to what's going down."[1] I have the feeling that this Bible will not catch on.

Not only do new words continually flow into the language, but old words change their meaning. In Shakespeare's day the word *shrewd* meant "wicked," not "clever" as it means today. *Courage* could mean "male sexual prowess," and a *queen* could be a prostitute. In my own boyhood on a farm in mountainous east Tennessee, people still used *prevent* to mean "go before" or "announce," just as the word is used in the King James Version of the Bible, where the psalmist tells us, "I prevented the dawning of the morning."

Some good words mysteriously pass out of the language altogether. When the English in the sixteenth century spoke of whispering, they used the word *rouning.* I like the word. It catches the low murmuring of some whispering, especially the kind that occurs in a crowd of people who do not so much whisper as grumble. But the word is gone. Our parents or grandparents talked about *swells* who put on a great show of wealth. From it they derived the adjective *swell* and spoke of having a *swell* time at a party, meaning "a time befitting the rich." The word is all but gone now. Other words, like *spiffy, zany, snazzy,* and *gosh,* are similarly in oblivion.

Now English usage is changing so swiftly that moderate conservatives like me want to slow it down a little. Our language is a currency of meaning; currencies work best when their values remain fairly constant. If too many words mean one thing today and another tomorrow, communication between generations breaks down. It is a great gift that an adolescent can enjoy Jonathan Swift's *Gulliver's Travels,* written over two centuries ago, and that the novels of Charles Dickens still live for readers more than a hundred years after Dickens died. American democracy rests on a constitution written generations ago that still makes sense to us.

In the novel *1984,* George Orwell invented the word *newspeak* to stand for the terrifying loss of the common meanings of words. Tyrants in this century have used a perverted language to subjugate their people. The former Soviet Union established satellite states called "people's democracies." But in these "democracies," the people dared not dissent from government edicts and no election was honest. When the Soviet Union collapsed and these false "democracies" were overthrown, people rushed into the streets singing and rejoicing.

A perverted language leads to cynicism and mistrust. In the United States, something called "national security" has enabled our own government to invade the privacy of its citizens, burgle their houses and offices, tap their telephone, limit their freedom of speech, and threaten them for having unpopular opinions.

Yet the conservative critics of language often express themselves foolishly. In my introduction to this book, I referred to the critic John Simon, who uttered these sentiments, apparently with a straight face:

> Why does language keep changing? Because it is a living thing, people will tell you. Something that you cannot press forever, like a dead flower, between the pages of a dictionary. Rather, it is a living organism that, like a live plant, sprouts new leaves and flowers. Alas, this lovely albeit trite image is—as I have said before and wish now to say with even greater emphasis—largely nonsense. Language, for the most part, changes out of ignorance.[2]

Simon is a priest in the self-constituted church of linguistic puritans who live in terror lest anyone appear to be enjoying language without obeying all the rules. But usage is king; English is, finally, what people speaking and writing it understand it to be. The language is no more in decay now than it was in Shakespeare's time, or even in the time of *Beowulf;* it is only changing. Ambrose Bierce, early in this century, defined *laundry* as "a place where clothing is washed." He added, "This word cannot mean, also, clothing sent there to be washed."[3] Richard Grant White, the Edwin Newman of his day, published *Words and Their Uses* in 1870 in the general conviction that English was going to the dogs. He disliked the word *editorial* for the essay editors wrote expressing their opinions in newspapers. He condemned the use of *execute* as a verb meaning "to put to death." He thought *ice water* and *ice cream* should be *iced water* and *iced cream.*[4] (I once had a friend who corrected me for ordering "ice tea" in a restaurant. "It's *'iced tea,'"* he said.) Not long ago, the only definition standard college dictionaries gave for the word *sweater* was "one who sweats."

Many purists become angry at usages of which they disapprove. With respect to the word *hopefully,* used as a synonym for "I hope" or "it is hoped," poet Phyllis McGinley is quoted as saying, "'Hopefully' so used is an abomination and its adherents should be lynched."[5] The linguistic puritans see language as the property of the educated, and a territorial imperative impels them to fight off invaders. Language to them is a measure of status, and it is hard to escape the feeling that they assault the common language of others as a means to exalt themselves.

Yet while I deplore the bad temper and nonsense of these puritans, I sympathize with their intuitions. Language should not be sterile, but it should be stable—not only because a stable language allows us to communicate across space in the present but also for the reason that I have already mentioned: A reasonably stable language allows us to communicate across generations and provides a tradition that, in a fine phrase by Saul Bellow, allows the living to break bread with the dead.

I find it also cogent to measure usage by the practice of good writers.

Ah, but who are the good writers? That, of course, is a matter of taste. I have my own canon of great writers, and I think most of them accept innovations carefully.

Some Lively Problems in Usage

In the following pages, I express some opinions about lively problems in usage. When readers looked at the first draft of this book, several commented with dismay that I was far too conservative and that the strictness of some of my definitions might make writing more difficult for the inexperienced. I am as aware as anyone that mine is the kind of list that a century from now may be ridiculed by as yet unborn readers who will see that many words that make me wince are by then completely accepted in the language. Usage commands, and at a certain point the most rabid purist must step aside. Usually nature herself intervenes, for purists die, and the language goes happily on without them. Even John Simon is mortal, though one would not think so from his divine tone of wrathful judge over the doom of English.

Since the first edition, I have changed my mind about some matters. For example, in the first edition I made a distinction between *ensure,* which means "to make sure," and *insure,* which means "to provide insurance." But I have noticed that *The New York Times* has folded the two meanings together into the word *insure,* and its headlines regularly speak of efforts to *insure* the peace or to insure lower prices or whatever. Earlier, I would have supposed that to "insure the peace," one would have to take out a policy so that if peace should be damaged or killed, someone would receive some sort of financial payment. But no, the *Times* means that someone is trying to make sure of peace. Who am I to stand against the august authority of *The New York Times?* I have dropped the distinction.

Yet my suggestions remain on the conservative side. Of course, many people will disagree with some of my readings. I freely admit that my commentary on usage—like all commentaries—reflects my own reading, experience, taste, and prejudices. I served on the usage panel for the third edition of the *American Heritage Dictionary*—a task I enjoyed despite its long questionnaires and demands for extended notes about my choices. I hope that I have read enough and thought enough about language to give my comments some authority, but no informed reader will agree with all of them. The *American Heritage Dictionary* provides percentages of the number of members of its panel who vote on controversial usages, and these votes are never unanimous. Even so, I believe that the majority of professional writers and editors share my views. Whether they will for long is another question.

Perhaps the greatest value of my list will be to make you check my views against what you read and your own. Look carefully at the prose in good magazines and popular nonfiction books to see how many times my rules are broken. This exercise will make you more conscious of language and more conscious of your own usage. To be aware that usage offers problems and requires choices is to start making the distinctions that make for good writing. It is also fun to study words closely, to see their origins, and to observe the connotations that hover about them. Every good writer I know loves to study words, to play with them, to compare their definitions in various dictionaries, and to see how other writers use them. We also love to learn new words or subtle meanings in old ones. If you are going to write well, you have to love words and take care of them. Perhaps the fallible list that follows will help you love words and their puzzles more.

All together/Altogether

If you say, "They gathered *all together* in one place," you mean that they were all present. If you say "They were *altogether* mad," you mean they were completely mad. The adverb *together* refers to some kind of collection; the adverb *altogether* refers to some kind of completeness.

Alot/A lot

This is a mysterious but common error. *Alot* is not a word, yet my students write *a lot* as one word time and time again as though it were *awhile*. Even the correct form, *a lot,* is usually too colloquial and too vague for my taste. It seems dull to say something like this: "Custer discovered that he had stirred up a lot of Indians." It's better to say, "Custer saw thousands of Indians riding down on him and realized he was in trouble."

Alright/All right

The spelling *alright* is not acceptable to most editors, although it turns up in thousands of student papers every year. Use two words: *all right.*

Alternative

Many purists say that we can use *alternative* only when we have but two choices in a matter. They reason that since the Latin word *alter* means "the other," implying only two, the derivative *alternative* can never be used when there are three or more choices. Common usage has long since buried this rigorous etymological logic, and we happily speak of three or four alternatives as we ponder a decision. But *at least* two choices must present themselves if *alternative* is to be used sensibly. If we say, "Our only alternative is to keep going," we are saying that there is *only one* choice, and that is no choice at all. If you say, "We can die; our only alternative is to keep going," then you are presenting two choices. You can also say, "Our only course is to keep going." That means what it says.

Amount/Number

The distinction between these words is similar to that between *less* and *fewer,* which you will encounter later in this list. You cannot divide an *amount* into units that you can count. You can count a *number* of things.

A large *number* of people applauded her performance. They left a large *amount* of litter on the floor.

Number has some idiomatic quirks. If we say, "the number of something," we use a singular verb.

The number of writers in any society *is* relatively small.

But if we say "a number of something," the verb is plural.

A number of his friends *were* arrested.

Anxious/Eager

The debate about this pair goes back at least a century. It seems better to use *anxious* to indicate fear or anxiety, *eager* to show pleasure in some expected occurrence.

I am *eager* to attend opening day in Fenway Park each April.
I am *anxious* to see if the Red Sox fold this year in May rather than in August.

Anymore/ Any more

The adverb *anymore* means *nowadays* and has traditionally been used only in negative constructions. You can say, "He doesn't smoke anymore," and everyone will understand that he once smoked but stopped and does not smoke now. Sometimes people say, "Anymore I drink tea rather than coffee." The positive construction of the verb confuses readers and hearers. On reflection, we can see that the speaker means she once drank coffee but now drinks tea. A negation is implied, but the implication confuses most people accustomed to the convention that *anymore* must follow a negative and come *after* the verb phrase. The more customary and clearer statement is this: "I don't drink coffee anymore; I drink tea instead."

Always make a distinction between *anymore* and *any more.*

I never see her *anymore.* [Adverb. I used to see her, but now I don't.]

I don't want to see *any more* friends today. [Adverb *any* + adjective *more.*]

Apt/Liable/Likely

To say that someone is *apt* is to remark on a skill, especially one that seems somewhat casual or general.

She is *apt* at good talk.

He is an *apt* student.

Strictly speaking, *liable* has a legal connotation, always unpleasant.

He was *liable* to be sued.

To say that someone is *likely* to do something is to remark that he or she will probably do something.

Roger Clemens will be interviewed tonight and will *likely* insult Red Sox fans again because they don't pay enough for his autographs.

As/Since

English writers commonly use these two words as synonyms. Charles Darwin did so in *The Origin of Species,* and Charles Dickens did the same in his novels. The American practice of differentiating between the two words seems preferable. *As,* used as a conjunction, connotates contemporary time, something happening while something else is happening. *Since* gives the sense of something happening *after* something else, quite often causing the later event.

These sentences do not confuse:

He waved at me *as* the boat pulled away from the dock.

Since her mother became ill, she seldom goes out of the house.

But a sentence like this one can be confusing:

As I commute to work by bicycle, the cuffs of my pants sometimes get blackened by oil.

Does commuting by bicycle *cause* my cuffs to be blackened by oil, or does the blackening happen mysteriously as I bike along?

Since conveys a stronger impression of causation than *as,* and the conjunction *because* conveys an even stronger impression.

Because I commute to work by bicycle, the cuffs of my pants sometimes get blackened by oil.

So my advice may seem somewhat perverse. If you wish to indicate causation, choose *since* over *as,* but choose *because* over both.

A while/Awhile

Awhile is an adverb used to modify verbs: "He stayed *awhile.* "

While is a noun expressing an unspecified but usually short period of time. It is often the subject of a preposition: "He stayed for *a while.* "

The sense of the two forms is so close that good writers often confuse them. The meaning given by most dictionaries for the adverb *while* is "for

❖

a while." Careful writers should make a distinction—if only to call attention to their care. It is an easy matter. When *while* follows a preposition—usually *in* or *for*—make two words: *a while;* when *while* is used with a verb and without an intervening preposition, use *awhile.*

Between/Among

The standard rule is that *between* should be used to speak of two things; *among* of more than two.

It was easy to make a distinction *between* the two words.
She moved gracefully *among* the guests in the room.

So far, so good. But the difference between the two words sometimes gets fuzzy. We don't speak of the infield on a baseball diamond as the space *among* the four bases, and we don't say that a treaty banning genocide was signed *among* most of the nations of the world. We say the treaty was made *between* the nations. If I am sitting with four friends at a table and wish to share a bit of gossip, I say, "Just between us, I think his best friends hate him." I somehow don't feel comfortable saying, "Just among us."

The best rule seems to be to let literate people follow their inclinations. We should not fear using *between* with more than two when the intent is to show some kind of active participation of every party following someone's lead—as in signing a treaty. We should not fear using *between* to refer to an enclosed space and its boundaries, no matter how numerous those boundaries are. Even these rules are not sufficient to cover all the ways we can use *between* when we speak of more than two.

But don't write *between you and I* or *between she and I* or *between he and she.* When I hear these constructions I wince. *Between* is a preposition here, and the objects of prepositions should be in the objective case. So you should say *between you and me* or *between her and me* or *between her and him.*

Avoid the phrase *between each,* as in this construction: "A wall was built between each of the rooms." *Each* is singular; *between* implies more than one. It does not make sense to say *between each* unless you add another parallel noun: "A wall was built between each room and the one adjacent to it."

Co-equals

This is a redundancy, like *irregardless.* Two captains in an army unit are not *co-*equal in authority; they are merely *equal.* But *co-* words are becoming common, probably in imitation of the word *copilot.* The problem is that we sometimes don't know whether *co-* signifies "equal to" or "assistant to." A copilot is an assistant to the pilot on an airplane. Some high school football teams have a captain and a *co-captain,* who, like a *copilot,* takes over when the captain is unable to function. Other teams have no captain at all and, instead, have co-captains, who are supposedly equal to one another. The *co-* scene is a mess, and I think it is better to abandon *co-* words, except when we speak of copilots. Fortunately, we don't have to speak of them very often.

Common/Mutual

Many writers, and even more speakers, have used these words as synonyms since at least the time of Shakespeare.

In 1658, the English writer George Starkey wrote of "our mutual friend," and in the nineteenth century, Charles Dickens wrote a novel called *Our Mutual Friend,* a title for which he has incurred the scorn of purists ever since. Yet people commonly speak of "mutual friends" today, although they are just as commonly silently condemned for doing so by many who hear them. Strictly speaking, we should use *mutual* to describe some reciprocal action, something going back and forth between two things or two persons. In *Measure for Measure,* Claudio comments wryly on "the stealth of our most mutual entertainment" that has made his lover, Julietta, pregnant. Sexual intercourse is indeed an example of the reciprocity implied in the more "correct" use of the word. People can also have mutual affection or mutual dislike for each other.

If they share something like an interest in photography, however, we should say, "They had a common interest in photography," or, simply, "They shared an interest in photography."

The term *mutual friend* has become so established in American and English habits of speech that it seems unfriendly to fight it; and no one will hang you if you say, "You and I have a mutual friend in Arkansas." Even so, I prefer, "You and I are both friends of Dee Post in Arkansas."

Comprise/Compose/Include

These three words often get mixed up. *Comprise* means "to embrace." So we say, "The Senate *comprises* 100 members." The 100 members do not *comprise* the Senate; they *compose* the Senate. They *include* lawyers, judges, farmers, business executives, and a fair number of people who will someday go to prison. You could not say the 100 members *embrace* the Senate. *Comprise* calls attention to all the parts. When you wish to call attention to only a few of the parts, use *include.*

Conditions

The high frequency with which this word is used may originate with TV meteorologists. They talk about "snowy conditions prevailing in Minnesota" or "stormy conditions over New England." They cannot bring themselves to say, "Snow is falling in Minnesota tonight" or "Thunderstorms are flooding Arizona." Now we have traffic "conditions," economic "conditions," and housing "conditions." When an Air Florida jet crashed during takeoff from Washington National Airport in 1982, one official was reported as saying, "Weather conditions are such that they are not conducive to rapid recovery." He apparently meant that it was too cold to recover bodies quickly from the icy Potomac River.

We should have snow, rain, weather, traffic, and housing; we should reserve *conditions* to mean "requirements." And here we should use *conditions,* not "preconditions." To speak of "preconditions" is like speaking of "hot heat" or "watery water."

Contact

Many writers object to the use of *contact* as a verb. Strunk and White, in their classic little book *The Elements of Style,* advise readers to telephone, write, or get in touch with someone but never to *contact* him. The objection sounds oddly genteel to me, a bit like the prohibition of the word *legs* in Victorian society even when speaking of the legs of a table. *Contact* means "touch," and to use *contact* as a verb probably seemed vulgar to some because it is more direct than *get in touch with.* But thoroughly respectable professional writers have been contacting people for decades, and few of us object if someone contacts us about next week's meeting—though we may object to the meeting itself. *Contact* means that some of us may be telephoned, others written to, and still others hailed on the street and invited to come.

Continuous/Continual

Something *continuous* goes on without interruption; something *continual* goes on at intervals.

The movement of blood through our bodies is *continuous* until death.

The Kennedy family in Massachusetts is a subject of *continual* interest.

Don't tell someone that you expect to be with him *continuously* unless you intend never to let him out of your sight.

Cope

People often use this word to give the impression that they are saying much more than they really are. If you *must* use the word, write "cope with" and follow the two words with some reasonable object.

Many Americans embrace conspiracy theories because they cannot *cope with* the reality that a murderous lunatic like Lee Harvey Oswald could have killed President Kennedy on a whim.

Cope conveys a vagueness that I don't like. If you must use it, be as specific as you can. To say "I can't cope" is to indicate some general debility, a frustration of some sort, but it does not locate the source of the frustration. It leaves readers and listeners, and perhaps the person using the word, in a state of general confusion. Usually the expression is so mild that the confusion is unimportant, especially in casual speech. But in writing, unimportant and confusing locutions are like mud on a bicycle chain. They provide an unnecessary drag on the motion of prose. Neither you nor your readers have the time or the energy for them.

Couldn't care less/Could care less

The original idiom, which had a certain force in my adolescence, was, "I couldn't care less." It seemed straightforward and emphatic. It meant that someone cared so little for a person or thing that he could not possibly feel *less* concerned. "I couldn't care less about Jackson" meant that Jackson was so insignificant that you could not have less feeling about him, no matter what he did.

Now the idiom has become convoluted into the nonsensical "I could care less." It seems to be everywhere, like the virus of the common cold. "I could care less about Jackson." If we take language seriously, this idiom means that the speaker does care something about Jackson. Perhaps she adores Jackson. Perhaps she hates him. Whatever her emotion, for some unspecified reason she *could* care less about him. We wonder what Jackson would have to do to provoke such a lowering of her esteem. With an idiom like "I could care less," language has become not communication but incantation.

The problem can be avoided by a simple, less hackneyed expression, direct and to the point: "I don't like Jackson." At best, even when used sensibly, "I couldn't care less about Jackson" has become a cliché, and we may as well bury it. Even so, the cliché that makes sense is better than the nonsensical phrase "I could care less."

Crafted/Handcrafted

These are advertising words with almost no meaning, part of the general dilution of language that advertising has brought about. They are, alas, in the language to stay, but if careful writers among us realize how empty they are, that recognition may clean up our language a bit. Supposedly *crafted* and *handcrafted* mean the same thing—that something has been made by hand using a combination of strength and skill and that the handwork guarantees that the object has a special quality. We often say that writing is a *craft,* meaning that writing is a manual activity—something we do skillfully with our hands, something we can improve by spending more time on it.

In fact, many crafted items these days are made by machine; and though a great many crafted or handcrafted items *are* made by hand, things made by hand can be good or bad. If you buy a handcrafted shirt, for example, you may be sure that the stitching was done on a sewing machine—probably by some sweat shop in Hong Kong. But even if the pieces of the shirt were cut out by a machine, somebody had to *operate* the machine, so advertising copy writers can still speak of "crafting." We could speak of the "crafting" of automobiles since so much of their manufacture is done by hand. But cars are probably more reliable if they are built by a robot. Robots don't have hangovers on Monday morning or rush to quit early on Friday afternoons.

Diametrically opposed

Here is another example of the inflation of good English into something puffy and formless. People who say they are "diametrically opposed" to something may imagine that they are on one side of a circle and their opponent is on the other, separated from each other at the widest point of the circle, its *diameter.* They are, in short, as opposed as they can possibly be. But I think the sense of the circle long ago passed out of the expression, leaving it with a meaningless emphasis for most people who use it. If you are opposed to something, just say so, and give your reasons. Once you begin to give reasons for your opposition—and when you consider your opponent's reasons—you may discover that the two of you are closer to agreement than you think.

Different from/Different than

Most writers use *different from* and consider *different than* to be bad diction, but the distinction seems to be fading. Most writers I know prefer to say, "His tastes in literature are *different from* mine. *Different than* is often used before a clause: "His tastes in literature are different *than* they used to be." I prefer *different from,* and most editors prefer this form. "His tastes in literature are different *from* what they used to be."

Dilemma

Properly speaking, a *dilemma* is a vexing problem that presents us with two equally unattractive alternatives and requires us to make a choice. Confirmed cigarette smokers face a dilemma: They can give up a habit that gives them much pleasure and suffer discomfort, prolonged nervousness, irritability, and perhaps a failure of concentration; or they can keep on smoking and die of lung cancer, if heart disease and emphysema do not kill them first, and while they smoke they will annoy most of their friends and many strangers.

Careless writers often use *dilemma* to indicate any serious problem, and the language is poorer in consequence. To ensure clarity, use *dilemma* only when speaking of the need to make a choice between painful alternatives; then tell what the contrary choices are. Don't use the word *dilemma* unless you tell us what the dilemma is—or was.

The Germans in 1914 faced a dilemma. They could refuse to support the Austro-Hungarian Empire in the Balkans and see their only ally in Europe progressively weakened by Russia and the south Slav peoples who hated the Austrians. Or they could support the Empire and risk a catastrophic war.

Disinterested/Uninterested

Perhaps we should retire *disinterested* from the language, substituting the word *impartial*. Much confusion might thereby be averted. Most of us take the disinterested person to have nothing to gain or lose no matter who wins an argument or contest. Juries, umpires, referees, judges, and teachers should be disinterested. Jonathan Edwards, the great American Puritan preacher of the eighteenth century, defined *love* as "disinterested benevolence," a benign feeling toward others that does not demand anything from them in return. But a judge should not go to sleep when a murder trial is going on under his nose; he should be interested and disinterested at the same time.

To be *uninterested* is to lack interest. I happen to be uninterested in chess, professional football, and books by Joyce Carol Oates.

The confusion of these words has been around for years, and it is unlikely to disappear soon. So it may be time to send *disinterested* into honorable retirement.

Dubious/Doubtful

Things are *dubious* when they cause doubt; people are doubtful about dubious things.

Many people wanted to believe the *dubious* story that Adolf Hitler kept a diary throughout his dictatorship of Nazi Germany.

But many became *doubtful* when chemical analysis showed that the paper on which the diaries were written was manufactured long after Hitler's death.

The distinction between these words has long been recognized though, since the seventeenth century, some have seen them as synonyms, and more do so now. I think it is a distinction worth preserving, and careful editors and writers still maintain it.

Due to/Because

Willis C. Tucker, one of the journalism professors to whom this book is dedicated, used to say that the only safe use of *due to* was in a sentence like this: "The train was *due to* arrive at two o'clock. He thereby neatly avoided the annoying complexity of the debate over this apparently simple little phrase when it is used with nouns. Purists hold that the phrase should be used only as an adjective, as in the sentences, "Her victory was *due to* her stamina" or "William Jennings Bryan's heart attack was *due to* overeating." In this "correct" sentence, *due to* is a synonym for *caused by*, and nearly everyone will accept it as grammatically correct. Purists object to using *due to* as a preposition synonymous with *owing to,* as in the sentences, "He won *due to* bribery," or "The mayor felt annoyed *due to* his jail sentence."

I object to the phrase even when it is formally "correct." For one thing, it leads to clumsy constructions, especially when it is used as a synonym for *because* at the opening of clauses: "She was late *due to* the fact that her car broke down." It is much simpler to say, "She was late because her car broke down."

For another, the use of *due to* often makes the statement of a sentence vague. "He was convicted *due to* the pistol." What pistol? Why? Perhaps the context will spell out these details. But it seems better to state the situation more specifically by writing another sentence entirely. "The jury found him guilty because ballistics proved that the murder weapon was the pistol that police found in his belt when they arrested him." Here is another example of the clarity you may add to a sentence by using enough words to state your meaning fully.

Even if *due to* is used as the purists demand, only as an adjective, it can be vague. He suffered a demotion *due to* incompetence. Whose incompetence? We want to know. Even the "correct" use of *due to* does not tell us. *Due to* often makes writers think they have said much more than they have in a sentence. Try to avoid the phrase.

Effect/Affect

This is a perennial problem! The word *effect* is usually a noun, as in the phrase *cause and effect:* "The *effect* of her decision was to create a boom in the computer business." *Affect* is usually a verb: "My attitude always *affects* my performance."

But occasionally *effect* is used as a verb meaning "to cause": "Luther's revolt against the Catholic church *effected* a revolution in western thought." *Effect* used as a verb carries with it the connotation of completeness, of having done something to the full.

Either/Both/Each

Either indicates choice between one or another, and it is most appropriately used with *or* where the choice is between two nouns. "You may choose *either* the roast beef *or* a vegetarian dinner." Sometimes *either* implies the *or:* "You can look at *either* candidate and see a man whose mother probably dislikes him." The sentence implies a choice between two candidates. This writer says that whichever choice we make is unlikely to be good.

For many people, the idea of choice becomes blurred, and *either*

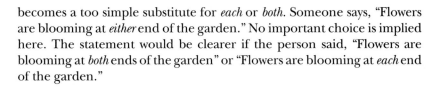

becomes a too simple substitute for *each* or *both*. Someone says, "Flowers are blooming at *either* end of the garden." No important choice is implied here. The statement would be clearer if the person said, "Flowers are blooming at *both* ends of the garden" or "Flowers are blooming at *each* end of the garden."

Enthuse/Enthusiastic

It is still not widely acceptable among professional writers and editors to use the word *enthuse* as a verb, as in the sentence "I am *enthused* at the prospect of teaching writing." It is much more acceptable to use the adjective *enthusiastic:* "I am *enthusiastic* over the prospect of living without television."

Factor

A much overused word, *factor* is a verbal signal that a paper will be dull. Like other such words, its chief fault is not that it is wrong but that it prevents us from making a more specific statement. It lets us shilly-shally: "His character was a *factor* in the breakup of our friendship." It's much better to say, "He was a liar and a cheat, and so I ended our friendship," or "He was much more successful than I was; so I decided I disliked him."

Factor is one of those words, like *implement* and *prioritize,* that substitute easy writing for the hard work of finding words to express our thoughts exactly. Though it is a different kind of word, it fails in the same way that intensifiers fail. It's better by far to ask yourself exactly what you want to say, say it, and forget about *factor.*

Feedback

This word, like *imput,* has come into the language from electronics and is probably here to stay, like the common mosquito. It originally denoted a circuit by which part of the output of a radio source was brought back to its origin. Sometimes this feedback was unintentional, and the result was a high electronic shriek in the loudspeaker when a speaker got too close to a microphone. To some of us, that sound is as reminiscent of high school as the smell of fetid clothes in the dressing rooms of the gym. Now *feedback* is commonly used as a synonym for *response* when people talk about other human beings. It is becoming increasingly common in all sorts of bureaucratic writing, but it seldom appears in well-edited books and magazines. I strongly object to mechanistic metaphors to describe things human beings should do with their brains. *Feedback* makes us sound like robots.

Feel bad/Feel badly

The confusion between these two is one of the most common errors in contemporary writing and speech. We *feel bad* when something makes us sorry or when we are unwell; we *feel badly* if we have burned our fingers or otherwise damaged our skin so that we have reduced our sense of touch. If I say, "Loretta *feels badly* because Leo lost their cat in a poker game," I mean that Leo's rash bet numbed her fingers. If I say she *feels bad* about the loss of her pet, I mean she is sorry to lose the family cat.

The verbs of sense used with several common linking verbs cause trouble because some writers and speakers mistake a predicate adjective for an adverb. A predicate adjective modifies the subject of a clause. We do not have any trouble with sentences like this one: "He looked healthy and happy." We understand that the meaning of the sentence is this: "He looked to be healthy and happy." No one would write, "He looked healthily and happily." We also say, "Mary sat still in the house." We do not say, "She sat stilly in the house." We say, "He felt damp after being caught in the rain." No one would say, "He felt damply after the shower." We write easily, "He walked into the room resolute and angry," knowing that it is not his walking that is resolute and angry but that *he* is resolute and angry. We should close a door *tight* because we mean it to be tight in its frame. If we close the door *tightly,* we imply that we are drunk—or at least *tight*—as we shut the door. We say we have our steak cooked *rare* because to say we have it cooked *rarely* would imply that most of the time we eat raw steak but that once in a great while we put it on the stove and cook it.

So we feel *bad* when something displeases us or when we do something foolish or thoughtless that we regret—just as we smell *bad* when we have not taken a bath in a while and smell *good* when we have just bathed with nice soap. We feel *good* when our team wins, *bad* when it loses.

Flaunt/Flout

To *flaunt* something means to wave it proudly, even arrogantly, for everyone to see. The implication is that some people will be displeased for all that waving, but the flaunter does not care.

> Saddam Hussein *flaunted* his contempt for the United Nations army led by the United States.

Flout means to disobey, to scorn, or to run in the face of some convention, and to do so flagrantly, openly, arrogantly.

> The Serbs *flouted* international standards of human decency by their policy of "ethnic cleansing" in Bosnia.

Both *flout* and *flaunt* imply pride or even arrogance. This pride, combined with the similar beginnings of both words, accounts for their confusion. Careful writers and nearly all editors preserve the distinction.

For free

Many advertising writers and journalists on small newspapers have recently begun using this form.

Senior citizens have been given their fishing licenses *for free.*

It's much better to use the simple and conventional *free.*

Senior citizens have been given free fishing licenses.

Former/Latter

Try to avoid using these words to refer to two preceding persons or things. When you do so, you require the reader to look back to see which is which.

> David Halberstam and Neil Sheehan both became celebrated for books they wrote about the Vietnam War, the former for *The Best and the Brightest* and the latter for *A Bright Shining Lie.*

A reader cruising through prose that contains this sentence has to stop, go back, see that Halberstam is the *former* and therefore author of *The Best and the Brightest* and that Sheehan is the *latter* and therefore author of *A Bright Shining Lie.*

It's better to say this:

> David Halberstam and Neil Sheehan both became celebrated for books they wrote about the Vietnam War, Halberstam for *The Best and the Brightest* and Sheehan for *A Bright Shining Lie.*

Fortuitous/Fortunate

Something that happens *fortuitously* happens by chance or by accident and may be good or bad.

> It was *fortuitous* that when the police raided the drug dealer's hotel room, they found the mayor there, and he ordered them to leave without making an arrest.

We can hardly argue that this event was *fortunate* for anybody, except perhaps for the mayor's enemies. *Fortuitous* suggests randomness, something happening entirely by chance.

> Some scientists think life on earth may have begun by the chemical reaction of a *fortuitous* burst of lightning in the soil.

Yet *fortuitous,* like *disinterested,* seems to have lost so much strength that you should consider using another word to avoid misunderstanding. I would not now write this sentence: "He happened to be home sick that day, and so his presence in the house at the moment of the burglary was entirely *fortuitous.*" I would say, "He happened to be home sick that day, and so it was entirely by chance that he was in the house when the burglars broke in."

Fulsome

Here is another word so often misused that its proper meaning may be irretrievably lost. Until recently, the common meaning of *fulsome praise* was praise so flattering that it could not possibly be sincere. *Fulsome* meant "disgusting" or "obsequious" or even "nauseating." Anyone who received fulsome praise without protest was taken to be blindly arrogant, and anyone who gave fulsome praise was a boot-licking sycophant. But now *fulsome* often means "great" or "enthusiastic."

It is a shame to lose the distinction, for our language will be impoverished by the loss of such an ironic and useful term. *Insincere* praise carries none of the scornful force of *fulsome* praise, but now the cult of exaggeration makes the simple offering of praise, or even lavish praise or high praise, seem inadequate. All our expressions must be inflated until they are sound and fury, signifying nothing much, depending on the exuberance with which they are delivered rather than on the plain meaning of the words. Writers and speakers who exaggerate everything are responsible for turning *fulsome* into yet another inflated adjective, and in their eagerness for emphatic utterance, they fail to see that the traditional and useful meaning stands opposite to their intention.

Head up

People now seldom *head* or *direct* or *lead* things. Instead, they *head up* committees, bands, groups, classes, and clinics on posture. I don't know what *up* adds to *head* except perhaps a specious bureaucratic importance.

Healthy/Healthful

Something is *healthy* if it enjoys good health, that is, if it is strong, vigorous, and alive.

Jack kept himself *healthy* by eating well and biking every day.
Marge had a *healthy* arrogance.

Something is *healthful* if it contributes to the health of someone or something else.

Oat bran is a *healthful* food.
Nuclear weapons are not *healthful* to children.

Hopefully/Hope

Few words provoke more antagonism and debate nowadays than *hopefully* used as a hanging adverb meaning "I hope" or "it is hoped." Writers and speakers have used the word for centuries to mean "in a hopeful spirit" when it, like other adverbs, modified a verb, an adjective, or another adverb. But since about 1932, it has developed this new and more general and objectionable meaning. The ninth edition of the Merriam-Webster *New Collegiate Dictionary* includes a scornful note against the "irrationally large amount of critical fire" drawn from the word when it is used as a synonym for "I hope" or "it is hoped," and it offers analogies with *interestingly, presumably,* and *fortunately,* which are often used as *sentence modifiers,* that is, modifiers of entire sentences.

While willing to admit that usage is king and that probably no great good is accomplished by opposing *hopefully,* I must nevertheless record some reservations that to me are compelling. For one thing, 76 percent of a usage panel assembled by Wright Morris, editor-in-chief of *The American Heritage Dictionary,* and Mary Morris, a distinguished authority on usage, said they would not use *hopefully* in the sense of "I hope" or "it is *hoped.*" That such a lopsided majority should oppose the word should make us hesitate to use it.

The words *interestingly, presumably,* and *fortunately,* cited by the editors of the Merriam-Webster dictionary, offer little of the ambiguity of *hopefully.* If we say, "Presumably, he joined the army," we know that the adverb does not modify the entire sentence but that it modifies the verb *joined,* and there is no ambiguity. It is presumed he joined the army; we do not know if he did or not. But if we say, *"Hopefully* he joined the army," we are left in confusion. Thanks to today's usage, we do not know if he joined the army with hope in his heart—the obvious grammatical meaning of the sentence—or if the writer of the sentence hopes he joined the army. It is just this ambiguity that makes foes of *hopefully*—including me—find the word unattractive.

Other adverbs are equally ambiguous. *"Briefly,* he was in prison for forty years." People use *briefly* in such a way to mean that they are going to be brief in their statement. But the statement would be far clearer if authors of such sentences left the *briefly* out. *"Unhappily,* the dog ate all the hors d'oeuvres before the guests arrived." Unhappily? Probably the hosts were unhappy, but I suspect the dog enjoyed himself immensely. *"Thankfully,* the terrorist died in a hail of bullets before he could injure anyone." The terrorist probably was not so thankful.

So it is with *hopefully,* as in the sentence, "Hopefully, the faculty will get a raise this year." Does the sentence mean that the faculty is certain to get a raise and that it will do so with hope in its collective heart? Or does it mean that the writer of the sentence hopes that the faculty will get a raise? The latter meaning is more in accord with current informal usage, although the administration may hope with all *its* collective heart that the faculty does not get a raise. Is it too much to ask writers to tell us where the hope originates? "The faculty hopes it will get a raise this year." "I hope the faculty will get a raise this year."

To use *hopefully* or any of its random children in the peculiar sense here under discussion creates another disadvantage. Adverbs cannot be inflected; they have only one form for present, past, and future. Nobody can say, "Hopefully, when I was young, I would be rich." We must say, "When I was young, I hoped to be rich." The verb *to hope* can be inflected to show when the hope goes on. If you want to use the past tense, you must say, "I hoped." Why not use the verb in the present tense as well and say, "I hope"?

But the main objection to *hopefully* is that it makes something abstract that is personal. Hope does not float around in the air like nitrogen; hope is an emotion we feel as persons, and we ought to locate its source and identify the people who have it. I hope readers will take seriously these comments on a common usage.

Illusion/Allusion

We make an *allusion* when we refer to something without mentioning it specifically. We create an *illusion* when we form an image that is not reality.

When he told me that he wanted nothing but to lie down in green pastures, he was making an *allusion* to the Twenty-third Psalm.

In our society, movies create *illusions* that take our minds off our troubles.

An allusion is always indirect. It is not the same as a mention or a citation or a quotation. Literary allusions enliven writing by calling to mind other things we have read. When we read, "All his ambitions were sound and fury," we recall Shakespeare's Macbeth and the hopelessness to which his ambitions led him, for Macbeth declares that life is a "tale, told by an idiot, full of sound and fury, but signifying nothing." A writer does not have to mention Macbeth by name; we would think him pedantic if he did so. The allusion is sufficient.

Impact/Impacted

For centuries *impact* was used only as a noun and *impacted* as an adjective. Our forebears spoke easily of the impact of hooves on cobble-stones or the impact of a new revelation about the government. They never said, "Victoria impacted her Parliaments but did not control them." The *Oxford English Dictionary* shows that John Wesley, in a 1791 sermon, used the word as an imperative. "Impact fire into iron by hammering it when red hot." Wesley was old then and probably in less control of his language than he had been earlier in his career. Every other usage that the *O.E.D.* gives under *impact* as a verb has the past participial form which, in English, may serve as an adjective. For centuries, the person who said "I am impacted" was saying "I am constipated."

But of late, *impact* has become a universal synonym for "influence." Polls impact elections. Reform movements impact welfare programs. Such usage is only another corruption of language spread by bureaucrats so uncertain of their own place in the world that they must devise strong-sounding language to convey the impression that they are doing more important tasks than, in fact, they are. Shun *impact* as a verb. It is a neologism of the worst and most pretentious sort.

Imply/Infer

Here is another confusion that has lasted for centuries, and I can express only the majority opinion, not a unanimous verdict. We *imply* something by conveying a meaning in some way other than a direct statement; we *infer* a conclusion by reasoning out the evidence, although that evidence may not deliver the solid proof we wish. The writer or the speaker *implies;* the reader or the hearer *infers.*

> By not mentioning South Korea as an area the United States would defend, President Truman *implied* that he would not oppose militarily a North Korean invasion.
> The North Koreans *inferred* as much and invaded—only to discover that they were wrong.

Cognates of *imply* and *infer* are *implication* and *inference.* Here we seldom find confusion. "I did not understand the implication of his words." That is, he implied something I could not grasp. "The inference I drew was that she did not want to tell me everything." That is, I inferred that she did not wish to tell me everything she knew.

Incredible/Incredulous

Something is *incredible* if we cannot believe it. We are *incredulous* if we cannot believe something incredible. (See also *Intensifiers.*)

> Some found it *incredible* that Oliver Stone could convince millions that his cynically dishonest movie "JFK" told the true story of the assassination of President Kennedy.
> Her remark that she had read all the works of Tolstoy in a week left me *incredulous.*

Indicate/Say

To indicate is much the same as to imply, though the connotation of *indicate* is usually stronger. That is, something indicated is nearly always true, but something implied may be true or false. Even this distinction between the two words is not always observed. *Indicate* is often used to show that something happens without any special intention on the part of the actor. *Imply* is customarily used when the actor wishes to convey some significance beyond the plain meaning of the words.

Smoke indicates fire. The smoke is impersonal; it has no intention. It is merely a sign that a fire is burning somewhere even though we cannot see flames. A woman, by laughing, indicates that she is happy. She may be laughing spontaneously without intending to show that she is happy, but she shows happiness whether she intends to or not.

Do not use *indicate* as a synonym for "say."

> "Tuition will go up by 14 percent next year," the president *said.*

She did not *indicate* that tuition was rising; she made a plain statement of fact, not to be softened by the weaker word *indicate*. But you can say this:

> When she was asked if tuition would rise next year, the president said, "No comment," indicating that it might.

Individual

A much overused word. Use *individual* only when you are making a deliberate comparison between a single person or object and a group.

> One of the great philosophical problems has always been to balance the rights of the *individual* against the rights of society as a whole.

It is stiff and pretentious to write, "Three *individuals* came to collect their bribes."

Sometimes, for no good reason, the word *individual* is used with the pronoun *each:* "*Each individual* house on the block has a porch and a garage." A little thought shows that "each individual" is redundant. You get the same meaning by saying "each house."

Intensifiers

Words like *very, absolutely, definitely, incredibly, basically, certainly, positively, fantastic, terrific, wonderful, marvelous, dreadful, horrible, fabulous,* and many more are *intensifiers*.

As I have said already, we live among hucksters screaming for our attention, a kind of Las Vegas mentality where gaudy and wildly moving electric signs deaden our senses—calling forth from their makers even more flamboyant displays. Few advertisers subtly bid for our attention; they scream at us. The habit has carried over into the language of daily discourse like some sickness infecting multitudes.

Intensifiers deaden prose. They sound like shouting, and if you use them over and over, people shut you off. Resist the trend.

Lay/Lie

Herein lies one of the most commonly violated distinctions. Both verbs are irregular in the past and in the past participle—a major reason for the confusion they cause writers and speakers. To complicate things still further, the past tense of *lie* is *lay*. No wonder even educated people mess them up!

> I *lie* on the floor to take a nap in the afternoon.
>
> I *lay* a paperback book under my head as a pillow.

The past tense is more troublesome.

> Yesterday I *lay* on the floor and took a nap.
>
> I *laid* a paperback book under my head as a pillow.

The past participle can also give trouble.

I have often *lain* on the floor to take a nap.

I have *laid* a paperback book under my head for a pillow.

The *lay/lie* affair gets more complicated when we consider some folk usages that come down to us from the time when English reflexive verbs were more common than they are now: "Now I *lay* me down to sleep; I pray the Lord my soul to keep." In modern idiom we might say, "Now I *lie* down to sleep."

To add still further to the confusion, *lay* and *lie* are both used as nouns to indicate how something is lying. The choice is entirely idiomatic; that is, it has no rules. We speak of the lay of the land but the lie of a golf ball. A friend tells me of playing golf with a new acquaintance who became nervous when he discovered that my friend was a high school English teacher. The acquaintance hit a ball off into the woods, was gone for a long time, and, when he emerged after hitting the ball out, apologized for taking so long. "I had a bad *lay* in there," the acquaintance said. He conveyed a different impression from the one he intended.

Despite the confusions, be careful with this one. The distinction is important, and people with an ear for language notice when others confuse the words.

Less/Fewer

Some authorities think this distinction has been lost, and it has, indeed, often been blurred, but most careful writers and editors preserve it. The distinction resembles that between *amount* and *number,* commented on earlier in this list. *Less* is used for quantities not counted by unit; *fewer* is used for quantities that can be counted. "There was *less* litter on the floor because *fewer* people used the room."

Some idioms call for *less* when we might at first suppose that *fewer* would be preferred.

She gave me *less* than ten dollars.

Today's highest temperature was ten degrees *less* than yesterday's.

In these idioms, we sense a unity of quantity in the money and in the temperature, and we use *less* to indicate our sense of the wholeness of what we describe.

Like/As if/Such as

This distinction is changing before our eyes. The supposed rule, followed by most editors and writers, is that *like* should never be used as a conjunction to join two clauses. But in speech and informal writing, many educated people have been using *like* as a conjunction for years.

Charles Darwin wrote, "Unfortunately, few have observed *like* you have done."[6] Not long ago, N. R. Kleinfield wrote, in the business pages of *The New York Times,* about the decline of an audience for televised professional football games.

> One result is that disgruntled advertisers, complaining that they are not getting the audience for commercials that they expected have been banging on the networks' doors, looking for restitution. And it looks like they will be successful.[7]

Many authorities want *like* to govern only nouns, pronouns, or a noun substitute, such as a gerund. No one could object to this sentence: "I felt *like* coming in the summer." *Coming* is a gerund, a noun substitute, and can be governed by *like.* But many will object if you write, "I felt *like* I might come in the summer." *Like* now becomes a conjunction, and to many this usage seems improper. Purists will prefer that you write, "I felt *as if* I would come in the summer."

You will be safe from attack if you use *as if* instead of *like* to introduce a clause. But to many ears, *like* is a simpler and even more pleasing choice. This is a place in the grammatical rule book where you should make up your own mind—knowing that if you do use *like* as a conjunction, many people will be annoyed.

The confusion between *like* and *as if* is not nearly so obnoxious as the ill-considered efforts of some dislikers of *like* to purge *like* from our vocabulary as if it were a tramp bringing shame on the club. It is correct to say, "The party included some distinguished guests, *like* the dean of the college and the president of the university." The fastidious will substitute *such as* for *like.* There is nothing wrong with *such as.* But there is nothing wrong with *like* either. The rule some writers follow in using *such as* is aptly phrased in one textbook, which gives this advice: "When you are using an example of something, use *such as* to indicate that the example is a representative of the thing mentioned, and use *like* to compare the example to the thing mentioned." This rule would give us these sentences: "The party included distinguished guests, *such as* the dean of the college" and "He aspired to be distinguished, *like* the dean of the college." The rule is harmless, but it is also not binding.

A somewhat more troublesome use of *like* is in comparisons like these: "She sings like a bird"; "He walks like an elephant." The fastidious say that these sentences imply a verb following the final noun: "She sings like a bird sings"; "He walks like an elephant walks." So if the verb were written, the sentences would be formally incorrect. In fact the verb is *not* written, and we can let her sing like a bird if she can and let him walk like an elephant if he must. It would be a false note to have her sing *as* a bird and heavy-handed at best to make him walk *as* an elephant.

❖

Literally

This word gives notice to your readers that you are not using metaphor or hyperbole. When you say, "My papers were *literally* scattered to the winds," you mean that a storm blew your papers in confusion down the street. When you say, "He *literally* did not have a dime to his name," you mean he could go through all his assets and not find ten cents.

Avoid using *literally* merely to be emphatic when you don't mean what you are saying. Don't say, "My blood literally boiled" unless your temperature rose to 212 degrees Fahrenheit and you started giving off red steam. Most of the time you can avoid the word. Instead of saying "Literally thousands gathered to hear her speak," you can say, "Thousands gathered to hear her speak."

Masterful/Masterly

This distinction has been all but lost, and I regret its passing. *Masterful* once meant "domineering" or "overbearing"—acting like a master ruling his slaves or apprentices. *Masterly* meant "with the skill of a master." If we say, "Coach Dixie did a *masterful* job preparing his team for the game with Alabama," we mean that he treated his team like a chain gang. If we say he did a *masterly* job arranging his schedule so his team would remain undefeated, we mean that he did supremely well what publicity-conscious football coaches do nowadays to ensure their teams national ranking. To confuse the words eliminates a fine distinction.

Me/I/Myself

We have already considered the phrase *between you and me* in the rubric dealing with *between*. The phrase should always be *between you and me*. *I* should never be a direct object or the object of a preposition in a sentence. Don't say, "He told Rocky and *I* that he would not fight the challenger" or "She sent Jill and *I* to the library for the book."

Oddly enough, just as *I* has become misused in the objective case, *me* is now often misused in the nominative, or subjective, case. Many young people say and write, "*Me* and Paul went to the movies Friday night."

The same failures in proper case often turn up in other ways. *Myself* is a *reflexive pronoun;* that is, it calls attention to a special emphasis on the subject *I* or indicates action by the subject on itself. So we can say:

I *myself* have often made that mistake.

I shot *myself* in the foot.

But don't say, "He invited Jean and *myself* to the party." Say, "He invited Jean and *me* to the party." And don't say, "*Myself* and Abigail invite you all to our party."

Medium/Media

The word *medium* is a singular noun that signifies anything that enables something else to work or appear. Until recently, its most common use was in the phrase "medium of exchange," which means money or anything else that allows people to carry on trade. In recent times, the plural form, *media,* has come to mean all the instruments of mass communication that serve society. The media include radio, television, newspapers, and magazines—though the word is most frequently used to mean television. A connotation of the word seems to be something ephemeral, something that does not remain important for long. Books are a medium of communication, but somehow they are usually excluded when we speak of "the media."

Two objections may be raised against the word *media:* It is less specific—and therefore less vivid—than the words it replaces, and it is often misused in that it appears with a singular form of verb or pronoun. You should not say, "The media *is* responsible for the shallowness of American politics." If you use the word, it should take a plural verb.

But we should rarely use the word at all. It seems far better to say something specific. "The effort of candidates to shape their pronouncements to fit the four-minute sound bite on television news has contributed to the shallowness of American politics. Few people can be profound, complex, or subtle in four minutes."

Militate against/Mitigate

Mitigate means "to lessen," often for good reason. If your neighbor sues you for driving your power lawn mower through her flower garden, your lawyer may claim the mitigating circumstance that you are allergic to petunias and that you could not sit in your yard when your neighbor's petunias bloomed without breaking out into hives. The judge may then mitigate the rigor of the law that applies to your case.

Militate is related to *military;* anything that militates against a position offers a strong reason not to accept it.

> Her declaration that she would rather go to the party with a cabbage than with him *militated against* his hope that she would marry him.

The common confusion of the expressions arises because people want a hard *g* sound to go with both words in the phrase *militate against.* So they use *mitigate against* when, in fact, the phrase makes no sense. Here is a rare instance in English where spoken rhythms, otherwise so desirable, may lead the unwary writer astray.

Model/Replica

A model duplicates the appearance of something else, but on a larger or smaller scale—usually so different in scale that there can be no confusion between the model and the real thing. A model railroad duplicates the appearance of a railroad but will fit on a table. A model of the DNA molecule is millions of times larger than the real thing.

A replica must be like the original in every detail, including size. The replica of the *Mayflower* in the harbor at Plymouth, Massachusetts, is exactly like the original ship. At least it is exactly what we know of the original.

The term *exact replica* is redundant. A *replica* is exact by definition.

More important/More importantly

It is incorrect to say, "The Yankees lost the pennant, but, more importantly, they lost money." In constructions like this one, a clause is implied—*What is more important.* This elliptical clause (we call it *elliptical* because some of its words are omitted) works as a noun rather than an adverb. In this sentence, a *Time* writer uses the correct expression:

> *More important,* he sat at Stengel's side, learning the game from one of its managerial geniuses.

Also avoid *firstly, secondly, thirdly, fourthly,* and so on. Say, *first, second, third,* and *fourth.*

Nauseous/Nauseated

When you are sick at your stomach and ready to vomit, you are *nauseated.* If you come on a dead horse and get sick at the sight and the smell, the horse is *nauseous.* Something *nauseous* makes you feel *nauseated.* So don't say "I'm nauseous" unless people habitually throw their hands over their mouths, make gasping noises, and run for the toilet whenever you walk into a crowd.

Ongoing

A bureaucratic synonym for "continuing." *Ongoing* is another of those flat, dull words that usually signal bad prose to come.

Oriented/Orientation

We live in a wealth-*oriented* society.
He was success-*oriented* as a youth but leisure-*oriented* as an adult.

The suffix *-oriented* and the noun *orientation* turn up all over the place now. We hear that MacDougal is success-oriented or that he has an orientation toward wealth. They are vague and colorless, keeping us and our readers from concrete thought. It is much better to say, We live in a society that seeks wealth and admires it too much in people." It's more concrete to say, "As a young man, MacDougal aspired to work hard and earn a hundred thousand dollars a year; but when he grew older he wanted only to drink beer, play golf, watch television, and read trashy novels."

Parameters

This word has become a synonym for *limits,* a good, strong word that says everything most people mean by *parameters* and says it without pretense.

The only generally accepted meaning of *parameter* is as a constant in mathematics that may be applied to variable situations. It is most common in speaking of computers. For example, you can set the parameters of a computer to give you sixty-six characters on a line and twenty-nine lines to a page, and the computer will paginate for you according to that setting, no matter how many pages you write or what file you choose to work on. If you figure compound interest at 18.5 percent per annum, your parameter is the figure 18.5, no matter what transaction you are considering.

Parameters may well be used on occasion in nonmathematical discourse. I can imagine saying, "Grace and courtesy have always been *parameters* of social success" or "Creativity is the intellectual *parameter* for all the great disciplines." But it is only pretension that makes some people say, "We want to carry out this construction project within certain *parameters.*"

Posture

This has become a word much like *conditions* and *case* and the intensifiers *definitely, absolutely,* and *incredible.* It is popular—and says almost nothing that cannot be said more simply and more vigorously in other words. Instead of saying, "They adopted a defensive *posture,*" why not say, "They became defensive" or "They went on the defensive"?

Preplanning/Advanced planning

Both these terms are *tautological;* that is, they say the same thing twice. Preplanning must take place before the thing that is planned. Since planning comes before the act that is planned, it is an unnecessary inflation to add the prefix *pre-* or the modifier *advanced* as if some kinds of planning will go on after the occasion being planned for.

Presently/Currently/Now

The adverb *presently* most properly denotes something about to happen: "The actors will appear *presently.*"

Recently the word *presently* has become a grandiose synonym for *now* or *currently* so that pilots come on the intercom to tell us, "We are presently flying over Tuscaloosa, Alabama." It seems better to hold to the older meaning of *presently* and to use either *now* or *currently* or, better still, let the present tense stand by itself to express something happening now. "We are flying over Tuscaloosa, Alabama."

Yet *presently* as an inflated synonym for *now* may be here to stay. In the first edition of this work, somebody in production wrote of me in the note "About the Author" that I was "presently working on another novel." I groaned within and without.

Principal/Principle

Principal has always had the connotation of "first." It is most often an adjective meaning "the first" or "the most important."

> The *principal* reason for her irritation with me was that I had run over her cat.

But it is also sometimes used as a noun to designate a person of primary authority.

> The *principals* in the final drama of the Civil War were Ulysses S. Grant and Robert E. Lee.

Principle refers to an ideal standard of conduct or an underlying system that helps explain some things we may see only in a superficial way until we think about them.

> Coach Dixie told us that the *principle* of fair play is great so long as it does not cause us to lose football games.
>
> The *principle* behind the mercury thermometer is that mercury expands with heat and contracts with cold.

Quotation/Quote

Quotation is a noun; *quote* is a verb, although lately it has begun to be used more and more as a noun. I still think it bad form to write a sentence like this: "His *quotes* from the Bible prove that Faulkner knew it well." I prefer this: "His *quotations* from the Bible prove that Faulkner knew it well."

Since *quote* is a verb, you can write like this:

> He *quoted* a price that I found excessive.
>
> Dickens frequently *quoted* Shakespeare.

Respective/Respectively

Use these words only when some major confusion might result without them.

> The winners of the first and second prizes were Jack Rowdy and Meg Loader *respectively*.

Otherwise, someone might suppose that Jack and Meg had somehow shared the two prizes. It is probably better to write, "Jack Rowdy won first prize, and Meg Loader took second."

Simple/Simplistic

Something simple is uncomplicated. People, machines, novels, poems, and plans can be simple. Only ideas or utterances can be simplistic. The connotation of *simplistic* is always bad, implying that the person with, say, a simplistic idea has not thought out all the consequences.

A simple way to raise enough money to repair the American highway system might be to impose an additional tax of fifty cents a gallon on gasoline and diesel fuel. A simplistic idea might be to turn all the highways into toll roads. This idea would be simplistic because the person advancing it would not have thought of how much money it would cost to build and operate the toll booths, how many accidents they would cause, and how much they would increase fuel consumption by making cars stop and start again.

That

This excellent and useful word has lately been pressed into service as a synonym for the adverb *very*. *Very* is a weak adverb; *that* seems to be stronger. So we get sentences like this one: "The game wasn't *that* close." The usage seems always to be in the negative, and the logical question is to ask what the referent of *that* might be. We can readily understand the word if it occurs in a sentence like this: "I have been sunburned through a shirt, but my son's skin is not *that* sensitive."

The first statement, about the speaker's sunburn, gives some context to the statement that the son's skin is not that sensitive. But what of this sentence standing without a referent? "His skin was not *that* sensitive." How sensitive? As sensitive as a baby's? As the skin of a rhinoceros? We have no context to tell us.

Perhaps the original idiom was *all that good* or *all that bad* and, by ellipses, we shortened it to *that*. It was not a good idiom in the first place, and shortening it made it worse.

This

Now and then you can get away with a vague *this* in your prose if your context is clear.

> Frederick Bazille and Claude Monet started painting in the open air; *this* was the real beginning of French impressionist art.

The *this* in the sentence above refers to the act of painting in the open air, described in the first independent clause. We have no trouble understanding the reference. But the vague *this* often leads to confusion.

> In their war plans of 1914, the Germans assumed that they would have to fight a hard war against the Russians but that they would have an easy time with the French, especially if they could send an overpowering army crashing through Belgium to capture Paris within weeks after the outbreak of hostilities. With France quickly defeated, the Germans could turn all their force against the Russians. This was why a local conflict so quickly became a European war.

In a text this complicated, the vague *this* causes all sorts of trouble to the reader who does not already know the story. Always try to have *this* refer to a noun or pronoun.

> This German military thinking explains why a local conflict so quickly became a European war.

Thrust

This is another lazy word, like *factor,* used by writers who wobble and weasel. We read of "the *thrust* of an article" or "the *thrust* of an argument." Writers telling us of the *thrust* are usually trying to tell us that they are so clever that they see many different issues but that by their superior wisdom, they have picked out the main line of discourse. They protect themselves from the accusation that they have missed the point, and they provide room for themselves to whirl around and run the other way should anyone challenge them. Don't weasel and wobble. Don't use *thrust.*

Tragedy/Calamity

Strictly speaking, a *tragedy* is a drama played out in life or on the stage in which a great human being is brought down to defeat by forces beyond his control—forces either within himself or in the world around him. Macbeth is tragic; so is Othello. Macbeth cannot control his ambition, and Othello cannot control his jealousy. Tragedy has always been part of the human experience because it reveals the glory and depravity in even the greatest of human beings and comforts us with the assurance that we are not alone in finding both glory and depravity within ourselves.

But the rise of modern sensational journalism has confused *tragedy* with *calamity, misfortune, disaster,* and *accident.* In consequence, the tragic sense, having nearly vanished from our language, may be in danger of vanishing from our sensibilities. Now an airplane crash is a *tragedy,* as is the wreck of a truck that kills somebody. *Tragedy* should be restored to its original noble meaning, and other words should be used to describe the consequences of accidents that originate primarily from simple carelessness or mechanical failure. But the word may have been already diluted beyond the power of restoration.

Transpire/Occur

Transpire originally meant "to sweat," a meaning the French word *transpirer* keeps. From this meaning, *transpire* evolved into the sense of "passing from the hidden to the open," a useful concept in sentences like these:

> It *transpired* that high officials in the United States government knew by 1967 that Americans could not win the Vietnam War.

> It *transpired,* after they had talked for a little while, that they had been in college at the same time thirty years before.

To use the word *transpire* as a synonym for *happen* or *occur* is portentous discourse, as in this sentence: "The game *transpired* on a golden autumn afternoon before 96,000 screaming fans in Knoxville."

Try and/Try to

The proper idiom is *try to,* although in speaking many people say *try and.* "I will *try to* attend the concert tonight." *Try* takes an infinitive when it is used with another verb.

Unique

Unique means "one of a kind," and it can be modified only by words like *nearly* or *almost.* You cannot logically say that something is "very unique" or "rather unique" or "the most unique" or "somewhat unique." Something is either unique or it is not. If something is *not* unique, you can say that it is *rare, uncommon,* or *unusual,* or you can say that it is *almost* or *nearly* unique.

Varying/Various

The distinction between these two words gives unusual trouble. If we are discussing changes in the same thing from one time or place to another, the word to use is *varying.* If we are discussing different things with attention to the differences between them, the word is *various.* *Varying* is used before a singular noun, *various* before a plural. These sentences use *varying* correctly:

> Her love was *varying,* depending on whether she saw the mess I made around the house or the devotion I felt to her.

> The *varying* weather made the day interesting, though not especially pleasant.

The following sentences use *various* correctly—with a plural noun:

> *Various* friends told her she was correct.

> The responses to my proposal were *various.*

> *Various* black musicians created jazz.

Viable options/Viable alternatives

Both expressions are inflated discourse designed to deceive readers into believing that something important is being said. Are *nonviable options* really options at all? If not, why should we bother to speak of *viable* options? The word *viable* should be reserved for its proper meaning, as in the phrase *viable seeds,* meaning seeds that will germinate if we plant them.

Verbal/Oral

A strange confusion has grown up about these words, making them synonyms. I hear people say and write something like this: "I made a *verbal* agreement with Congressman McPork not to tell how much money our coal company paid him to vote for strip mining in Yellowstone National Park." The writer or speaker seems to mean that the agreement was not put down on paper. But if so, the agreement is *oral;* an agreement put down on paper is still *verbal;* that is, it is cast in words. So if you do not put an agreement or a contract down on paper, it is *both* "oral" and "verbal."

Violent/Vehement

If you hit somebody with your fists or with a club, you are *violent;* if you attack only with words, you are *vehement.* A violent protest against an umpire's call in a baseball game is running out onto the field and hitting him; a *vehement* protest is screaming at him, suggesting an oculist, or profanely discussing his Mafia connections.

While/Although

Some writers use *while* as a synonym for *although,* with confusing results: "While MacDougal was an athlete in college, he became as fat as a keg after graduation." What does this sentence mean? It could mean that although MacDougal was an athlete in college, he stopped taking exercise after graduation and became as fat as a keg. Some might suppose that during the time MacDougal was an athlete in college, he stopped taking exercise and became as fat as a keg—but still remained an athlete. The example may be extreme, although if MacDougal was a baseball pitcher, it is plausible. *While* conveys a brief confusion any time it is used as a synonym for *although,* and good writers should protect readers from brief confusions.

Which

In my chapter on false rules (Chapter Ten), I reject the that/which rule, and readers interested in that oft-inflated subject may seek enlightenment there. But *which* causes another difficulty, similar to that of the vague *this* discussed earlier in this list. When it does not refer to a clear antecedent, the reader often feels an absence that may create bafflement.

> In many universities, writing teachers love teaching but often work only part-time, without adequate benefits, at low salaries, and without much contact with the rest of the teaching faculty, *which* accounts for the low morale many of them feel.

The *which* clause here has no clear antecedent. We can grasp the meaning only if we assume that the *which* clause does not apply to the statement that "writing teachers love teaching." Morale may be low because of these other facts mentioned in the sentence. The sentence could be fixed by adding this to the clause: "disadvantages which account for the low morale many of them feel."

Which should always have a clear antecedent expressed as a noun or a pronoun. Such clarity will save readers the trouble of backing up and reading again to see if they missed anything.

Who/Whom

This distinction provokes much acrimonious debate among writers and grammarians. Some want to get rid of *whom* altogether, or use it only immediately after a preposition. Then we would have sentences like these:

We did not care *who* he chose to represent us.

She did not know to *whom* she spoke.

Whom appears to be withering away. My friend Richard A. Lanham, U.C.L.A.'s distinguished authority on grammar, begins one chapter of a good book with the title "Who's Kicking Who?" He says "who's kicking whom" sounds stilted to him. It does not sound stilted to me, and other conservative grammarians agree. You must make up your own mind. Many people will object if you fail to use *whom* in its traditional place; no one will object if you use it in the traditional way.

If *whom* sounds stilted to your ear, revise your sentence to get rid of it. *Who* and *whom* clauses are not frequent in journalistic styles. You can read page after page of *Sports Illustrated, Time, Smithsonian,* or *National Geographic* without encountering a single clause introduced by *who* or *whom.* Many serious books use such clauses rarely. Richard Ellmann's *James Joyce* goes for many pages without using a *who* or *whom* clause. It may be that good writers sense that such clauses introduce distracting elements in sentences. Everybody uses them now and then, but when you write one in a first draft, consider changing it.

As in the great debate over *like* and *as,* some people want to preserve the distinction between *who* and *whom* but, unfortunately, do not know what the distinction is. They use *whom* when *who* is proper. The rule is this: Use *who* or *whom* according to how the pronoun is used in the clause where it appears. If it is used as the subject of the clause, use *who;* if it is used as the object of the clause, use *whom.* This rule sounds more complicated than it is. Don't write this:

The university wanted a football coach *whom* the president said could break NCAA rules without being caught.

The writer of this sentence saw that *coach* was a direct object. He assumed that the clause modifying *coach* should begin with *whom,* in the objective case. But the sentence should read like this:

> The university wanted a football coach *who* the president said could break NCAA rules without being caught.

In the dependent clause modifying *coach, who* is the subject of the verb *could.* Therefore *who* must be in the subjective case. The short clause *the president said* is parenthetical, inserted in the *who* clause but not governing the subject *who.* You can check such clauses by trying to replace the *who* or *whom* with *he* or *him* in a sentence constructed from the clause. You can say, *"He* would be able to break NCAA rules without being caught." You cannot say, *"Him* would be able to break NCAA rules without being caught."

In the illustrative sentence we used above, *whom* is correct. "We did not care *whom* he chose to represent us." Here *whom* is a direct object. "He chose *whom.*" We could say correctly, "He chose *him.*" We could not say, "He chose *he.*"

It's important to remember that parenthetical elements such as *he said* within a *who* or *whom* clause do not govern the pronoun. These sentences are correct:

> The candidate *who* the committee thought would be the best librarian was rejected by the chancellor for wanting to buy more books.

> The assistant coach *whom* they believed Coach Dixie would choose lost his chance when he was arrested for gambling.

> The trustees fired the president, *who* had been beloved by the faculty, because he had insisted that football players attend classes.

> The woman *whom* they chose to replace the president promised to be guided in all her academic decisions by Coach Dixie.

Whom is always used if it is the object of an infinitive; that is, the recipient of the action described by the infinitive of a transitive verb.

> They wondered *whom* to send as their representative.

The greatest problem with *whom* seems to come in the use of its associated pronoun *whomever.* Here is a sentence that appeared recently in a good book published by Yale University Press:

> Haskell sold land to *whomever* would buy.

The author and the editors at Yale Press must both have seen the preposition *to* and remembered the rule that the object of a preposition should be in the objective case. They forgot that the entire clause following *to* serves as the object of the preposition and that within that clause the pronoun is governed by how it is used in relation to the verb. The sentence should have read: "Haskell sold land to *whoever* would buy." *Whoever* governs the verb *would buy* and must be in the subjective case.

Who or *whom* should always be used to refer to persons. You should not say, "The German generals that planned the war later tried to blame it all on Hitler." You should say, "The German generals *who* planned the war . . ."

These rules may seem so complex that you will be tempted to accept Richard Lanham's advice and throw *whom* onto the garbage dump of language along with other obsolete words. I would say only that *whom* is not obsolete yet; and if you want your work to be respected by the educated, you're better off with *whom* than without it. The *"whom*less" writer may find it difficult to gain attention.

Whose/Of which

Some conservative authorities insist that the possessive *whose* be used only when the antecedent is a person or a group of persons. They object to any use of *whose* to refer to an impersonal antecedent. But even H. W. Fowler, a conservative authority, ridicules this notion. It would require us to write sentences like this: "The aircraft, the tail *of which* fell off on the approach to the runway, landed safely." Most of us would write, "The aircraft *whose* tail fell off on the approach to the runway landed safely." Of course, we may rewrite the sentence to avoid the problem altogether: "The aircraft lost its tail on the approach to the runway but landed safely." But often such rewriting is neither feasible nor important, and we must choose between *whose* and *of which*. Whenever we do have this choice, we should let the rhythm of the sentence dictate our solution. That will usually be to use *whose*.

-wise

I'm in no hurry *time-framewise*.

Pricewise, German cars failed to compete with Japanese cars, and *saleswise,* the Japanese began taking over the American import market.

Sticking *-wise* onto the ends of nouns to turn them into adverbs has become a virus much like tacking *-ize* onto nouns to make them verbs. It represents a lazy mind, and you should avoid it.

With

With should not be used loosely with the sense of *and* or *in addition*. Don't write this: "Chip took first place, *with* Yoke coming in second." Write this: "Chip took first place, and Yoke was second."

Nine

Figurative Language

F*igurative language* is language that uses words in any but their literal sense. If I say, "She floated easily on her back in the swimming pool," I am using the word *floated* in its literal sense. But if I say, "She floated gracefully from guest to guest at her party, making everyone feel like an intimate friend," I am using *floated* in a figurative sense. If I say, "The water boiled for tea," I mean that the water was heated to 212 degrees Fahrenheit, that it bubbled violently, and that it began to turn to steam. If someone says, "His condescending attitude made my blood boil," *boil* is being used figuratively. This particular device we call *hyperbole*—exaggerated speech used to make a point emphatically.

Figurative language must do three things: (1) it must draw on some common experience that binds the writer to the audience; (2) it must be fresh and engaging—often surprising; and (3) it must be appropriate to the context in which it is used.

Similes and Metaphors

Similes and metaphors are among the most common figurative devices. They join two experiences so that one is illuminated by the other. In the writing program I direct, we have a metaphor for a certain kind of research paper filled with quotations, demonstrating hours of hard work but lacking any ideas from the student writer. We call this the "model-plane essay." You can buy such a model at a hobby shop and spend hours or even weeks putting it together until you have an impressive object on your dining room table. The finished model looks exactly like the picture on the box. You have contributed nothing of your own to it except your labor and your dexterity.

We want papers that show careful labor, but we also want original thought, some fresh insight. We want writers to do more than paste sources together; we want them to bring the design of their paper out of their own experience, their own struggle with the ideas and information in the sources. The model-plane metaphor helps students understand the difference between writing merely a formally correct paper and producing one that shows that the writer has become deeply engaged with the material.

Specialists in rhetoric often make an unnecessarily sharp disctinction between *metaphor* and *simile*. Similes and metaphors differ in their construction. A simile is a kind of metaphor. A *metaphor* speaks of something as if it were something else: "Johnson was a bulldog in argument." A *simile* tells us that something is *like* something else. We could say, "Johnson is like a bulldog in argument" or "Johnson is as tenacious as a bulldog in argument." In both cases we isolate a quality of bulldogs—their legendary tenacity—and apply it to Johnson. We don't apply every quality of bulldogs to Johnson. He does not, for example, walk on all fours and bark and eat dog food and bury bones in the backyard and chase the letter carrier. He is tenacious; that is the only point we want to make in the metaphor or simile.

Both metaphors and similes depend on some shared experience between writer and reader. When I say, "Johnson is a bulldog in argument," I assume that my readers know something about bulldogs—or at least that they *think* they know something about bulldogs. (Bulldogs are, in fact, gentle and loving creatures.) Their knowledge of bulldogs helps me tell them something about Johnson. If my readers were Siberian nomads who had never seen or heard of a bulldog, my metaphor would be ineffective.

The balance between the reader's knowledge and the writer's intent is delicate. Suppose I said, "Johnson is a salmon in argument." Most readers could not think of anything about salmon that would apply to arguments; so the metaphor would fail. I might expand: "Johnson is a salmon in argument; he starts in one place and goes all around the world and comes back to where he began, no matter what contrary views we put in his way." Now the metaphor is extended, and it works a little better. But it is still clumsy. Good metaphors work a little like jokes: They make a sudden and vivid impression. Jokes and metaphors that must be explained are awkward. Like good jokes, good metaphors depend on common experience. Most of us have failed to get a joke that convulses everyone else in a group. We don't get the joke because we lack the common experience that makes it funny to others. Unless we make metaphors out of the common experience of our readers, they will not get the point.

THREE KINDS OF METAPHOR

Most metaphors may be classified under one of three general headings.

1. The *descriptive metaphor* helps us understand one concrete object by reference to another.

2. The *abstract metaphor* helps us understand an abstraction by reference to a concrete object.
3. The *embedded metaphor* substitutes metaphorical language for literal reporting.

Metaphors that help us see one concrete entity by reference to another help us describe things; metaphors that use a concrete reference to illuminate an abstraction help us explain ideas; embedded metaphors brighten our language in more subtle ways.

The descriptive metaphor   Descriptive metaphors help us imagine scenes. Loren Eiseley describes a flight of birds like this:

> It was then that I saw the flight coming on. It was moving like a little close-knit body of black specks that danced and darted and closed again. It was pouring from the north and heading toward me with the undeviating relentlessness of a compass needle.[1]

One concrete metaphor in this passage speaks of "a little close-knit body of black specks." The other speaks of the "undeviating relentlessness of a compass needle." Each metaphor refers to something we commonly know—specks and a compass needle—and applies it to the flight of birds to help us see better what Eiseley saw.

Here is a metaphorical passage from *National Geographic* describing lightning:

> It is a river of electricity rushing through a canyon of air. Careering as fast as 100,000 miles a second, lightning sears wild and unstoppable through twisted channels as long as ten miles.[2]

Always, the descriptive metaphor uses something readers know to help them see something else vividly. Eiseley assumes that we have seen enough black specks to understand what a distant but undefined group of them look like, and he thinks we know that a compass needle always points north. In describing lightning, William R. Newcott assumes that we know something about rivers, canyons, and channels, and he uses this knowledge to begin an article that will help explain lightning to us.

The descriptive metaphor can be used in any kind of writing, fiction or nonfiction. Sometimes metaphors can add powerful effects that become more intense the more we think of them. Philip Caputo, writing about his days as a Marine in the Vietnam War, describes the heat:

> It was noon, without a breath of wind, and the sky seemed like a blazing aluminum lid clamped over the world.[3]

Caputo's metaphor calls up a metallic, whitish sky of a sort that those who have experienced hot summers know is a sign of torrid heat. But his "aluminum lid" has deeper meaning; it reminds us of pans placed on the heat of stoves. The heat in Vietnam makes this soldier feel that he has been placed on a stove with the heat turned up, and the metaphor makes us think not only of the heat of summer but of the more deadly heat of flame baking us in a skillet. The metaphor with extended meanings gives us a remarkable sentence.

The abstract metaphor   A different kind of metaphor, and perhaps the most powerful, helps explain ideas by attributing a concrete reality to an abstraction, thereby making the abstraction more manageable. Such metaphors have been used for centuries, often in religion, where the essence is worship of an invisible God. In Psalms we read, "My cup runneth over." In this statement, the writer, feeling the blessings of God, uses the cup as a metaphor for the life that can receive God's goodness. "In Proverbs we read, "The candle of the wicked shall be put out." The "wicked" in this scriptural text walk by a man-made light that will be extinguished, leaving them in darkness. Some people speak of "bearing a cross," meaning a suffering they endure through no fault of their own. Sometimes we speak of death as a person, recalling both the apostle Paul's personification of death in his epistles and the figure of the Grim Reaper with his scythe that has been with us since the Renaissance. A famous metaphor in economics was Adam Smith's "invisible hand," a term he used to explain how supply and demand work in the marketplace.

This kind of metaphor—the abstract metaphor—easily translates into political cartoons. Hunger becomes an emaciated skeleton devouring the world. War becomes a cruel warrior in classical Roman armor. Such metaphors have a long history. When Southerners claimed, before the Civil War, that every state had the right to *nullify*, or disregard, laws made by the United States Congress, Daniel Webster replied that if Southerners were correct, the federal union was no more than a "rope of sand." Abraham Lincoln some years later used a biblical metaphor when he spoke ominously of a country part slave and part free, declaring that "a house divided against itself cannot stand." In our own century, when Franklin D. Roosevelt proclaimed that his administration would give a "new deal" to the American people, the metaphor became one of the most powerful in American history. Millions suffering from the Great Depression felt they had been dealt an unlucky hand. The image of a "new deal" made them think that they might now have another chance, another deal of the cards of life. The metaphor suffered the fate of many good metaphors: It became a cliché. Now the term *New Deal* simply calls up the Roosevelt administration, and hearing it, few think of a new deal in a card game where every player gets another chance.

A good metaphor may help us think. As aids to thinking, metaphors are important—perhaps necessary—to modern science. Some argue that without metaphor, some current scientific thinking could scarcely go on. Albert Einstein's theory of relativity deals with phenomena so removed from commonsense experience that most people can scarcely begin to understand it. Early in Einstein's career, the *London Times* called his theory "an affront of common sense." Metaphors have helped explain it to the nonscientific mind.

Einstein tried to imagine how the universe would look to someone traveling at the speed of light; he made a pictorial leap in his mind similar to the kind of leap we make when we read a good metaphor. He began with the notion that the speed of light is constant, seen from any vantage point in the universe, whether the light is moving toward us or away from us. Einstein taught that nothing in the universe could move faster than the speed of light and that anything in motion at that speed creates a set of relations with other objects that is radically different from the relations of anything in motion at a lesser speed. The idea, so alien to common sense, called forth from English philosopher Bertrand Russell this metaphorical utterance:

> Everybody knows that if you are on an escalator you reach the top sooner if you walk up than if you stand still. But if the escalator moved with the velocity of light, you would reach the top at exactly the same moment whether you walked up or stood still.[4]

Because we experience motion at much lesser speeds than the speed of light, scientists and science writers after Einstein have had to use figurative language to enable the rest of us to understand what they are talking about.

The embedded metaphor   The embedded metaphor is perhaps the most common metaphor—so common, in fact, that we may not even recognize it as a metaphor. The *embedded metaphor* uses a verb or a noun in something other than its literal meaning.

Suppose I write, "The fire devoured the house." I could say "The fire burned the house" or "The fire destroyed the house." When I use the word *devoured,* I employ an embedded metaphor to suggest that the fire is like a ravenous animal eating something up. The metaphor *devoured* treats the fire as if it were an animal.

Norman Mailer, writing of the police riot in Chicago during the 1968 Democratic convention, writes a passage rich with metaphor.

> The police cut through the crowd one way, then cut through them another. They chased people into the park, ran them down, beat them up; they cut through the intersection at Michigan and Balbo like a razor cutting a channel through a head of hair, and then drove columns of new police into the channel who in turn pushed out, clubs flailing, on each side, to cut new channels, and new ones again.[5]

Mailer gives a group of human beings the quality of an inanimate cutting instrument, and eventually he extends the metaphor into a full-fledged simile so that the police cut "like a razor cutting a channel through a head of hair."

The interplay of metaphor takes place in much good writing—though it can be overdone. At times living things are likened to inanimate objects; at other times inanimate objects are given the qualities of living things. The purpose of the metaphor is always to make us bring two parts of our experience together so that the immediate object of our attention becomes much more vivid. The pleasures of a good metaphor are probably as great to the writer who creates the metaphor as they are to the reader. Metaphors provide another example of how writing sharpens thoughts that might otherwise be dull and commonplace.

METAPHORS AND ATMOSPHERE

Atmosphere, tone, and *voice* all refer to the complex and sometimes only partly conscious emotional response a piece of writing sets out to create in readers. How do we feel when we read something? Metaphors may condition our response. Suppose you wish to call attention to how thin someone is. One metaphor can create an impression of unhealthiness.

Mr. Murray was so thin that he looked like a patient in a cancer ward.

Another can create a more positive impression.

Mr. Murray was so thin that he looked like a long-distance runner.

Some writers create atmosphere with stunning metaphorical power. Study the metaphors (I have italicized them for emphasis) in the following passage by Joseph Conrad, a master of the metaphorical art. Conrad's metaphors create a mood of awe and foreboding.

You know how these squalls come up there about this time of year. First you see a darkening of the horizon—no more; then a cloud rises *opaque like a wall.* A *straight edge* of vapour lined with *sickly* whitish gleams *flies up* from the southwest, *swallowing* the stars in whole constellations; its shadow *flies* over the waters and *confounds* sea and sky into one *abyss* of obscurity. And all is still. No thunder, no wind, no sound; not a flicker of lightning. Then in the tenebrous immensity a livid arch appears; a swell or two like undulations of the very darkness run past, and suddenly wind and rain strike together with a peculiar impetuosity as if they had burst through something solid.[6]

Few writers today would dare duplicate this rich and subtle use of metaphor. The first image is of a cloud rising "opaque like a wall," then of a "straight edge"—a ruler—of vapor lined with "sickly whitish gleams," as if the stormy sky were a person sick with some tumultuous disease. Next the passage tells of the vapor flying up, and we easily imagine some monstrous bird "swallowing the stars in whole constellations." Then its "shadow flies over the waters," giving us another image of a bird of prey swooping over the sea after something—perhaps a helpless ship—that it may find floating there. Afterward a swell or two of the sea runs "like undulations of the very darkness." Those familiar with the first chapter of the book of Genesis, as most literate people were in Conrad's day, remember the chaotic and utter darkness at the beginning when "the earth was without form and void, and darkness was on the face of the deep"—an image we are prepared to meet in Conrad's words "confounds" and "abyss," which recall the primordial universe before God created light.

Conrad gives us two worlds, the world of the storm on the sea and the eerie world of imaginary association called up in his mind by the storm—a world he transmits to us with his metaphors. The association includes in it not only what we may have experienced of violent tempests but also what we have read and thought about the biblical story of creation, where God struggles against the chaos at the dawn of time. Conrad creates in us something of the primitive fear that probably lurks in the subconscious of most of us, a legacy of the terror of our remote ancestors before the forces of nature. Without this string of metaphors, Conrad's prose would not accomplish these effects. The metaphors are numerous, but we accept them because they are consistent and because they work together to create an atmosphere of awe and gloom. It is a view of a storm different from the one we might see on the evening television news, where a brightly painted meteorologist gestures at a colored map and tells us that a hurricane is coming.

In his inaugural address of January 20, 1961, President Kennedy included a series of metaphors that conveyed vigorous energy and made his audience believe that a young and vigorous administration was about to lead the United States. He said:

> Let the word go forth from this time and place, to friend and foe alike, that the torch has been passed to a new generation of Americans, born in this century, tempered by war, disciplined by a hard and bitter peace, proud of our ancient heritage and unwilling to witness or permit the slow undoing of those human rights to which this nation has always been committed and to which we are committed today at home and around the world.

Reading or hearing Kennedy's image of a torch passed, we think of Olympic runners carrying the flame from one to another across countries and the world until they arrive at the place where the games are held. The new generation of Americans is described as "tempered," which recalls the process of making steel stronger by first heating it and then plunging it into cool water. We are told that these Americans have been "disciplined by a hard and bitter peace," and we think of soldiers or athletes trained by hardship to do their duty. We are told that Americans will not allow "the slow undoing of . . . human rights," and we think of a carefully knitted garment being unraveled before our eyes by a perverse child or malicious adult.

So it goes through the speech, one vigorous metaphor after another conveying a total image of strength, vitality, endurance, and courage. Presidents provide some sense of what they think of themselves and their administrations when they use metaphors. You can read their speeches and get some idea of what they believed about their own leadership and about the people they tried to lead. In your writing, the metaphors you use will tell readers much about what you think of yourself and of them.

CAUTIONS ABOUT METAPHORS

Metaphors should make one point sharply. Long extended metaphors seldom interest readers. You may think it clever to create an extended metaphor that likens getting a college education to climbing a mountain. Admission is like arriving at the base of the mountain; enrolling in your first class is like putting on your helmet and climbing tentatively over the first rocks; college social life is like rain on the side of the mountain (a little of it is refreshing, but too much may wash you off the cliffs). You can go on and on with such metaphors, but after a while they become tedious. Their worst quality is that they don't enlighten anyone about the college experience or about anything else. By the time you get to the top of your mountain, most readers have left you. In Britain, an overextended metaphor is said to be walking "on all fours." This scornful expression mocks metaphors that try to do too much and so become contrived and boring.

Don't base your arguments on metaphors. To convert a metaphor into an argument may be inappropriate and dangerous. The so-called organic metaphor has long been popular in the study of history: Plants and other organisms are born; they enjoy youth; they pass into maturity and then into old age; finally they die. Edward Gibbon's eighteenth-century masterpiece, *The Decline and Fall of the Roman Empire,* accustomed generations of literate readers to thinking of the final centuries of the Roman Empire in the West as a decline, a sickness, much like the aging and death of a human being.

In itself, Gibbon's metaphor did no special harm. But more recent historians, such as Oswald Spengler and Arnold Toynbee, made the organic metaphor into an argument. From it, they constructed elaborate patterns that they said human history followed. Both frequently twisted the historical evidence to make events conform to the design they had imposed on the past. Spengler, in particular, wrenched history into a plantlike cycle whereby all civilizations are seen as passing through the same stages, every stage likened to a similar stage in the development of an organism. He provided a design for history in which no individual striving could make much difference and no collective effort could change the implacable pattern of rise and fall. In his view, history repeats itself just as the life cycle of a plant repeats itself again and again in the members of a species. Because Spengler believed that the twentieth century represented the last stage in the organic life of western civilization, he provided no hope for the future. Toynbee, although more moderate in his judgment, fell into much the same trap.

Metaphors may *illustrate* arguments, but they should not *become* arguments. Metaphors help us express ideas, but they should not take over our minds or our writing. In a fundamental way, metaphors are not *real*. In *Antony and Cleopatra,* Shakespeare gave this description of Cleopatra's barge:

> The barge she sat in, like a burnish'd throne
> Burn'd on the water.

We are supposed to imagine that Cleopatra's stage barge was so polished that it *seemed* to burn like fire on the water of the Nile. As one scholar remarked, if we supposed that Cleopatra's barge were literally on fire and that she and her sailors were leaping into the water to escape the flames, we would have no metaphor.[7] When we make metaphors, we use our imaginations. We play with words. We take part of one thing and make it intensify our sense of another. But a metaphor takes *only* a part; it does not take the whole. Human history is not like a plant in all its particulars; to make the metaphor of growth, maturity, and decline an ironclad rule for how human societies develop is to confuse a metaphor with an argument.

Avoid packing your prose with so many metaphors that they become confusing or ridiculous. *The New Yorker* frequently runs a little feature called "Block That Metaphor," a passage from a writer who has solemnly jumbled metaphors together without thinking of their total effect—like this passage from a review of James Michener's novel *Alaska:*

> Perhaps the problem is Michener has grown "formula" in preparing such all-encompassing works. But here at least, the fluffy snowdrifts thaw, exposing a permafrost of substance.
>
> To survive the long polar night of prose, readers must dig in and await spring when the narrative thaws and the verbal tundra becomes hospitable. It takes a gold miner's stamina, though, to pan away, discard the trivial tailings, and be rewarded—not by a mother lode of meaning but by precious flecks of literary gold.[8]

What can this passage mean? I think the reviewer intends to say that in all the trivia of Michener's enormous novel, one may find a few interesting things. But the language in the review becomes so pompous with grandiose metaphors that it is easy to lose track of the reviewer's intention.

Metaphors should make sense. Work on your metaphors carefully. Think about them. Practice writing them in your notebook.

APPROPRIATE METAPHORS

Metaphors should be appropriate to the topic at hand. Here, exercise good taste. Some writers feel comfortable using metaphors and similes that annoy others. I would not like to read that "Robert E. Lee's theory of battle was to crash into his foes as if he were trying to drive a bulldozer through a brick wall." General Lee never saw a bulldozer in his life; and a careful reader, considering the incongruity of such a simile, might be annoyed by it.

In making similes and metaphors fit your subject, use your wit. Here is an instructive simile from an article in *Time* about computer software:

> A computer without software is like a car without gasoline, a camera without film, a stereo without records.[9]

You can make yourself sound ridiculous by mixing metaphors. A memo handed out in my university a few years ago urged the faculty "to grapple with the burning issues." I rather hoped the administration would issue insulated gloves so the issues would not scald me. I once heard an inspirational speaker tell an audience of high school seniors that they could "climb the ladder of success only by keeping their noses to the grindstone." I thought of how painful it was going to be for these young people, lugging that heavy grindstone up the ladder while keeping their noses pressed to it. *The New Yorker* picked up a hilarious string of mixed metaphors uttered in solemn seriousness by another speaker.

> But a fellow user pushing for stricter security counters: "Perhaps I am flogging a straw herring in midstream, but in light of what is known about the ubiquity of security vulnerabilities, it seems vastly too dangerous for university folks to run with their heads in the sand."[10]

You *can* use a series of metaphors effectively, as long as they do not clash. Here is Irving Howe describing the Jewish immigrant housewife in turn-of-the-century New York:

> It was from her place in the kitchen that the Jewish housewife became the looming figure who would inspire, haunt, and devastate generations of sons. She realized intuitively that insofar as the outer world tyrannized and wore down her men, reducing them to postures of docility, she alone could create an oasis of order. It was she who would cling to received values and resist the pressures of dispersion; she who would sustain the morale of all around her, mediating quarrels, soothing hurts, drawing a circle of safety in which her children could breathe, and sometimes, as time went on, crushing her loved ones under the weight of her affection.[11]

Howe's metaphors come so naturally that we may not at first recognize them as metaphors. But then we identify "oasis of order," "circle of safety," and the metaphorical phrase "crushing her loved ones under the weight of her affection."

Match your metaphors and similes to the tone and content of your essay. These examples drawn from Howe nicely fit his subject, the development of the Jewish mother. It is a serious subject but not a somber one. His metaphors convey that tone. Here is Norman Mailer describing his safe and elevated view of the Chicago police riot during the Democratic National Convention in 1968. Metaphors burst in his prose like lightning.

> Let us escape to the street. The reporter, watching in safety from the nineteenth floor, could understand now how Mussolini's son-in-law had once been able to find the bombs he dropped from his airplane beautiful as they burst. Yes, children, and youths, and middle-aged men and women were being pounded and clubbed and gassed and beaten, hunted and driven, sent scattering in all directions by teams of policemen who had exploded out of their restraints like the bursting of a boil, and nonetheless he felt a sense of calm and beauty, void even of the desire to be down there, as if in years to come there would be beatings enough, some chosen, some from nowhere, but it was as if the war had finally begun, and this was therefore a great and solemn moment, as if indeed the gods of history had come together from each side to choose the very front of the Hilton Hotel before the television cameras of the world and the eyes of the campaign workers and the delegates' wives, yes, there before the eyes of half the principals at the convention was this drama played, as if the military spine of a great liberal party had finally separated itself from the skin, as if, no metaphor large enough to suffice, the Democratic Party had here broken in two before the eyes of a nation like Melville's whale charging right out of the sea.[12]

This passage from Mailer illustrates some of the glories and dangers of metaphors. It is cast in the wild, bare style typical of Mailer now for many years. Parts of it are confused. He assumes that all the delegates to the Democratic Convention of 1968 were men because he speaks of the "delegates' wives" rather than their "spouses." In Melville's *Moby Dick,* the whale did not break in two; rather the whale broke Captain Ahab's ship in two. Even so, the paragraph conveys the tumult of the streets and Mailer's tumultuous thoughts as he watched from the safety of a hotel room and tried to describe what happened.

Don't force your metaphors; don't make them overwrought and unnatural. Don't crowd your prose with them. But do use them.

Other Forms of Figurative Language

Metaphors form the broadest class of figurative language, but other forms are also important. The classical rhetoricians called these forms *tropes,* from the Greek word for "manner," as in "manner of speaking." Now and then they can enliven your work, but all have their dangers, and you should use them with brave caution. Many tropes overlap.

HYPERBOLE

Hyperbole is exaggeration so great that no one can take it literally. We have already mentioned the cliché "He made my blood boil." That is hyperbole. No one expects the person who says such a thing to emit red steam. Mailer's paragraph on watching the Chicago riot from his hotel room is filled with hyperbole. Note his comment on the "gods of history."

American humor often depends on hyperbole. Here is Texas journalist Molly Ivins giving her impression of the invasion of Grenada in 1983. President Reagan said he was sending in the troops to protect American medical students in a school on Grenada. Maurice Bishop was prime minister; he was arrested and put to death by his army, which may have had support from Cuba. Mocking various events of the Reagan administration, Molly Ivins writes:

> My personal favorite: On October 25, 1983, the United States of America (population 250 million), the mightest nation on earth, invaded the island of Grenada (pop. 86,000) by air, land, and sea. And we whipped those suckers in a fair fight. We sent in almost 7,000 fighting men, armed to the teeth, along with ships, planes, guns, missiles, and tanks, to face a situation that we had (1) helped create by ignoring Maurice Bishop's pleas for help, (2) was none of our business anyway, (3) did not involve American medical students, who neither needed nor wanted our help, and (4) at worst could have been handled by a couple of Texas Rangers. The local population was mostly armed with sticks, and the 800 Cuban construction workers who were supposed to be commie soldiers either dropped their guns or never got to them at all. According to the Pentagon's own postinvasion analysis, none of the sixteen Americans killed in the invasion died by enemy fire; they all died by accident. The press, for the first time in the history of the nation, was not permitted to accompany U.S. troops into action—and only would have reported that we had bombed the local mental hospital anyway. President Reagan slept through the whole thing, as was his wont in moments of national crisis. Nevertheless, he went on television that night, after we had defeated the entire military might of Grenada, a place smaller than Cleveland, and his voice trembled with emotion as he said, "This—is our finest hour." The army later gave out 8,612 medals for heroism in the great Grenadan invasion, even though fewer than 7,000 men took part.[13]

UNDERSTATEMENT

Understatement is the opposite of hyperbole. Understatement is effective in writing about passion-filled issues; because it seems slightly out of place, it is often humorous. In writing of Adam Smith, whose *Wealth of Nations,* published in 1776, gave a theoretical justification for modern competitive capitalism, John Kenneth Galbraith said:

> After the local school Adam Smith went on to the University of Glasgow and then to Balliol College, Oxford, an experience that he celebrates in *Wealth of Nations* with a stern rebuke for the public professors, as they then were called, those whose salary was independent of the size of their classes or the enthusiasm of their students. Thus relieved of incentive, these professors, he alleged, put forth little effort, did little work. Much better, he thought, that they be paid, as he himself would be later at Glasgow, in accordance with the number of students they attracted. Smith's views on this matter would not be well received in a modern American university.[14]

Galbraith's last sentence is an understatement poking fun at modern university professors, who might riot if any administrator suggested that they be paid according to the number of students who signed up for their courses.

IRONY

Irony is a deliberate effort to say something that will be taken in a sense opposite to the literal meaning of the words. It is, I think, the most difficult of the tropes, the one most likely to be misunderstood; and if it is misunderstood, irony loses its point.

Irony involves contradiction. The person who has a flat tire on her way to the airport and knows that it means she will miss her plane and an important meeting may say, "This is a fine state of affairs." Her statement is simple irony, meaning the opposite of what she feels. If I say "The President took a courageous stand against burning the flag," the statement is ironic because it takes little courage to condemn flag burning in the United States. I may actually mean that the President was trying to *look* courageous by making brave-sounding remarks that carried no risk to him at all.

We speak also of the irony of events. Romeo and Juliet die because of a scheme intended to help them escape their families and marry each other. The secret tape recordings of conversations in his office that Richard Nixon intended to preserve as a record of his presidency led to his forced resignation. Writers can call attention to ironic events, but the irony of figurative language is the rhetorical device that concerns us here.

Ironic statements have been with us for centuries. Jesus, speaking of those who pray loudly in public to impress others with their show of piety, said, "Truly I say to you, they have their reward." He meant that their reward was that people saw them, not that God heard them.

Irony can be a simple statement, or it can be an extended work of prose or poetry. Probably the best-known ironic work in English is Jonathan Swift's essay "A Modest Proposal for Preventing the Children of

Poor People in Ireland from Being a Burden to Their Parents or Country, and for Making Them Beneficial to the Public." Swift, writing in the eighteenth century and appalled by the desperate poverty of rural people in Ireland, where he lived, proposed that poor Irish children be raised as food for the wealthy. "I have been assured by a very knowing American of my acquaintance in London, that a young healthy child well nursed is at a year old a most delicious, nourishing and wholesome food, whether stewed, roasted, baked, or boiled, and I make no doubt that it will equally serve in a fricassee, or a ragout."[15]

Mike Barnicle, a columnist for the Boston *Globe* and one of my favorite writers, is a master of irony, often mixed with hyperbole. Here he is commenting on the first rumors that his newspaper was about to be sold to *The New York Times*—a rumor verified a few days after this column appeared:

> As we left my new club after lunch yesterday, The Century on West 43d Street in Manhattan, Mr. Arthur Sulzberger Jr. of New Paltz, N.Y., young genius publisher of the Mother Paper—the *New York Times*—suggested, quite amiably, that I transfer what cash I had on me from my pants pocket to my shoe. At first, I was fairly confused. "It's simply a matter of being street-smart," Mr. Sulzberger told me. "With your money in your shoe, they will not be able to rob your corpse after they shoot you dead on the sidewalk. Remember, this is New York."
>
> I was dining with Mr. Sulzberger because of reports that he and his marvelous publishing family could soon be purchasing the Boston *Globe*. Naturally, hearing this I flew immediately to the big city in order to grovel and see if I could not buff my new boss's boots while seeking an answer to the ultimate question of our age: What about me?
>
> At the *Times,* I was first refused admittance because I was not dressed properly nor had I soaked my head in cement. This procedure is a tradition at the paper of record, aimed at diminishing any imagination within a potential employee.[16]

It's clear in this piece from the start that Barnicle does not like New York and that he does not like the idea of the stuffy *New York Times* taking over his beloved Boston newspaper. The difficulty of irony is that though it must take the *form* of serious, literal statement, readers must know that the author is playing with them, saying something that contradicts the literal meaning of the words. In other words, readers must see the art. Some student writers in my classes have written essays that they intended to be ironic but that I took literally because the irony was not sharp enough for me to see. I recall once reading what seemed to me to be a racist tirade, only to be told by the student that it was intended as an ironic attack on racism. This is irony that shoots itself in the foot.

If you mean the opposite of what you say, but your audience does not see your meaning, then you are working against your purpose. That is the difficulty the nineteenth-century English writer Thomas Carlyle referred to when he wrote to his friend John Stuart Mill, "Irony is a sharp instrument; but ill to handle without cutting *yourself.*" When intelligent readers take your irony literally, you have failed. Yet despite its dangers, irony is one of the great tropes, and a paper that uses it successfully can be memorable.

Irony often points to an outrageous reality. When Swift wrote that poor Irish children should be raised as food for the wealthy, he called attention to rich English landlords in Ireland who worked their Irish tenant farmers into misery and starvation. In a metaphorical sense, these wealthy English aristocrats were "devouring" Ireland. When Swift proposed a *literal* devouring—cannibalism—he hoped to make readers think of the devastating economic devouring going on under the color of Christian morality.

The ironic statement can provide a dash of wit to an argument. *Time* writer Michael Kinsley wrote ironically in an essay on the 1989 Supreme Court decision that opened the way for state legislators to debate what kind of abortion laws they would have.

> The disaster facing America's state legislators, and potentially its national legislators, is that they may have to address an issue of public policy on which many of their constituents have strong and irreconcilable opinions. This they hate to do and are skilled at avoiding, even though it is what they are paid for. They would far rather pass laws against burning the flag.[17]

Ironies abound in this short passage. As the essay develops, it becomes clear that Kinsley thinks the national debate about abortion will be a good thing. He does not mean that it is a disaster at all. But it is a disaster in the minds of legislators, who, he implies, would much rather come out strong about uncontroversial issues such as protecting the flag than about bitterly contested matters such as abortion. The notion that our representatives are "skilled at avoiding . . . what they are paid for" is an ironic comment on politics. Members of Congress like to pretend that they are brave; Kinsley implies that they are cowardly. They do not like to do what their jobs demand they must.

Irony can be subtle—so subtle that some readers or hearers may not grasp it while others, who do understand, laugh both at the irony and at the ignorance of those who take it seriously. In that respect, irony is often treated by ethical philosophers as a moral problem. Should one mock others with ironies they do not understand? The only answer a writer can give to such a question is that indeed irony has often been used as a form of mockery. One must consider these moral issues when one uses the trope.

OTHER FIGURES OF SPEECH

Other figures of speech enliven English poetry and prose. In *synecdoche* we make a part stand for the whole. For example, we speak of thirty *head* of cattle. (*Head* here is an idiomatic plural.) The book of Deuteronomy in the Bible tells us that we do not live "by bread alone," making bread stand for food in general.

In *metonymy* we use some attribute to indicate the whole. We speak of the "top brass" when we mean the highest military officers, who used to wear brass emblems on their lapels to indicate their rank. We write of the "Blue" to indicate the Union Army and the "Gray" to indicate the Confederate Army during the Civil War. We speak of the "Big Orange" to indicate the University of Tennessee football team because its dominant color is orange.

Be on the lookout for figures of speech in your reading. Try to make figures on your own. Don't be extravagant, but don't be so fearful that you fail to use some of the rich figurative devices available in our language.

Clichés

Figurative language should make your writing vigorous; the opposite of vigorous writing is prose filled with clichés, expressions as predictable as a funeral sermon. A good metaphor surprises us. But when we hear the first word of a cliché, we know the whole expression. "The plan was as dead as a _____." We fill in the blank with "doornail" as we hear the first part of the sentence.

But what is a *doornail?* And what awful calamity killed it? We don't know. When we say "as dead as a doornail," we repeat a strong consonant *d* sound, and English is fond of such repetitions. In speaking, we might put some emphasis into the phrase. But it means nothing, no matter how we say it; it does not create a picture in our minds of a poor little doornail lying dead on the ground with its feet in the air.

"The author waxed eloquent on the glories of his book." Why do people "wax eloquent"? No one knows. They seem to wax eloquent more often than they wax anything else except possibly their new cars. *Wax,* as it is used in *wax eloquent,* means "to increase." So we know that people "waxing eloquent" are becoming *more* eloquent. People in the sixteenth century used to "wax old." The moon still waxes and wanes. But in modern prose, people seem only to wax eloquent.

"The cold, hard facts are these; it will be a cold day in July before I pull his chestnuts out of the fire." Why must disagreeable facts always be cold and hard? The expression must have had some power once. Facts may have seemed like cold pieces of steel—perhaps steel with which people made daggers. Unpleasant facts would not be warm and cuddly.

But now everybody trying to sound tough and worldly uses the expression "cold, hard facts."

So it is with "a cold day in July." The expression might have seemed funny to someone living in a Tennessee valley, where July is like an open furnace. But it long ago ceased to be either amusing or striking. And it makes no sense in the mountains of northern Vermont, where July days can be chilly.

And what living reader has never pulled somebody else's chestnuts out of a fire, risking burned fingers or a scorched face? Chestnuts are still around, and a few people may roast them in fireplaces. But I doubt it. (This cliché was a favorite of Joseph Stalin, the tyrant of the former Soviet Union. It's best to let it lie dead and buried with him.)

Writers use clichés out of weariness or uncertainty or hesitancy. A writer sits at a desk, struggling to put something on paper (or on the screen), realizing, as we all do, that writing is hard work and that sometimes words don't come easily. A cliché pops up. "We want our university to be on the cutting edge" of research. The writer grabs "cutting edge" because it is there. No matter that it's as tasteless as secondhand chewing gum. It's there; it takes up space; it even conveys a rough sort of meaning. The writer uses it—and the prose where it lies sinks just a little under its dull weight.

A young reporter covers a congressional hearing where the president of a cement company urges construction of an interstate highway through Glacier National Park so that more motorists can see the grizzly bears. The reporter writes that the company president "has his own ax to grind." Neither the reporter nor her readers will think of the company president, bringing his ax to the community grindstone, forgetting all the other tool owners in the village, and concentrating only on his own task. No reader of this story has ever ground an ax; the reporter may have seen an ax only on TV. But the phrase pops up, and it feels comfortable. So down it goes—and down sinks the prose.

We know that someone who "has his own ax to grind" is someone who is motivated by greed to advocate high, even noble causes. Most clichés convey meaning; what they don't convey is images. They are dead metaphors—dead because they create no pictures in our minds. Clichés open no windows, let in no fresh air, provide no revelations, give us nothing to remember.

Good writing gives an impression of a bright mind thinking seriously, but not necessarily somberly, about a topic and saying something worth reading. We heed such writing because we enjoy it. Clichés, on the other hand, grind us down and erode our respect for the writer.

Clichés come in two packages. Some are dead metaphors vainly puffing to call up an image; others are common phrases, including fad words and formulas. Dead metaphors include *tight as a drum, fit as a fiddle, sound as a dollar, white as snow, blue as the sky, quick as lightning, sharp as a tack, neat as a pin.* Common clichéd phrases include expressions such as *add insult to injury, pick and choose, tried and true, a deep, dark secret, an undercurrent of excitement, an agony of suspense, bustling city, brutal murder,* and *tragic death*—and row on row of others stacked up like counterfeit money in the vaults of our minds.

Fad words come and go like pockets of unpredictable air turbulence. Suddenly people start using them to show that they know what's going on. *Parameter* seems to have receded as a synonym for "limit" or "perimeter." But *feedback, input,* and *bottom line* cling to our language like chronic diseases. Football coaches still tell us that the "name of the game" is defense or scoring touchdowns or good blocking or good tackling or whatever else the name of the game happens to be on a given weekend. I always thought the name of the game was *football.* Coaches hold onto clichés the way some children hold onto teddy bears—and for the same reason. Coaches say, "When the going gets tough, the tough get going." They say "We came to play" when we thought they might have come to drink tea. Good players give "110 percent." Why not 130 percent? I don't know. Since we are now a computer-driven society, we hear that scholars in the English department must *interface* with people who teach writing. We also hear that some people are *programmed* for success and others for failure. Since the Watergate scandal in 1973 and 1974, we cannot say "at that time"; we seem driven to pretend to be more precise: "at that *point* in time."

Clichés ooze out of newspaper columns, academic essays, student papers, and memos that pass from office to office. The "tip of the iceberg" rises menacingly in Washington, D.C., almost every week. "Read my lips!" George Bush cried in the 1988 presidential campaign, promising not to raise taxes. What on earth does the expression "read my lips" mean? Whatever it was, voters in 1992 read Bush out of office.

Yet you will not find clichés often in slick-paper magazines such as *The New Yorker, Time, Atlantic, Newsweek, Smithsonian, National Geographic, Popular Mechanics,* and others. You do not even find them often in *Sports Illustrated,* except when reporters are quoting coaches and athletes. These magazines must be carefully edited for a literate public if they are to survive. Editors know that clichés kill prose and that dead prose does not sell. Here again, we may look to good journalists and essayists as models for our own writing. Such writers mush try to seduce readers into spending time with them, and intelligent people are not seduced by worn-out old lines.

How do we know when a cliché jumps into our fingers as we write? They are so pervasive that we cannot always avoid them. But some inexperienced writers cannot even recognize them. I have given one clue already: Many clichés give themselves away because they are so familiar that the first word or two calls up the rest of the phrase automatically. When you start to use such a phrase, sit for a few moments and think of another expression.

Weigh the words you use. We read in the morning paper that a thug shot someone in the street, and we are told that it was a "brutal murder." The reporter wishes to convey horror and outrage. But do we need the worn-out adjective *brutal?* Can we imagine a *gentle* murder? Perhaps a "gentle murder" is committed by putting rat poison in somebody's hot milk.

On my bicycle trip through the Pacific Northwest in 1993, I came upon a stuffed female grizzly bear in a glass case in a hotel lobby in St. Mary, Montana. A sign told me that this bear had been guilty of several "brutal cattle killings" and had therefore been shot to death. I thought, "If only that poor bear had killed those cattle courteously and gently, the way we do it with hammers in slaughterhouses, she might still be alive."

And what of those declarations that someone is a "personal friend." Are there *impersonal* friends? When flight attendants tell us to collect all our "personal belongings," do they mean that we should take our children with us but leave *impersonal* belongings like our bags behind? And what of those historians of the Renaissance who tell us again and again of those "bustling cities" in Italy! The term is used so frequently in history texts that we may imagine cart drivers, merchants, bankers, lawyers, priests, courtiers, prostitutes, beggars, and princes hurrying about in the streets shouting "bustle, bustle, bustle, bustle, bustle."

Couples living together without benefit of marriage tell us they have "a meaningful relationship," and when they break up, they tell us that their love affair was "a learning experience." Young people who learn their profession by apprenticeship are said to have *hands-on* experience. We hear that laptop computers are "selling like hotcakes," and we do not stop to think that most cakes we buy today are cold.

All this is to say that writing requires attention. We must examine every word, measure every sentence, and tailor our expressions to fit our thoughts. When we revise, we should pull our clichés out of a text as we might weed a garden.

The simplest way to deal with a cliché is to turn it into ordinary language. Cities don't have to *bustle;* they can thrive. We don't have to say that a murder was *brutal.* We can describe it and let our readers decide whether it was nice. We don't have to look at the *bottom line.* We can consider the consequences or decide what the most important issue might be.

No book can settle the problem of dead language. But to be a good writer you must make your words stir a response in the minds of your readers. Good figurative language creates images, both for you and for your audience. Dead language cannot create those images or the resultant desired responses. Now and then we may all use a cliché without being hanged for it. But too many clichés will smother your prose, and your readers will conduct your literary funeral by refusing to read your work.

Appendix Two of this book provides a short list of clichés. You will not find every cliché there, but you can open the book to these pages when you feel tempted to use a phrase and do not know whether it is a cliché or not. If the phrase is in my list, use a different expression.

Conclusion

Use figurative language when it seems appropriate. Try to make it come out of your own experience; do not put an expression on paper merely because you have heard it before and because everybody seems to be using it. If you reflect on language and experience, notebook in hand, you can develop a talent for figurative language. It takes time. So does everything else about writing.

Remember always that the most important quality of writing is its substance. To use figurative language in an essay that has nothing to say is like trying to ride a painting of a horse. It's not going to get you anywhere.

I have read with enormous pleasure David McCullough's biography *Truman*. McCullough is one of our best and most popular writers. He uses metaphors and similes rarely; and he seldom uses understatement, hyperbole, or irony. He achieves his effects by prodigious research and a sure eye for detail and by writing simple declarative sentences filled with facts. I read his work with the feeling that here is an honest writer leading me with great authority through ground that he has carefully explored. He has worked hard to learn something, and he wants to tell me what he has learned. Most of what he tells us comes in the strongest kind of prose in the English language—the simple declarative sentence. You can be a great writer if you apply the same conscientious standards to your own work.

Ten

False Rules and What Is True about Them

*E*nglish has rules established by centuries of habit. They were not written by the moving finger of God on tablets of stone. Some of them are irrational. But break them and you make it hard for readers and yourself. When you violate the rules, readers may think you are ignorant and therefore not worth their time. Yes, that attitude is unfair, but as John F. Kennedy said, life is unfair.

The good news is that the rules of English are much less complicated than most people think. When my students make mistakes, I often find that their minds were running faster than their hands. They were thinking ahead to the next word, the next phrase, the next sentence while they wrote. As a result, they lost their concentration and made errors they could easily catch if they reread their work—especially if they read it aloud. When I work carefully over my own early drafts, I find all sorts of dumb mistakes. I laugh at myself and correct them.

Alas, many people—including too many teachers—complicate matters by making up false rules. I once asked a group of writing teachers to tell me the most annoying mistakes made by their students. One teacher said, "I just hate it when my students use 'pretty' as an adverb." I said, "In English it's pretty hard to avoid doing that."

False rules oppress writers and can make prose sound stilted and somehow wrong. Any examination of published prose will show that professional writers break these false "rules" all the time. Yet these rules have a vigorous life. Writing is a complicated business, one of the most difficult acts of the human brain. False rules seem to grant security, to reduce writing to a formula that anybody can understand, to make it less threatening. The people who tout false rules are like astrologers; they can always find an audience even if experience proves them wrong.

Writing is more than obeying the rules; it is observation and imagination, order and revelation, style and form. It means making a subject part of yourself. And it always involves risk. Multiplying false rules is much like welding armor onto a car; it may make the car safe, but it may also make it too heavy to move.

Although false rules are wrongly expressed, they may have substance buried deep inside them. People have devised them to deal with some real problems. We should take this substance into account even as we reject the silliness and the pedantry of the extremes.

Common False Rules

Here are some common false rules, with a few notes about what may be true about them.

1. Don't use the first person.

Every college freshman knows this one because so many high school teachers order their students never to say *I* or *we*. So instead of the first person, we get impersonal stiff constructions like these:

> It is the opinion of this writer that . . .
>
> This writer would be forced to agree . . .
>
> This writer has shown . . .
>
> The reader is made to feel . . .
>
> This writer was hit by a truck when she . . .

The best argument for the first person is that we see it in all kinds of professional prose. It is used in reviews of books and movies to avoid the tedious repetition of phrases such as "the reader" or "the audience." Walter Jackson Bate, writing about Samuel Johnson, demonstrates the graceful use of the first person without recourse to the tiresome impersonality of "the reader."

> Even if we knew nothing of the state of mind he was forced to battle during this psychological crisis, the edition of Shakespeare—viewed with historical understanding of what it involved in 1765—could seem a remarkable feat; and we are not speaking of just the great *Preface*. To see it in perspective, we have only to remind ourselves what Johnson brought to it—an assemblage of almost every qualification we should ideally like to have brought to this kind of work with the single exception of patience; and at least some control of his impatience, if not the quality of patience itself, might have been passable if this period of his life had not been so distressing.[1]

The first person is often used in accounts of events the writer has observed even when he or she has not been a part of them. *New York Times* reporter Neil Sheehan's *A Bright Shining Lie: John Paul Vann and America in Vietnam* tells the tragic story of a Marine Lieutenant Colonel whose self-delusion stands as a symbol of the entire American experience during the Vietnam War. Because Sheehan covered the war and knew Vann, he sometimes interjects his own memories and speaks in the first person.

> We picked up news of the dimensions of the Viet Cong buildup in the Delta—in retrospect, the first stage in the creation of the second Viet Minh—at the beginning of August. We would have learned about it sooner but we had all been unable to leave Saigon for a look at the war since June because of the Buddhist street demonstrations and the constant threat of another suicide. Mert Perry of *Time* heard of a big fight in Kien Hoa Province in July in which eleven helicopters had been hit. I knew the captain who was the advisor of the 7th Division battalion involved in the battle from a march through the rice paddies long before. He came to Saigon at the beginning of August for a weekend leave, and I ran into him by chance on the street.[2]

One may read hundreds of pages in this large book without encountering Sheehan's use of the first person, but where his own experience intersects his subject, he uses the first person without hesitation.

Writers expressing opinions about a controversial subject use the first person to avoid any ambiguity about where they stand or as a means of noting their opinions in a controversial field—an opinion that has weight because of the writer's experience and authority. Here is Stephen Jay Gould in an essay about women's brains and their relation to women's intelligence as people thought about these matters in the nineteenth century. He considers the argument made by a French scientist named Gustave Le Bon that women's brains are so small compared to the brains of men that women should not receive higher education. Le Bon was following data on brain size gathered by another Frenchman, Paul Broca. Here is a paragraph from his essay:

> In 1888, Topinard published Broca's more extensive data on the Parisian hospitals. Since Broca recorded height and age as well as brain size, we may use modern statistics to remove their effect. Brain weight decreases with age, and Broca's women were, on average, considerably older than his men. Brain weight increases with height, and his average man was almost half a foot taller than his average woman. I used multiple regression, a technique that allowed me to assess simultaneously the influence of height and age upon brain size. In an analysis of the data for women, I found that, at average male height and age, a woman's brain would weigh 1,212 grams. Correction for height and age reduces Broca's measured difference of 181 grams by more than a third, to 113 grams.[3]

Gould uses the first person to tell us about work he has done with Broca's statistics. You can often use the first person to describe your own work on the problem you are writing about.

Yet modern writers do not use the first person indiscriminately. When you write, ask yourself, Am I writing about myself, or is my subject something else? Don't get in the way of your subject. Professional writers do not say, "In my opinion, the Middle East is the most dangerous place in the world." They say simply, "The Middle East is the most dangerous place in the world." If a writer signs her name to an article, every reader with common sense will understand that the assertions in the article represent the writer's considered opinion and not some universal truth agreed on by all.

Inexperienced writers sometimes seem to think that nothing is worth writing unless it demonstrates some powerful emotional transformation in the writer. Sometimes they add an emotional commentary at the end of a paper. They want me to know that their hearts are in the right place. Writing about passion has its place now and then. But most of the time the facts standing alone—sometimes starkly alone—have such weight and power that for the writer to add his or her emotions would be trivial and distracting. In the following paragraph, social historian Robert Proctor writes about Nazi Germany's medical policy of putting to death those children judged to be incurably ill or handicapped. The children were removed from their homes supposedly for special and improved treatment, but instead they were killed. Says Proctor:

> Methods of killing included injections of morphine, tablets, and gassing with cyanide or chemical warfare agents. Children at Idstein, Katenhof, Görden, and Eichberg were not gassed but were killed by injection; poisons were commonly administered slowly, over several days or even weeks, so that the cause of death could be disguised as pneumonia, bronchitis, or some other complication induced by the injections. Hermann Pfannmüller of the hospital at Eglfing-Haar slowly starved the children entrusted to his care until they died of "natural causes." This method, he boasted, was least likely to incur criticism from the foreign press or from "the gentlemen in Switzerland" (The Red Cross). Others simply left their institutions without heat, and patients died of exposure. Nazi medical men could thus argue that their actions were not technically murder, for they were simply withholding care and "letting nature take its course." Parents were informed with a standardized letter, used at all institutions, that their daughter or son had died suddenly and unexpectedly of brain edema, appendicitis, or other fabricated cause; parents were also informed that, owing to the danger of an epidemic, the body had to be cremated immediately.[4]

Proctor would have ruined the force of this stark paragraph had he interjected his opinion that killing infirm children represented savagery. These cruel details in themselves constitute a moral judgment. He trusts us to know what side he stands on, and he does not insult us by assuming that we have to be coached about the correct emotions to have before these horrors. He keeps the focus on his true subject—Nazi medicine—and not on himself.

Wayne C. Booth's "implied author" should come to mind here. Never write to show readers how noble you are. Don't brag, even about your modesty. Don't show off; avoid drawing unnecessary attention to yourself. Stick to the business of telling readers what you know. When we blatantly insert ourselves into our story, we are like thoughtless people who invite friends to a movie and then spend so much time talking that they can't enjoy the show.

Avoid giving the impression that when you say "I think" or "in my opinion," you are installing yourself in an impregnable fortress, immune to any counterargument. Many Americans suppose that all opinions are equal and that those who express themselves vehemently enough and sincerely enough deserve respect and even admiration. These people imagine that others are guilty of bad taste, or at least discourtesy, if they disagree with opinions strongly stated. Many an argument ends with the offhand and sometimes surly remark, "Well, you have your opinion, and I have mine." Implied in a remark like this is often another: "Don't bother me with the evidence."

Thank God we live in a free society, where people can say any silly thing they please. But if you are going to influence thoughtful and fair-minded people, you must be able to defend your opinions by reasoning about them. Don't use the first person to avoid an argument. If you command evidence, you can argue your case without using the first person at all. Eugene D. Genovese, in his classic book about slavery in the South before the Civil War, writes about the music of the slaves.

> The slaves' talent for improvisation, as well as their deep religious conviction, drew expressions of wonder and admiration from almost everyone who heard them sing.[5]

Genovese then quotes from his sources. He is not compelled to place an "I think" before this opinion; he summons up evidence, and the evidence convinces us without a needless first-person pronouncement that would call more attention to Genovese than to what he is saying about slaves.

When you deliver yourself of an "I think" before a judgment in writing, you appear to be granting that other people can think anything they want. But if you present evidence for your assertions, you convey an impression of confidence that your audience will take seriously.

So the false rule about the first person contains some truth. Avoid using the first person except when it is clearly called for. In the following instances, use of the first person may be in order.

When you deliberately assume a conversational tone, as in a regular newspaper column, a letter, or a book like this one, you may use the first person. The conversational tone may help you create intimacy with your readers. Most books about writing share the assumption that we all perform the same task and that the author has something to share with others who write. Most books like this one are chatty—perhaps too much so. E. B. White, John McPhee, George Orwell, Joan Didion, Ann Tyler, and many other modern writers use the first person as a matter of course when they write essays. They are writing about things that happened to them, reactions, their conclusions. They are sharing their experiences with us to enlarge our own. Some subjects lend themselves to informality; some do not. You will not find a chatty medical book on brain surgery or leukemia. For such subjects, informality would be in bad taste—unless the author happens to be writing about his or her experiences as a victim of either affliction.

For serious subjects, use the first person only if your experiences are essential to your essay. If you report on research that you have done alone or with colleagues, you may use the first person or the passive, depending on your own taste. Most scientific journals use the passive.

> One thousand people were questioned about their preferences for automobiles. They were asked whether performance was more important than economy, whether they needed a large back seat, and whether color might influence their choice of a new car. They were asked whether they had more confidence in American cars or in Japanese makes.

Some writers use the first person in such reports to make their prose more informal and lively. That is the style of *Consumer Reports,* the nation's most popular and most respected consumer magazine. Here is a paragraph from an article about tests on strollers for young children:

> Parents and other adults do the most to keep the perils at bay, of course, but they should have an ally in the manufacturer. Unfortunately, the companies whose strollers we tested for this report don't always bear their fair share of the load. Although baby strollers have been significantly improved in recent years, more than 10,000 babies and children under five are injured seriously enough every year in carriages and strollers to require emergency hospital treatment.[6]

If you sign your name to a formal essay or report, you may venture an occasional comment in the first person. You may wish to assert your own choice among conflicting opinions. You cannot use the first person singular if you have not signed the essay. If you write a memo to represent the views of your university on a controversial issue like hate speech, you may use the editorial *we* to show that your thoughts represent the official policy of your institution. But you cannot say *I* because no one knows who you are if your name is not on the piece.

2. Never write a sentence fragment.

This false rule should be amended to read, "Never write a sentence fragment unless you know what you are doing." If you cannot tell the difference between a sentence and a sentence fragment, get yourself a

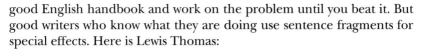

good English handbook and work on the problem until you beat it. But good writers who know what they are doing use sentence fragments for special effects. Here is Lewis Thomas:

> Now all that has changed. I cannot think that way anymore. Not while those things are still in place, aimed everywhere, ready for launching.[7]

And here is part of a *Time* story on terrorism:

> Just since the World Trade Center bombing, at least 36 car bombs have exploded around the world, killing more than 300 people and wounding more than 800, according to Brian Jenkins, one of the world's leading terrorism experts.
>
>   Which indicates that the new terrorism could be even deadlier than the old. Harder to combat too, precisely because the perpetrators are less organized than their forebears and thus more difficult to spot, track, and intercept.[8]

We can scarcely read any modern writer without running into sentence fragments. They provide a rapid pace, especially effective in the context of a series of events or thoughts or described objects. If the context is clear, fragments are both readable and efficient. They move readers quickly from place to place.

Sometimes you can begin with a series of fragments—a rapid-fire collection of facts that set the tone and theme for your essay. Most fragments depend for meaning on the sentences that come just before them. They can usually be joined to the preceding sentence by a comma, a dash, or a colon. Instead of forbidding you to use them at all, teachers should tell you to use them with care. Care includes being sure that the fragment does not become tiresome because you use it too often or that it does not become confusing because you use it out of a proper context.

3. Don't split infinitives.

Before we talk about split infinitives, we should be sure we know what they are. An infinitive can be split only by inserting a word or phrase between the infinitive marker *to* and the verb that makes the infinitive. The split infinitives below are in italics:

> General Manager Lou Gorman begged his Red Sox team *to really and truly try* not to fold until August this year.
>
> McDougal's daily exercise was *to strenuously and rapidly lift* a 4-pound chocolate cake from his plate to his mouth until the cake was consumed.

These are *not* split infinitives:

> *To be truly understood,* Paul wanted his life to be an open book.
>
> Unfortunately, the pages were far too dull *to be read carefully* by anyone with taste.

Many people who know nothing else about grammar know about split infinitives and don't like them. For their dislike they reckon on a literalistic understanding of the infinitive form. In most languages, the infinitive is one word. *Hacer, faire,* and *facere* are infinitives meaning "to do" in Spanish, French, and Latin respectively. Each is one word. Rigorists insist that an infinitive in English should be considered one word and that to split an infinitive is barbaric. Their reasoning seems confirmed by our use of infinitives in English, especially by our habit of referring to an infinitive with the pronoun *it:* "To write was everything to her; it was a compulsion that sometimes alarmed her friends." The pronoun *it* refers to the infinitive *to write,* a singular entity used as a noun. Rigorists believe that splitting an infinitive violates the integrity of the noun the infinitive represents.

Nevertheless, common sense tells us that English infinitives are not one word but two, and even the most casual observation reveals that good writers occasionally split infinitives. Here is a paragraph from *Time* about the disappearance of a Japanese explorer, Naomi Uemura, who vanished during a mountain-climbing expedition:

> He became a national hero in 1970 when, as a member of the first Japanese team *to successfully climb* Mount Everest, he was the first to reach the 29,028-ft. peak.[9]

Writing is governed by flexible standards set by editors. Most editors nowadays publish split infinitives, and I find it futile to rave against split infinitives as if they represented decadence and sloth.

Still, moderation is in order. Although professional writers split infinitives, they do so only occasionally. Several split infinitives in a short essay begin to sound clumsy. They seem to break down the natural rhythms of speech that make for clear writing and easy reading. We rarely split infinitives when we speak; we should be moderate in splitting them when we write.

And beyond rhythm is efficiency. Most split infinitives are bad not because they violate a sacrosanct rule but because the adverb that splits the infinitive is unnecessary. Suppose you wrote, "He wanted to really work hard." You could drop *really* and have a better sentence. *Really* is a pointless intensifier in the sentence. The same is true in most split infinitives; the adverb that does the splitting is unnecessary, and dropping it would make the sentence stronger.

Remember, too, that many people detest split infinitives with an irrational passion. I once knew a university president who scorned any letter to him that split an infinitive. He never wrote a book in his life, but he was convinced that anyone who split an infinitive was ignorant. People like him are surprisingly numerous in this world, and you should at least know that they exist when you write.

I don't split infinitives. Split infinitives disturb some delicate sentence balance in my head. Perhaps my reluctance arises from a lingering memory of the sweet-tempered seventh-grade English teacher, Mrs. Hattie Simmons Witt, in my rural Tennessee school. She believed firmly in God, brushed teeth, soap, and unsplit infinitives; and we loved her. Whatever caused it, my aversion to the split infinitive is so strong and so habitual that I do not fight it. I revise sentences to eliminate split infinitives, and something old-fashioned in me makes me notice when others split them—although I don't correct them on student papers.

You are much more likely to find split infinitives in journalism—newspaper and magazine writing—than in trade books. The more time editors take with a manuscript, the more likely they are to eliminate split infinitives. But the split infinitive is so common nowadays in so many things we read that writing teachers appear a little foolish when they become vehement about enforcing this rule.

4. Don't end a sentence with a preposition.

Prepositions are short words that never change their form no matter how they are used; they connect nouns or pronouns in prepositional phrases that serve as adjectives or adverbs in a sentence. Prepositions allow the strength of nouns and pronouns to modify other elements in a sentence.

> *In the night,* he dreamed *of horses.*

The prepositional phrase *In the night* works as an adverb modifying the verb *dreamed;* so does the prepositional phrase *of horses.* Without prepositions, we could not easily express these ideas. *Nightly he dreamed horsely,* we might say. Some scholar might reveal the meaning of such a sentence, but it would be difficult.

> The dictionary *on my desk* is my favorite book.

The prepositional phrase *on my desk* serves as an adjective modifying *dictionary,* a noun.

To place a preposition before its object is to follow the general rule of English syntax that related elements in a sentence should be as close to each other as possible. To end a sentence with a preposition is to deprive that preposition of a natural object on which to rest, and this apparent disorder may be unsettling. "The committee voted *against.*" Against what? "The hamburger came *with.*" With what?

But sometimes it seems unnatural to be strictly formal about keeping prepositions before their objects. You can change "That was the decision I fought *against*" to "That was the decision *against* which I fought," but only a robot or a flight attendant talks like that. You could also revise the sentence to read, "I fought *against* that decision"; but if you have been talking about several decisions and want to identify the particular one you have fought against, the most natural way to do it is to say, *"That* was the decision I fought *against."*

In developing our style, we choose between alternatives that sometimes differ only slightly from each other. There is a difference in emphasis between "That was the decision I fought *against"* and "I fought *against* that decision." Context would determine which one I used, but I would quickly use the former if I found it convenient.

5. Don't begin a sentence with a conjunction.

I once received an angry letter reproaching me for this sin. Conjunctions join sentence elements—words, phrases, or clauses. The common coordinating conjunctions—*and, but, for,* and *or*—join equal elements. Other conjunctions, such as *if, although, whether,* and *even,* join dependent elements.

I do not know the origin of the rule that sentences should never begin with a conjunction, but it is quoted to me frequently, usually by men over 60. Yet any glance at a newspaper or magazine shows that professional writers frequently begin sentences with conjunctions. John F. Kennedy used conjunctions to begin fifteen sentences in his short inaugural address in 1961. E. B. White, one of the finest essayists of our time, uses conjunctions to begin many of his sentences. So does Lewis Thomas, one of our best writers about science. So the false rule appears to have little validity among those who write English best.

Using a conjunction to begin a sentence emphasizes the connection between the thoughts of two consecutive sentences. When you use a conjunction to open a sentence, you say something like this: "Pay attention. This sentence is closely related to the thought in the sentence immediately before it. But it is important enough to stand by itself, to begin with a capital letter, so take careful note of it."

As I pointed out earlier, most sentences develop some thought in the sentence immediately preceding them. Although you may wish to emphasize such connections now and then, your readers will become immune to the effect if you use the device too often. Too many conjunctions begin to look like a verbal tic, an eccentricity of style that can become as annoying as the steady kick of a restless child behind you against your seat at the movies. Used with circumspection, the device of beginning an occasional sentence with a conjunction can make your prose a little more fluid. But remember the implacable habit of most writers: Around 80 percent of all sentences begin with the subject.

6. Avoid the pronoun *you.*

If you have read this far, you know I have violated this false rule again and again—for a reason. I have written these pages in an informal, conversational style; and in conversation we address listeners as *you.* We do the same in letters.

In more formal writing, to say *you* may seem out of place. No good writer would produce this sentence in a formal essay on cancer: "If *you* study cancer long enough, *you* discover that it is not one disease but a large group of diseases that share certain lethal qualities." It's much better to say this: "Cancer is not one disease but a group of related diseases." Nor do professional historians use the pronoun *you* in essays about history: "*You* have to sympathize with the Germans in World War I, facing as they did powerful enemies in both the east and the west." They are more likely to say something like this: "In World War I, Germany faced powerful enemies in both the east and the west."

Even in informal writing, the second person should be used sparingly. I dislike sentences like this: "To serve in one of the first submarines, *you* had to be brave or foolish or both." Your readers did not serve in one of the first submarines; you cannot meaningfully include them in your sentence. Say this instead: "Crew members on the first submarines had to be brave or foolish or both." Nor can you say this: "When *you* have been a famous athlete most of your life, *you* sometimes feel miserable when the cheering stops." Most readers have not been famous athletes all their lives. Write this instead: "Famous athletes sometimes feel miserable when the cheering stops."

It's all right to say *you* in various informal contexts. Articles that give advice or describe processes often use *you:*

> Most of the cameras give *you* no say in the exposure. A few, however, have a backlight switch, which lets *you* correct the exposure when strong light is coming from behind a subject.[10]

Personal essays also often address the reader. Here is Alice Walker writing about the Reverend Martin Luther King, Jr.:

> *You* know, if *you* have read his books, that his is a complex and revolutionary philosophy that few people are capable of understanding fully or have the patience to embody in themselves.[11]

7. Avoid contractions.

Here, much of the advice about use of the pronoun *you* can be repeated. Contractions do well in informal or semiformal prose—like the prose in this book. You may sometimes loosen stiff prose by using contractions. Most teachers accept contractions in college papers, and contractions serve well enough in letters or personal essays.

They serve less well in formal essays. I feel uncomfortable using them in scholarly books and articles because I find them a little too conversational, a little too informal for a subject that I want to be viewed seriously by the reader. I do not see contractions in dissertations, in formal books about history or philosophy or literary criticism, in business reports, or in articles in medical journals. Less formal publications, such as *Sports*

Illustrated, use them—but not excessively. Of course, when quoting a source that uses contractions, quote exactly as the words were written.

8. Use *that* to introduce restrictive clauses, *which* to introduce nonrestrictive clauses.

Restrictive clauses add essential information to the core statement of a sentence; *nonrestrictive clauses* add information that may be interesting and valuable but are not essential to the meaning the writer is trying to convey. You cannot leave a restrictive clause out and preserve the meaning of a core statement; you *may* omit a nonrestrictive clause without damaging the core statement. The restrictive clause in the following sentence is in italics:

> Of all my teachers, the one *who gave me the lowest grades* taught me the most.

If you leave out the italicized clause, you have nonsense. Grammarians call the clause *restrictive* because it restricts the noun it modifies. We are not talking about just *any* teacher; we are talking about the teacher *who gave me the lowest grades.*

Here is a nonrestrictive clause, one that does not restrict the meaning of the noun it modifies but merely adds some information:

> My English teacher, *who was also my next-door neighbor,* knew me from the time I was born.

Now we have a clause that can be deleted from the sentence without doing harm to the main statement. The clause is *parenthetical;* it adds interesting but unessential information. It does not restrict the noun *teacher.*

Many people, especially those over 65, believe that restrictive clauses should be introduced with *that* and nonrestrictive clauses should be introduced with *which.* At times they become irate when anyone suggests that this rule is only a foolish and cumbersome false rule that few writers observe or even think about. We have just seen that in clauses that refer to people, *who* can introduce both restrictive and nonrestrictive types. Why all the fuss?

Back in 1906, the English grammarian H. W. Fowler hit on the idea of using *that* to introduce restrictive clauses and *which* to introduce nonrestrictive clauses. He rightly believed that writers should make a clear distinction between the two types. Fowler wanted people to write sentences like these:

> The song that Sam played in the movie *Casablanca* was called "As Time Goes By."

> The ocean, which we could see from our house, changed color according to the shifting light of the sun through the clouds.

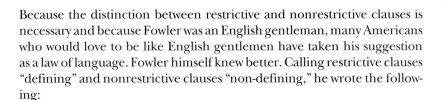

Because the distinction between restrictive and nonrestrictive clauses is necessary and because Fowler was an English gentleman, many Americans who would love to be like English gentlemen have taken his suggestion as a law of language. Fowler himself knew better. Calling restrictive clauses "defining" and nonrestrictive clauses "non-defining," he wrote the following:

> If writers would agree to regard *that* as the defining relative pronoun, and *which* as the non-defining, there would be much gain both in lucidity and in ease. Some there are who follow this principle now; but it would be idle to pretend that it is the practice of either most or the best writers.

Fowler was being much more charitable than his modern disciples, who have turned the *that/which* "rule" into a fetish. After the first edition of this book appeared, some outraged readers called my office to express their fierce indignation that a writing teacher should be so decadent as to deny the "rule" any authority. The fact remains that few writers and editors care much about it. We use *that* or *which* according to some indefinable sense of which one sounds better in the sentence. The rule is impossible to observe in sentences such as the one immediately preceding this one or in a sentence such as this: *"That which* makes the rule invalid is its impossibility." Neither can the "rule" hold in *who/whom* clauses, and it cannot help us in restrictive or nonrestrictive phrases.

But recall the motive of the "rule": You must make a distinction between the two kinds of clauses. The only sure way is by proper punctuation. Restrictive clauses are not set off by any kind of punctuation; nonrestrictive clauses are usually set off by commas, although you can also use parentheses or dashes.

On occasion, the meaning of a sentence will change according to whether the writer has used commas to make the clause nonrestrictive or has *not* used them to make the clause restrictive. Here is an example:

> The novel, *which* he wrote in Virginia, sold more than 30,000 copies.

Here is a nonrestrictive clause, one that gives added information about the novel under discussion. *He* seems to have written only one novel. He wrote it in Virginia. But here is the sentence with the nonrestrictive clause turned into a restrictive clause by the omission of the commas.

> The novel which he wrote in Virginia sold more than 30,000 copies.

Now we are talking about one novel among many. Other novels, *not* written in Virginia, may have sold more or fewer copies. The one written in Virginia, however, sold more than 30,000 copies. The restrictive clause marks off this novel from others.

The *that/which* rule is false, and few writers observe it. But you must be conscious of whether your clauses are restrictive or nonrestrictive, and you must punctuate accordingly. Otherwise you may confuse your readers by obscuring your meaning.

Concluding Remarks on False Rules

Don't be seduced by false rules, but don't go to the other extreme and suppose that English has no rules at all. Consider the motives behind the false rules, and observe the cautions that I have mentioned here. Always be aware of your audience. If, for example, you don't know if your teacher—or editor—will accept contractions, ask her. Try to be efficient in your writing. That is, use as few words as possible to express as clearly as you can the meaning you want to convey. That principle will help you cut needless intensifiers out of your prose—especially those that split infinitives. Read carefully and thoughtfully to learn the practices of other writers. Use common sense.

Eleven

Grammar and Mechanics

*M*ost Americans, given half a chance, will moan loudly about their ignorance of English grammar, sometimes in tones that smack suspiciously of pride. To some, grammar seems almost effete, a collection of puritanical rules that ought to be ignored by hearty men and women. Others take an opposite view. They believe that grammar is the soul of writing and that schools ought to be marching students through grammar drills in lockstep.

In both views of grammar there are chunks of truth. On one side, we have to say that grammar drills isolated from writing itself accomplish almost nothing. The soul of writing is having something to say. If you have nothing to say, no one will read your prose merely to admire its flawless grammar. Students of every age gain much more by forming the habit of writing than they do from grammar drills and filling in the blanks of workbooks. But on the other side, we know that writers ruin their prose when they make mistakes in grammar. Readers lose respect for them, and their writing becomes confusing.

Most of us know more grammar than we admit. We start learning grammar as we learn to talk. When our grammar works, we communicate with our families. When we communicate, we get what we want. As we succeed, we remember the speech patterns that gave us success and we use these patterns again to satisfy our next desire. Most of us continue to use the grammar we picked up as children. We may not recall the technical terms. Not many educated people can name the parts of speech, but they use them well enough. Few can make a lightning distinction between a conjunctive adverb and a conjunction, but they use, without difficulty, conjunctive adverbs like *moreover* and conjunctions like *and*.

Since about 1890, the grammar of literary English has been remarkably stable. It works in print and on radio and television and in our daily utterances. We can understand Australian movies and English newspapers. A few differences crop up. The English may write: "If one persists on betting on the horses, *one* will lose *one's* shirt," where an American will write: "If one persists on betting on the horses, *he* will lose *his* shirt." The English use plural verbs with many collective nouns. They'll say: "The committee *are* undecided," where Americans will say, "The committee *is* undecided." Yet Americans will also say, "The majority *are* sure of themselves." These slight variations do not seriously harm communication between Americans and Australians, New Zealanders, the English, the Scots, or the Irish.

Grammar cannot be a science; like the rest of language, it is a collection of proved conventions and patterns that allow communication. Despite the best efforts of scholars on linguistics, we do not know just how those patterns developed. Why have we rejected *ain't* as a contraction for *am not* or *is not?* Why is *he don't* wrong and *he doesn't* right? Why can't we write, "Thomas Jefferson and Karl Marx was both heirs to John Locke"? The only worthwhile answer is that the "erroneous" sentences are contrary to conventions developed over the centuries.

These conventions used to be much looser than they are now. The coming of mass literacy and the newspapers and magazines that feed literacy have created a much less flexible grammar than Shakespeare or Chaucer used. Mass production requires standardization. Standard forms are easier to teach and easier to learn and also easier to recognize. When only a few people could read and when readers read aloud—as they did in the late Middle Ages when modern English was developing—grammar could be much more flexible. But when readers rapidly scan print in silence, irregularities trip them up and make them go back to read a line again before they can understand it. A standard grammar—like standard tools of all kinds—helps a mass society work.

A few writing experts contend that to enforce the conventions of grammar smacks of elitism. They say that conventional English is only one dialect among many and that all dialects are equal. No humane person could suggest that we scorn those whose dialect learned at home is different from conventional English. But it is a serious misreading of both past and present to say that all dialects, including conventional English, are equal in a large and literate society. Those who do not learn to use conventional English are at a lifelong disadvantage.

Television and other mass media are homogenizing the conventions even more. In the rural South where I grew up, the word *ain't* is fading. Neighbors my age still use it; their children use it less. Why is it going? I suspect that it is passing away because people are not hearing it on television, and the thousands of hours the average American child spends before the tube affects language more than all the English teachers in America combined.

Students may have problems with grammar because writing is so different from speaking. They get lost in the physical process of writing—

of moving a pen or a pencil laboriously across the page—so that the brain runs off and leaves the hand. Writing goes so slowly and painfully for them that they lose track of their sentences. If you have problems in grammar, try reading your work aloud to yourself. You will pick up most of your errors. Writing with a computer liberates us from much of the physical toil of writing and allows us to see errors better and revise them away.

You can also buy yourself a good handbook, such as *The McGraw-Hill College Handbook* that I have written with Harvey Wiener. Handbooks usually summarize all the major conventions of grammar and provide an index that lets you find items quickly. But the best way to learn to write is to write. No one becomes a good baseball player solely by studying the baseball rule book. We learn baseball by playing the game. We learn grammar by writing, discovering our flaws as we go along, and by correcting them as we continue.

This chapter is devoted to a list of problems in grammar and punctuation that trouble my students. (Punctuation is part of grammar in that it is one of the forces that holds sentences together and helps us arrange them.) It is not an exhaustive study. But it will help you overcome some common errors.

I hope something else will happen as you study this section. I hope that you gain the confidence to use English with more variety. It's a shame, for example, that many people avoid the subjunctive mood of verbs altogether because they are afraid that they will use it incorrectly. The subjunctive is uncommon in English, but now and then it adds elegance to the language. You can get away with using the simple past tense for verbs, but using the various perfect tenses can add subtlety to your thought and thus make your work more interesting.

Punctuation seems unimportant to most of my students—a matter of dots and squiggles on a page. Why bother with it? But conventional punctuation holds sentences together as mortar keeps a brick wall from tumbling down. Bad punctuation may confuse and irritate readers. In my recommendations, I have followed the advice of *The Chicago Manual of Style,* published by the University of Chicago Press. The looming authority of this celebrated work is so great it should be included in every writer's library.

1. Make the subject and verb agree in number.

If the subject of a sentence is singular, it must take a singular verb; if the subject is plural, the verb must be plural. In nearly all verbs, except the irregular *to be* and *to have* verbs *(am, are, is; was, were; has, have),* the only variation between singular and plural forms is in the third-person singular of the present tense. We say, "I dance, you dance, we dance, they dance," but "she *dances.*" The simple past of most verbs uses the same form for both singular and plural: "I *danced;* he *danced;* they *danced.*" Helping verbs will vary like the present tense, but since the most common helping verbs are *to be* and *to have,* we don't need to learn many special forms. In this regard, English is simpler than languages that do not use helping verbs. So we can be grateful for some simplicity in our complicated tongue.

We are most likely to make errors in subject-verb agreement when we insert a clause or phrase between a subject and a verb. The danger becomes acute when the phrase is a preposition with a plural object. That happens in sentences like this: "Each of the cars *were* fast." *Each,* the subject of the sentence, is singular. The prepositional phrase *of the cars* throws the writer off so that here we have the plural verb *were.* The sentence should read like this: "Each of the cars *was* fast. *Anybody, everybody, anyone, each, every, neither, nobody,* and *someone* are all singular and take a singular verb.

> *Each* of the players *is* eligible until final exams.
>
> *Every* one of the coaches *chews* gum.
>
> *Nobody goes* there any more; it's too crowded.
>
> *Everybody* in the audience *is* applauding.
>
> *Each* of the choices *is* possible; *neither is* desirable.

Now and then, a compound subject considered as a unit takes a singular verb.

> Cops and robbers is an old American children's game.

But don't assume that readers will see the unity you see in a compound subject. You may write, "The *gathering and classifying* of data *goes* on relentlessly in all the sciences." In your mind, *gathering* and *classifying* may be a single act, and so you may use the singular verb *goes*. But many readers will assume that they are two acts, and you will confuse them by using a singular verb. Except in a few idiomatic expressions, use the plural verb with a compound subject.

Some collective nouns occupy a shadowy borderland. In American English, we use a plural verb in the following sentences with singular subjects: "A number of movies produced last year *were* filled with violence and sex"; "A majority of the team *were* unable to graduate."

2. When two singular nouns in the subject of a sentence are joined by *or* or *nor*, the verb should be in the singular.

> Neither economics *nor* history *is* an exact science.
>
> A tub *or* a shower *is* in every room.

3. When a plural noun in a compound subject is joined by *or* or *nor* to a singular noun, the verb agrees with the nearest noun.

> Neither the singer nor her *managers are* happy.
>
> Neither her managers nor the *singer is* happy.

Try to revise sentences like these to eliminate the unpleasant awkwardness of the constructions: "The singer *and* her manager *are* unhappy."

4. Use the correct verb form after the adverb *there*. In a sentence beginning with *there*, the verb must agree with the subject, which usually comes immediately after the verb.

Don't say, *"There is singing and laughter* upstairs tonight." Say instead, *"There are singing and laughter* upstairs tonight."

5. Use the nominative case for a pronoun subject of a dependent clause, even if the clause itself serves as an object.

Don't say, "He was prepared for whomever might ask a question." Say, "He was prepared for whoever might ask a question." *Whoever* is the subject of the verb *might ask* and so must be in the nominative case.

Don't be confused by parenthetical clauses within dependent clauses. A parenthetical clause has no *grammatical* effect on the subject of a dependent clause of which it is a part. Therefore don't say, "The woman *whom* he believed was drunk was in a coma." The *he believed* is a parenthetical clause. Say this: "The woman *who* he believed was drunk was in a coma." The pronoun *who* governs the verb *was*.

His aunt, *who* he said had known Virginia Woolf, kept a detailed diary.

Now complications enter. When you write a pronoun that is the subject of an infinitive, the pronoun is in the objective case.

She supposed *him* to be a friend. We imagined *her* to be wise and good.

The pronoun is in the objective case even if the infinitive is understood rather than written.

She supposed *him* a friend. She thought *her* beautiful.

The subject of an infinitive acts as the agent of action the infinitive describes. Any subject of an infinitive always follows a transitive verb, one that takes a direct object. Infinitives themselves are nonfinite verbs; we sometimes call them *verbals*. A nonfinite verb cannot express past or present time by itself. To express time, a verbal must be joined to a finite verb: "He wanted to be famous." The past tense of the verb *wanted* adds time to the infinitive *to be*, which has no time of its own. We could as easily say "He wants to be famous" or "He will want to be famous." If the infinitive has a subject, the subject becomes part of an infinitive phrase and serves as the direct object of the preceding transitive verb.

They told *us* to be careful.

6. Use the objective case for a pronoun that serves as a direct object, an indirect object, or the object of a preposition. Do not use the objective case for a pronoun that serves as a subject.

The confusion between subjective and objective case in pronouns is probably the most common single error in student writing and common speech.

Don't say, "Just between you and I, his poetry is terrible." Say this instead: "Just between you and me, I stop my ears when he reads." Don't say, "He laughed at Clara and I." Say, "He laughed at Clara and me." Don't say, "Me and Wilma spoke to them last night." Say, "Wilma and I spoke to them last night." Don't say, "Her and me decided to bicycle in France." Say, "She and I decided to bicycle in France." Don't say, "Myself and Richard invite you to the staff party." Say, "Richard and I invite you to the party."

7. Form the possessive case correctly.

My students have more trouble with the apostrophe marking the possessive case than with any other mark of punctuation. About half of them cannot form the possessive in accordance with the conventions of English. To form the possessive, you must use the apostrophe (').

To form the possessive of singular nouns, add *'s* at the end (Ann's job; Gertrude's voice; Doc's friendship; the hotel's buffet; Israel's troubles; the superintendent's office).

Use *'s* even when the singular noun ends in *s* (Burriss's house; Erasmus's first book; Charles's pen).

This rule is *not* observed in some traditional phrases (for goodness sake! in Jesus' name).

Be sure to add *'s* to words that end in *z* or *x* (Groucho Marx's films; Berlioz's music).

To form the plural possessive, use the simple apostrophe after words whose plurals end in *s* (the Joneses' street; the dogs' door).

If the noun has an irregular plural that does not end in *s*, form the possessive by adding *'s* just as you would if the noun were singular (children's literature; men's clothing; women's rights).

8. Use the correct verb tense.

Tense is the *time* of a verb. English has six tenses.

Present: I play.

Simple past: I played.

Simple future: I will play.

Present perfect: I have played.

Past perfect: I had played.

Future perfect: I will have played.

Each tense has a *progressive* form that expresses continuing, or progressive, action within the time noted in the tense.

Present progressive: I am playing.

Past progressive (imperfect): I was playing.

Future progressive: I will be playing.

Present perfect progressive: I have been playing.

Past perfect progressive: I had been playing.

Future perfect progressive: I will have been playing.

The present tense can do several things. It reports habitual action.

Birds *migrate* every year.

The sun *rises* every morning.

Wars *are caused* by stupidity.

Habitual action extends to verbs that describe the action in literature because the written word is assumed to be always speaking.

David Copperfield *is* not as interesting as other characters in the book.

Socrates *teaches* that the way to wisdom begins with the command, "Know thyself."

The Constitution *links* the right to keep and bear arms to serving in the militia—what we today call the National Guard.

The present progressive tense is the most idiomatic way we have of speaking of something happening right now.

She *is coming* down the street.

They *are repaving* the highway between Boston and Lynn.

The present progressive can become a future tense by adding an adverb of future time.

She is coming *tomorrow.*

They are playing softball *next Sunday.*

Adding *do* or *does* shows emphasis. The present emphatic is used in negations.

I *do not* like snakes.

She *does not* like people who *do not* like snakes.

The present emphatic is also used to affirm something that someone else has denied. For example, someone accuses you of disliking rock music, and, if you have any hearing left, you say, "I *do* like rock music."

The present tense may create confusion for writers who get carried away with the sense of action conveyed by the present. These writers often use the present tense to describe past action, especially when they write about history or an exciting story.

Franklin Roosevelt is elected because he promises to do something about the Depression, and Hoover keeps saying that the Depression is almost over. Roosevelt takes over in March 1933, and, in his inaugural address, he promises bold action and tells the American people that the only thing they have to fear is fear itself. Hoover tells them that he was right all along and that the only thing they have to fear is Roosevelt.

Narration in the present tense is sometimes successful. Thomas Carlyle used it to great effect in *The French Revolution*. But, in general, avoid using the present tense when writing about the past. Professional historians in Britain and America write in the past tense. The present sounds strained in telling English-speaking readers about the past, and since it violates a common convention, it is also confusing.

The simple past is usually formed by adding *-ed* as a suffix to the present stem of the verb. "I play" becomes "I played." The past participle is formed in the same way. "I have played." But English is complicated by having about 300 irregular verbs. They are irregular because they form the past tense or the past participle in some way other than adding *-ed*. We say "I draw" but not "I drawed." We say "I drew" and "I have drawn." We say "I see" but not "I seed." We say "I see," "I saw," and "I have seen."

We usually learn irregular verbs as we learn to talk and hear others use them. In some regions of the country, people diverge from standard English. In the farming community where I grew up, people said, "I seen him when he done it," and "He drawed me a plan for the barn, and I taken a lot of time to study it over." These were intelligent, sensible people. Similar people in other regions today may use verbs in nonstandard forms. When you are in doubt, consult a dictionary—the most valuable tool a writer has. Any good dictionary lists the various standard forms of irregular verbs.

The simple future tense is formed with *shall* and *will*. Strict grammarians used to insist that *shall* be used with the first person and *will* with the second and third persons. American writers generally ignore this distinction. We nearly always say, "He will be fifty on his next birthday" and "We will be happy to see you at the party." Today, in American English, *shall* seems to indicate an emphatic statement. "They shall not pass." "I shall be there." It is almost as if *shall* were always in italics in our minds.

We should devote a few more words to the progressive form, showing action that continues. The past progressive, or *imperfect,* is the most common form. Use it to show action going on while something else is happening: "I *was traveling* west during June." The sentence means that while June was going by, I was traveling west. Here are other examples:

He *was sleeping* when the robbery occurred.

While the team *was holding* its postgame prayer meeting, the gamblers *were counting* the bribe money to be paid to the players for losing.

We call the past progressive the *imperfect* form because the end of the action is not described. That is, the action of sleeping continued as long as the robbery occurred, and the actions of holding the prayer meeting and counting went on for an indefinite period of time. We are not told how long any of these actions continued. Think of the progressive as duration. The action continues for a time—or continued or will continue. Don't use the progressive when the past will do.

9. Avoid illogical mixing of verb tenses.

The simple verb tenses are seldom difficult. We combine them logically. We would never think of saying, "I was there when you will come." We say, "I will come when you are there." We know that the present tense *(are)* in the second clause is governed by the future tense *(will come)* in the first. Sometimes we stumble when we consider how to join the past tense with the present, but a little thought usually leads us aright. We mix past and present in the following sentences when someone in the past made a statement that continues to be true for all time.

> Plato believed that the soul is immortal.
>
> Thomas More thought that death is not the worst fate.

Normally, the past tense in a first clause will demand a past tense in a second clause, and we usually join such clauses without difficulty.

> He played baseball because he loved the game, not because he was paid a high salary.
>
> Players for the Boston Red Sox thought he was crazy.

Problems with mixing tenses usually arise when the perfect tenses are used. The present perfect always conveys a sense of action that started in the past and continues to the present, where either the action itself or its effects continue. The present perfect tense is formed by using the present tense of the verb *to have* with the past participle of the main verb in the construction.

> We *have worked* since yesterday afternoon.

The work started in the past and is still going on at the time the sentence describes. The present perfect tense can easily be used in combination with the present tense.

> He *has been* a great baseball player, but his greatest days are behind him, and he is retiring at the end of this season.
>
> She *has been grinding* rust off the car all afternoon with the electric sander, and now she *is* tired.

The present perfect tense can be used with the future because both tenses join at the time when the statement about future action is made.

> They *have been traveling* all night, and they *will travel* all day today and tomorrow.

The past perfect tense uses the past tense *had* of the verb *to have* with the past participle of the main verb in the construction. It always implies that an action ended before or just as another action began.

They *had been waiting* an hour when the train *arrived*.

The waiting ended at the moment the train arrived; both actions took place in the past. The past perfect cannot be used before the present perfect. We cannot say, "Country music had been popular and has remained so." It had been popular before what? The past perfect sets up the expectation of an end point, and if you do not have an end point, you must provide one or change the sentence.

Country music *had been* popular before 1950, but in that year it *attracted* national attention.

Here, the prepositional phrase *before 1950* provides the end point that the past perfect leads us to expect, and the later clauses go on from that point to make another statement. Sometimes we imply the end point, especially in oral English. We may speak of a friend who came to an early-morning history class in a tuxedo. Someone says, "Did you know that John came to class this morning in a tuxedo?" You ask why, and your friend says, "He *had been* at an all-night party." From the last sentence spoken by your friend, you infer an end point already mentioned in an earlier sentence. The implied thought is this: "John had been at an all-night party and came to class in the morning in his tuxedo." The end point of the action *had been* is his arrival in class.

You also cannot properly use the past perfect with the present tense. You should not say, "He had to learn to walk before he learns to run." You should not use the past perfect as a substitute for the simple past. That is, don't say "Henry VIII *had been* born in 1491" unless you intend to follow that sentence with another related to it by the simple past. It is better to say, "Henry VIII *was* born in 1491." You may use the past perfect in a paragraph whose sentences lack a dependent clause only if the end point of the past perfect is clearly stated in another sentence.

Henry VIII came to the throne in 1509. He *had not been meant* to be king. He *had been born* the second son of Henry VII. His older brother, Arthur, *had been heir* to the throne, but Arthur died. A persistent legend holds that young Henry *had been destined* to become a priest, but Arthur's death changed that destiny and the destiny of England as well.

Here we have several sentences in the past perfect, all moving toward the end point stated in the first sentence. The past perfect tense is used too much, especially in the writing of history. Use the simple past unless the past perfect is clearly needed.

The future perfect tense describes a future act that must be concluded before or just as another future act begins.

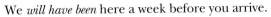

We *will have been* here a week before you arrive.

The apples *will have been picked* before then.

As is true of all perfect tenses, the future perfect makes you think of the time when one action will end and another begin. The action in the future perfect tense must end before some future moment or just as some future action begins. Always recall that perfect tenses imply a time considered as the end point of an action, a time when the action of the sentence is complete from the point of view of the sentence. You may say, "I have been waiting for an hour," using the present tense. You may go on waiting for another hour, or you may now be ending your wait, but neither possibility is the concern of this sentence. This sentence is concerned with the action that has gone on for an hour, and that hour is complete by the time the sentence is written or spoken.

A special problem sometimes arises with infinitives in the perfect tense. Some years ago, a submarine from the Soviet Union sank off the coast of Norway. Several American newspapers ran this line:

> "It must have been hellish to have been on that submarine," said Johan Joergen Holst, Norway's minister of defense.

The use of the perfect tense "to have been" is incorrect. The line should have been, "It must have been hellish to be on that submarine." "To be" is an infinitive; it takes the time of the finite verb that controls it. Therefore to write "must have been" presumes that the infinitive "to be" is controlled by the perfect tense of the main verb phrase.

10. Use the subjunctive form of the verb in dependent clauses that make a statement assumed to be contrary to fact.

I wish I *were* in the Caribbean.

I am not in the Caribbean; hence the subjunctive *were*.

If he *were* more tactful, he would have more friends.

He is not more tactful; so he does not have more friends.

Here is the most common use of the subjunctive—the form of the verb that is much more common in French or German or Greek than in English. We say that verbs are in either the *subjunctive* or the *indicative* mood. The *indicative* is used to represent simple statements of fact. The *subjunctive* carries with it always a mood of doubt or yearning or fear or command that in English lingers only in a few uses. Indeed it is used so seldom that the chief problem of the subjunctive is that insecure people afraid of being incorrect may use it when they should not.

The subjunctive is *not* used, for example, after every *if* in a sentence. Use the subjunctive only to make a statement clearly contrary to fact, as in the examples above. Don't use it for factual statements that may involve some uncertainty about the past. You should say this, "If what she said *was* true, he was guilty." This is a simple indicative statement. You do not know whether she spoke the truth or not. You merely make the statement that if she *did* speak the truth, he was guilty. That is a fact. The indicative is used in factual statements. If you knew beyond any doubt that she was lying, you would say this: "If what she said *were* true, he was guilty."

Had and *should* may express the subjunctive. "*Should* you win the Nobel Prize, I will help you spend the money." It is entirely uncertain that you will win the Nobel Prize. But if you do, I will help you spend the prize money. "*Had* the Germans not feared Russia so much in 1914, they might have beaten France quickly." The Germans did fear the Russians; they did not concentrate all their army in France; they not only did not win the war quickly; they did not win it at all. The subjunctive use of *had* introduces a condition clearly contrary to fact.

11. Use commas according to standard practice.

The comma appears more than any other punctuation mark in English. It is important for you to use it according to standard practice to avoid confusing readers.

A. Use the Comma *with a Coordinating Conjunction* to Separate Independent Clauses in a Sentence.

Independent clauses can usually stand alone as sentences. The coordinating conjunctions are *and, but, nor, for,* and sometimes *yet* and *so.* The comma and the conjunction bind such clauses together.

> Dolphins have brains bigger than humans, but they spend all their time in the water, *and* they can't even play checkers.

> The star quarterback of Sourmash State University could not read simple English after four years of college, *nor* could he find a pro team willing to hire him.

Do not use the comma alone to hold independent clauses together. Do not use a comma like this:

> Intercollegiate football games used to be for the participants, now the fans demand that teams win at any cost, even if they must cheat.

The absence of the coordinating conjunction *but* after the comma confuses us. For a moment, we think the participants are now the fans. We have to get to the end of the sentence to sort out its meaning. The fault here is called a *comma splice;* that is, the writer tried to splice the clauses together with a comma, but a comma alone cannot do the job. We must add a conjunction.

> Intercollegiate football games used to be for the participants, but now the fans demand that teams win at any cost, even if they must cheat.

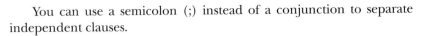

You can use a semicolon (;) instead of a conjunction to separate independent clauses.

> Coach Dixie was outraged; he thought local sports writers should be too loyal to reveal that he had hired a nonstudent to be quarterback.

B. Use a comma after a long introductory clause or phrase that precedes the subject of an independent clause.

Because the temperature on the highway was 115 degrees in the California desert, the air conditioning in the diner nearly knocked me flat.

Backed up against Antwerp, the Belgian army furiously counterattacked the Germans in September 1914.

Having failed to win peace in Massachusetts by negotiation and compromise, the British decided to use force.

C. Use commas to set off parenthetical clauses and phrases that add descriptive material not essential to the principal assertion of the sentence.

Here is a parenthetical phrase set off with commas.

> He kept the fountain pen, *a gift from his father,* for the rest of his long life.

The phrase *a gift from his father* adds information to the sentence but is not essential to the main assertion of the sentence. The writer might choose to develop something from the detail that the fountain pen was a gift from father to son. But the main assertion of this sentence is that *He* kept the pen for the rest of his long life. The assertion would remain the same without the phrase; so the phrase is set off by commas.

Here is a parenthetical (or nonrestrictive) clause set off by commas.

> The personal computer, *which was unknown only a decade ago,* is now an indispensable tool for thousands of writers.

The parenthetical clause adds an interesting detail, that a device as common as the personal computer was unknown only ten years ago. But it is not essential to the core assertion of the sentence, that the personal computer is now an indispensable tool for thousands of writers.

Do not set off clauses and phrases that are indispensable to the main assertion. Here is an essential clause not set off by commas:

> The churchmen *who opposed Galileo* feared that his teachings would undermine the faith.

The clause here is essential to the main assertion. The writer is not speaking of all churchmen but only those who opposed Galileo. Without the clause, the main assertion of the sentence would not make sense. At least it would not make the sense that the writer intended.

Be careful here. You can change the meaning of a sentence by setting off a clause or phrase with commas. Suppose you say this:

Faculty members *who are slipshod and lazy* rob their students.

This sentence means that only faculty members who are slipshod and lazy rob their students. By not setting off the dependent clause with commas, you indicate that it is essential to the meaning of your sentence. You are writing about one kind of faculty member. But suppose you say this:

Faculty members, who are slipshod and lazy, rob their students.

The commas tell us that you mean that *all* faculty members rob their students. You happen to add the information that faculty members are also slipshod and lazy, and so you deliver a double insult. You condemn the teaching profession for robbing students, and you announce that all members of that profession are slipshod and lazy.

Some writers set off all appositives with commas, but this habit may lead to confusion. Suppose you write this sentence:

In his novel, *For Whom the Bell Tolls,* Ernest Hemingway made a tragedy of the Spanish Civil War.

The commas make the title parenthetical, something that could be left out without damaging the meaning of the sentence. They tell readers that the main assertion is this: "In his novel, Ernest Hemingway made a tragedy of the Spanish Civil War." The sentence now implies that Hemingway wrote only one novel and that it was called *For Whom the Bell Tolls.* In fact, he wrote many novels, and the writer should not set off the title of the book with commas.

D. Use the comma to separate adjectives that modify the same noun if the adjectives can be connected by the word *and.*

You may say this: "Johnson was the strong, silent type." You could also say, "Johnson was the strong and silent type." So to replace *and,* use a comma. But you would not use a comma to separate adjectives in this sentence: "The large old oak trees cast a deep shade on the lawn." You would not say, "The large and old and oak trees cast a deep shade on the lawn." Therefore omit commas between the adjectives.

E. Use the comma to set off interjections or transitive adverbs at the beginning of a sentence.

Consequently, we thought Johnson was boring. Indeed, his wife thought Johnson was boring.

F. Use the comma to separate words or phrases in a series of three or more elements.

She wrote books, articles, and poems.

Lincoln's mighty words in the Gettysburg Address made the Civil War a struggle for government "of the people, by the people, and for the people."

G. Use a comma to set off direct quotations when introduced by an expression such as *he said* or *she said*.

John Lyly said, "If one write never so well, he cannot please all, and write he never so ill, he shall please some."

H. Use a comma correctly with other punctuation.

A comma at the end of quoted material goes inside the quotation marks.

"Hating people is like burning down your own house to get rid of a rat," said Harry Emerson Fosdick, one of the greatest of Protestant preachers.

But a comma goes outside parentheses or brackets at the end of the material so set off.

In hard times (the thought is from Euripides), friends show whether they are to be trusted or not.

She wrote me that she hated my "mispellings" [sic], but that my content was fairly good.

12. Use the dash circumspectly.

Many writers love the dash. It helps add seemingly spontaneous thoughts that break into our minds while we are writing a sentence. It provides a sense of telegraphic style. It allows us to digress slightly or to signal readers that we want to them to pay special attention to what follows.

The first thing to do with a dash is to make it correctly. On a typewriter or a computer, the dash is composed of two hyphens without a space between them, typed with no space between the word before the dash and the first hyphen or between the last hyphen and the first word after the dash—like this. If you use one hyphen - like this, you will confuse readers and upset the people who set your work into type. Use the dash to set off an emphatic phrase.

Baseball players now charge for their autographs—up to $25.00 a signature!

You can also use the dash to set off an emphatic clause.

> Longstreet surveyed the field at Gettysburg before Pickett's Charge and wanted to withdraw, and events proved him right. But he could not get his way for one reason—Robert E. Lee wanted to attack, and Lee was in command.

Dashes, like parentheses, sometimes set off slight digressions or definitions within a sentence. Dashes seem to be a little more emphatic than parentheses, though that depends on the writer.

> Renaissance painting—assuming there was such a thing as the Renaissance—emphasized the human figure and a somewhat idealized human expression.

Sometimes, for emphasis, you may want to write a compound subject, follow it with a dash, and make a statement about that subject with a clause.

> Beethoven, Chopin, and Liszt—these are perhaps the greatest of the romantic composers.

It's not good to use dashes to set off more than one element in a sentence. Writer's occasionally do so, but the effect is confusing. Be circumspect. You can often use a colon, parentheses, or a simple comma to set off elements that you might also set off with a dash. Too many dashes in a piece of prose always give me the uncomfortable feeling that the writer has a case of hypernervosity and wants to emphasize everything. The effect is a little like being yelled at.

13. Use standard American forms for quotations.

Use double quotation marks to set off direct quotations. If material you are quoting includes material in quotation marks, use single quotation marks (the apostrophe key on the typewriter) to set off the words in quotation marks within the original.

> Speaking of Sioux chief Sitting Bull, Evan S. Connell says, "A feminine element very often radiates from sexually powerful males and in the case of Sitting Bull this was so unmistakable that one journalist, fascinated by the oval face between long braids, spoke of his 'manhood and womanliness.'"[1]

English practice is the opposite of American practice. English publishers use single quotation marks where we use the double marks and the double marks where we use the single marks. Follow American practice. Commas go within closing quotation marks; semicolons and colons go outside.

> "You write in water," said Erasmus of work that had no result.
>
> "Hell will never be full until you be in it"; such was a Scottish proverbial insult.
>
> "Whom the gods love dies young": John F. Kennedy died when he was 46 years old.

Do *not* put quotation marks around block quotations. Use indented blocks for quotations more than four or five lines long. In typed or computer-generated manuscripts, the blocks should be indented five spaces from the left margin. The indention of a block of text is indication enough that you are quoting. If you add quotation marks, readers will assume you are beginning the quotation with a quotation from someone else.

The lines in the block quotation should be double-spaced. Within the block quotation, use quotation marks exactly as they appear in the quoted material. Elsewhere in this book, I recommended that you not use block quotations if you can avoid them. It is usually better to paraphrase and to quote smaller sections of a text than one quotes in a block. But in books such as this one, block quotations are necessary, and everyone has to use them now and then. When you use them, study the examples in this book if you have questions about the right form.

Do not use quotation marks to set off slang, clichés, or other words that you wish to apologize for. Only inexperienced writers use these apologetic quotation marks. They seem to say, "I know this is a cliché or some other lazy language, but at least I have put it in quotation marks to let you know that I know I'm being lazy." When you are tempted to put quotation marks around a cliché, try, instead, to think of some better expression. Obey your better impulse.

But do use quotation marks to indicate a usage by others that you do not share yourself.

> In the "People's Republic" of China, the people have no voice in their government.

For decades, the practice of writers in using direct quotations has been to change capitalization when adapting them to their own texts. Here is the original quotation:

> Persistent melancholy is one of the fundamental themes of Southern literature.

And here is the standard way of adapting that quotation:

> McDougal has called "persistent melancholy" a quality of Southern literature.

The *P* in the original is silently changed to *p* in the quotation to fit the sentence where the quotation is used. But of late a new typographical barbarism has been infecting publishers and writers with a foolish pedantry that would give us this version:

> McDougal has called "[p]ersistent melancholy" a quality of Southern literature.

The pedant wants us to know that in the original, the *p* in *persistent* was capitalized, but he has made it lowercase. The result is ugliness on the page and simple nonsense. Use the standard practice of silent change from lower case to capital or from capital to lower case.

14. Use ellipsis marks correctly.

My students have trouble using ellipses correctly. Ellipsis marks indicate that some words have been left out—usually out of a quotation. Make elipsis marks by using the period key on your typewriter or computer. Leave a space after the last word before the ellipsis, type a dot, leave a space, type a second dot, space again, the third dot, space again, and then resume the quotation. You should not make ellipsis marks without spaces between the marks, like this (...). Ellipsis marks should always have spaces between them like this (. . .). Otherwise the rapid reader will stumble and have to back up and reconsider what you have written.

Here are a few sentences from Paul Fussell's book *The Great War and Modern Memory:*

> Recourse to the pastoral is an English mode of both fully gauging the calamities of the Great War and imaginatively protecting oneself against them. Pastoral reference, whether to literature or to actual rural localities and objects, is a way of invoking a code to hint by antithesis at the indescribable; at the same time, it is a comfort in itself, like rum, a deep dugout, or a woolly vest.[2]

Here is part of a paper that quotes from this text, using ellipses to indicate some omitted words:

> Fussell argues that English troops in World War I used the pastoral tradition as an anodyne against the horrors they met in the trenches. He says, "Pastoral reference . . . is a way of invoking a code to hint by antithesis at the indescribable; at the same time, it is a comfort in itself."

The ellipsis marks show that words have been omitted between *reference* and *is;* by checking the original, you can see what those words were. Notice that there is a space between *reference* and the first dot and a space after each of the dots, including the space between the last one and the word *is.* Notice, too, that there are no ellipsis marks after *itself,* although it is not the last word in Fussell's sentence. The quotation marks are sufficient to show readers that the writer has stopped quoting. Any reader assumes that Fussell's text goes on; no reader needs ellipsis marks to understand that you are not quoting everything Fussell says.

Neither do you need ellipsis marks at the beginning of a quotation, even if you are quoting only part of a sentence. The quotation marks tell them that you are quoting, and they assume that you cannot quote all of your source. You don't need to create typographical monstrosities like this:

> Lincoln said that the Civil War was fought so that ". . . government of the people, by the people, and for the people . . ." might endure.

Remember always that the function of ellipsis marks is to show that you are leaving something out between your first quotation marks and your last. They certify your honesty, showing readers that you are not quoting something exactly as the author wrote it. The quotation marks themselves set off your quotation from what you choose not to quote in your source.

Sometimes you may leave out a whole sentence, several whole sentences, or an entire paragraph from a long quotation. Then you must punctuate the last sentence before the ellipsis marks. You put the period at the end of that sentence, make a space, and write the ellipsis marks according to standard practice.

> David Donald speaks of the difficulties a man as large as Thomas Wolfe had when he wrote. "He tried to keep to a fixed schedule. He began working on his book about midnight and, because no chairs or tables were ever quite comfortable for a man of his height, he usually stood while he wrote, using the top of the refrigerator as his desk. . . . Often in the early afternoon Abe Smith, his former student at New York University, now a young, married businessman, came by to type his interminable manuscript."[3]

The writer quotes David Donald, Wolfe's biographer, and the ellipsis marks show that words have been omitted after the sentence ending with *desk*. That sentence is punctuated with a period. Then there is a space, an ellipsis dot, another space, a second dot, another space, a third dot, and another space before the quotation takes up again.

15. Use a colon before a list or an amplification of a statement made in an independent clause.

Sometimes you may wish to make a list after a statement.

> Coach Dixie valued three things: winning football games, drawing the largest salary in the Southeastern Conference, and drilling his players on the split infinitive.

Note that the colon comes at the end of an independent clause. A colon should not break into an independent clause. You should not say "She wanted: a good job, respect, and loyal friends." You can see from the many examples in this book that colons frequently come just before a block quotation. Colons can also join independent clauses when the second clause is meant to be a consequence or a clarification of the first.

> Jackson was furious: Someone had given him a monkey for Christmas, and he hated pets.

Sometimes you may wish to amplify a statement.

> Coach Dixie lived by one principle: He never broke the rules if he thought he might be caught.

16. Observe the rules for parallelism.

Parallel grammatical forms can add power to your writing. The most simple parallelism is the series. "Churchill said, 'I have nothing to offer but *blood, toil, tears, and sweat.*'" But phrases and clauses can also make parallel forms. Parallel forms are joined by the coordinating conjunctions *and, but, or, for,* and *nor.* The words, phrases, and clauses joined by these conjunctions must be equal in form. In the example from Churchill above, the conjunction *and* helps join four nouns—*blood, toil, tears,* and *sweat.*

> I have heard the chimes at midnight and seen the sun at dawn.
>
> He liked neither beer nor wine.
>
> I shall sing a song, for I am happy.

The most common errors in parallelism are in a series. Here is a faulty parallelism:

> We came home, ate dinner, and we watched the All-Star game.

The correct form is this:

> We came home, ate dinner, and watched the All-Star game.

Appendix One

Avoiding Discrimination

Women

Fair-minded writers are not mean-spirited in their prose. They do not insult minorities or express prejudices against women. Sometimes inexperienced writers use terms they do not recognize as insulting or degrading. Weed such language out of your writing.

One of the most persistent discriminations in language has been against women. For centuries, ordinary English seemed to imply that only men were important. Now women vigorously and justly demand equality, not only in jobs and education and social life, but also in language. The consequences for writing have been confusing. I cannot clear up all those confusions, for they are still being vigorously debated. But perhaps I can clarify some of the issues and help you avoid sexism in language while, at the same time, preserving the natural fluency that good writing requires.

The most troublesome problem in sexist language is this: What do we do with the English custom of using *he, his,* or *him* when we need an indefinite singular noun or pronoun that can indicate either a male or a female? In common English, we have for years written this: "What do we want our reader to think about our writing? We want him to believe that we know what we are talking about." We know that "our reader" may include males or females or both. How do we express ourselves now?

With this example, the solution is easy. We turn the singular into the plural. "What do we want our readers to think about us? We want them to believe that we know what we're talking about." I always try to use plural forms when I can so that I do not exclude women.

But then sometimes we must use the singular. "The thief entered the house by breaking a pane of glass in the back door, cutting himself in the process, and leaving a trail of blood through the kitchen. The wound must not have been serious since he stole not only all my Dolly Parton records but came back for my life-sized painting of Elvis on black velvet."

Now what are we to do? In some sentences, we can write both the feminine and the masculine pronoun, but in these sentences the effect, to me at least, seems clumsy. "The thief entered the house by breaking a pane of glass in the back door, cutting himself or herself in the process and leaving a trail of blood through the kitchen. The wound must not have been serious since he or she not only stole all my Dolly Parton records but came back for my life-sized painting of Elvis on black velvet."

The constant repetition of *he or she* is the problem. We can use both the masculine and feminine pronouns easily enough when repetition is unnecessary. We can write, "The company promised to give the first-prize winner a case of any deodorant he or she may choose." But we get into trouble when we write this: "The company promised to give the first-prize winner a week's stay in any hotel in Hawaii that he or she may choose and promised also that he or she might take along a companion and that he or she would also be given free use of a rental car for the week and free meals in the restaurant of his or her choice." Here we can avoid sexist language only by extensive revision. "First prize was a week's stay in any hotel in Hawaii for the winner and a companion, a free rental car for a week, and free meals in any restaurant in the islands."

Occasionally we can use the pronoun *one* as a substitute for *he* or *she*. "Anyone who works the night shift for twenty years will discover that *one*'s view of life changes in ways incomprehensible to *one*'s neighbors." To many, such usage is uncomfortable.

I believe that the ultimate solution to the problem will be to use the pronouns *they, their,* or *them* as nonsexist substitutes for sexist pronouns. I now often hear educated people say things like this: "Anybody who works the night shift for twenty years will discover that their view of life changes in ways incomprehensible to their neighbors." This solution is not grammatically correct, and it makes me wince, perhaps because I'm so old. It seems not to offend younger people. I do not expect it to be adopted soon by most editors and professional writers, but who can tell? I see it now and then in advertising and even in slick-paper magazines. *Anyone* who says English cannot change to accept uncomfortable usage does not know what *they are* talking about.

Even the ungrammatical use of *their* to refer to a single person is much better than *he/she* or, worse, the *s/he* that I see occasionally in memos. We should be able to read writing aloud, and I do not see how we can read *he/she* or *s/he* aloud in any sensible way. It also looks wretched on the page.

My own solution, used in this book, is first to do my best to revise away the problem. Most editors of books and magazines seem to have adopted this procedure. You sit there and think and rewrite and use a plural instead of a singular, or you change your text even more. When I have to use a singular form, I vary the pronoun, using *he* sometimes and *she* sometimes. In my observation, many writers have now adopted this usage.

Yet to many it seems awkward, and woman writers as diverse as Barbara Tuchman and Mina Shaughnessy have used the traditional *he* without feeling that they were betraying their sex. But then their lives ended before the last decade, when sensibilities among women became much stronger.

I find myself torn. I don't want to offend an audience; an offended audience, for whatever reason, will not take your work seriously. And hardly any subject related to writing offends people more than the issue of sexist language. And alas! Some people are going to be offended no matter what we do. If we sound clumsy in our efforts to avoid sexist language, we offend traditionalists, of whom there are many. If we refuse to take note of social change and go on using *he* and *him* as if everyone on earth worthy of consideration were born male, we offend the large and rapidly growing number of men and women who believe that clumsiness of language is a small price to pay for sexual equality.

Aside from the difficulties with pronouns, we can easily avoid some of the traditional offenses of sexist language. You don't have to say *policeman;* you can say *police officer.* I have no problem writing *chairperson* or *chair* rather than the traditional *chairman.* And I now regularly say *spokesperson* rather than *spokesman. Freshperson* seems unbearably clumsy as a substitute for *freshman,* but we can always say *first-year student* instead.

Where once we spoke of *mankind,* we now speak of *humankind.* Where once we wrote "the average man," we now say "the average person." Instead of saying, "Man is the highest form of life," we can say, "The human species is the highest form of life." Whenever you are tempted to use a word that seems to show superiority of men over women, pause to think of another, sex-neutral word. You can nearly always find one.

Some words should be abandoned. *Poetess* for a woman now seems degrading—though *actress* does not. Women should never be referred to as "the fair sex" or "the distaff side," as if the only interesting quality of a woman were appearance and her only job in the home. A wife should never be called her husband's "better half," a term patronizing at best. The word *lady* now has a negative connotation, for many feel that it sets women apart and implies that they are worthwhile only if they act like characters in a nineteenth-century etiquette book. The word *woman* is better.

Above all, readers should not be addressed as though the only important people among them were men. Never identify women by telling who their husbands are unless that information has some special importance. A few years ago I received a notice about a conference on Thomas More where Mary Ellen Bork, president of the St. Thomas More Society of Washington, D.C., was to be one of the speakers. The circular identified her as the "wife of Judge Robert Bork." The conference was sponsored by a conservative religious group—perhaps a reason for labeling Ms. Bork in a manner so offensive to feminists and others often taken to be radical. Ms. Bork happens to have a long and distinguished career of activity related to the study of Thomas More, and having met her, I find her gracious and intelligent. It seems gratuitous indeed to identify her by reference to her husband, no matter how celebrated—or notorious—he may be or may have been. In a news story, that information might have been placed far down in the text, for it would interest some people curious to know if Ms. Bork was related to the judge. But it is demeaning as a primary identification.

Take care also with the proper titles of women. The term *Ms.* is now common, and I use it regularly to address correspondence to women. A few women object to the title and prefer the more traditional *Mrs.* if they are married and *Miss* if they are not. Courtesy requires that you call people what they want to be called, but though I might write to a woman as *Mrs.* if she prefers that title, I use *Ms.* regularly in speaking and writing in the third person.

African Americans

Next to women, blacks have suffered the worst abuses of language in our society. They have naturally rebelled. For many years, the polite way to refer to blacks was as "colored people" or "people of color." We still have the National Association for the Advancement of Colored People. The word "Negro," spelled with a capital N, was also used regularly for many decades, even in the 1960s during the civil rights movement. Dr. Martin Luther King, Jr., always spoke of "Negro" and "Negroes."

At some point in the 1960s, blacks began to object to the word "Negro" because white Southerners often used the word to show that they were not prejudiced when, in fact, they kept right on resisting the integration of schools, libraries, transportation, and other institutions of public life in the South. Blacks found the use of "Negro" offensive and hypocritical, and in the 1970s it seemed to vanish almost overnight in public discourse, replaced by the simple "black."

Recently, another issue arose. A great many people of color are not black but brown. Some people started using the hyphenated adjective, "Afro-American." But then Jesse Jackson, a black political leader, suggested a few years ago that the term "African American" be used in an effort to take the emphasis off color and put it on origin and to certify the completely American quality of people of color. This usage seems to be catching on in the public discourse of universities and sometimes in popular magazines such as *Time*.

Yet a poll in *The New York Times* a couple of years ago showed that 70 percent of Americans of African descent still prefer to be called "blacks" rather than "African Americans." I think the term "African American" is unlikely to endure simply because it is such a mouthful. But we shall see. In the meantime, I have not known any person of color to be offended by use of the term "black." The issue is not yet resolved, and it will not be for a long time.

Native Americans

Much the same process of change has gone on among American Indians. To many people, they are now "Native Americans." Yet one of the most aggressive organizations furthering American-Indian rights is the American Indian Movement. My university happens to offer many special scholarships to American Indians, and those I have known refer to themselves as "Indians" without self-consciousness.

Sexual Preference

Sexual preference is another area where language is difficult. We seem to have no choice at all in whether we are sexually drawn to people of the opposite sex or to those of the same sex. It is cruel to use language that demeans people who are what they are because they are born with certain preferences. "Homosexual" is still, to most people, a neutral term applying to both sexes, though to some homosexuals it has pejorative connotations. Increasingly, the term "gay" is used for male homosexuals, although it can apply to both males and females. Usually people now speak of "gays and lesbians," using "lesbian" as the nonpejorative term for females.

"Political Correctness"

All these matters are difficult. They require a willingness to change and a broad-mindedness about language. Academics are often attacked these days for sins committed in the name of "political correctness." These sins involve language. Usually, when I hear somebody talking about the crime of "political correctness," I find bigotry lurking just under the surface. But it is true that at any moment of great change, especially change driven by a moral impulse, some silliness may result. At an annual conference of writing teachers this March, a woman told me with great indignation that a couple of years ago her university had denied her the Ph.D. degree until she changed every *he* in her dissertation to *he or she.* That seems excessive. The efforts of some to substitute terms like "income disadvantaged" for "poor" or "physically disadvantaged" for "handicapped" eventually become silly both inside and outside academe.

But the occasional foolishness does not invalidate the genuine need we all have to examine our language to make it more sensitive to the community in which we live. Women are equal to men. They ought to be treated with equality, for to do otherwise is to demean men as well as women. The same is true for other groups within our society. When we demean them with language, we become less worthy human beings ourselves. The English-speaking world is democratic, and our language should reflect the ideals we profess.

Appendix Two

Clichés

Study the following list, and avoid the expressions you find there. They have been worked to death. They may have had some power once, but it has long since turned to dust. On occasion, you may find some special reason to use one of the phrases; and when we are pressed, we are all likely to tumble into using some of them because they come so easily to mind. That is just what is wrong with them. Although no one will hang you or beat you for letting one creep into your prose, it's a good idea to change the cliché into simple English whenever you can. Instead of calling a marathon an "acid test," you can say that it is a test of stamina and character. That says more specifically what you might want to say in the cliché "acid test."

abreast of the times

absolute truth

acid test

across a wide [broad] spectrum

across the spectrum

add insult to injury

after all is said and done

against the current

agony of defeat

agree to disagree

all walks of life

a man [or woman] for all seasons

at this point in time

avoid like the plague

[the] ball's in his court

basic needs

basic truth

beat a hasty retreat

be that as it may

better half

better late than never

better part of valor

beyond a shadow of doubt

[the] birds and the bees

bite the dust

bitter end
black as night
bloody but unbowed
blue as the sky
bolt from the blue
bottom line
bottom of my [her, his] heart
bottom of the barrel
bottom of the deck
brainchild
brave as a lion
bright as a new penny
bring down the house
bring home the bacon
broad array
broad daylight
brown as a nut
brutally frank
brutal murder
burn the midnight oil
bustling cities
by the same token

calm, cool, and collected
cat on a hot tin roof
chip off the old block
cloud nine
cold as ice
cold, hard facts
cold light of day
come to grips with
communicate effectively
consensus of opinion
conspicuous by his absence
cool as a cucumber
could have knocked me over
　　with a feather

crack of dawn
crisis of confidence
critical juncture
crowning glory
crying on the inside
cut and dried

dead as a doornail
deaf as a post
deep as the ocean
deep, dark secret
diabolical skill
distaff side
doomed to disappointment
do or die
down and out
down but not out
down for the count
down the primrose path
dry as dust
dyed in the wool

each and every
[to] each his own
easy as falling off a log
every dog has its day
every tub on its own bottom

face the music
factor
facts of life
fatal flaw
few and far between
filthy lucre
first and foremost
fit as a fiddle
fleecy clouds
fond memories

fond recollections
fresh as a daisy
frozen north

get the lead out
gone but not forgotten
go over like a lead balloon
go over with a fine-tooth
    comb
grave danger
green with envy
gutless wonder

hail fellow well met
hale and hearty
hands-on
happy as a clam
happy as a lark
happy medium
hard row to hoe
head up [the committee]
heady mixture
hearts and minds
heave a sigh of relief
higher than a kite
highest priority
high spirits
hit me like a ton of bricks
hit the nail on the head
hopes dashed
hotter than hell [Hades]
hush fell over the crowd
hustle and bustle

imminent danger
implement
in a nutshell
in a very real sense

innocent as a newborn babe
in some cases
integral part
in terms of
in the final analysis
in this day and age
it goes without saying
it is incumbent upon
it is interesting to note
it stands to reason

ladder of success
larger than life
last but not least
last-ditch [anything]
last straw
learning experience
lick and a promise
light as a feather
like father, like son
little lady
live and learn
live from hand to mouth
live like a king
lying in her teeth

mad as a hatter
make a shambles of
man about town
meaningful experience
meaningful relationship
method in her madness
mind like a steel trap
miss is as good as a mile
mitigate against [not only a
    cliché but incorrect]
more sinned against than
    sinning

more than meets the eye
murmur of approval

neat as a pin
needle in a haystack
nip and tuck
nip in the bud
nose to the grindstone
no sooner said than done
nuclear holocaust
nothing ventured, nothing
    gained
not too distant future

off his rocker
off the beaten track
off the track
off the wall
once and for all
one hundred and ten percent
one rotten apple spoils the
    barrel
ongoing
only time will tell
on the fast track
on this planet
other side of the coin
out of the blue

painfully obvious
paint the town red
paramount importance
pass the buck
pave the way
pebble on the beach
pencil thin
pertinent facts
pick and choose
pivotal figure

plain as the nose on your face
plain Jane
pleased as punch
poor but happy
poor but honest
precondition
preplanning
pride and joy
primrose path
prioritize
proof is in the pudding
proud owner
proud possessor
put your best foot forward
put your foot in it

quick as a flash
quick as a wink
quick as lightning

raise [rear] its ugly head
rank and file
rather unique
raving lunatic
rude awakening

sadder but wiser
scarce as hens' teeth
sell like hot cakes
sharp as a razor
sharp as a tack
short and sweet
short end of the stick
shot in the arm
shoulder to the wheel
sigh of relief
silver platter
simple as salt
sink or swim

skeleton in the closet
skin of your teeth
slow but sure
smart as a whip
smelling like a rose
sneaking suspicion
sober as a judge
soft place in my heart
sound as a dollar
spread like wildfire
stick out like a sore thumb
stock in trade
straight and narrow
straw that broke the camel's
    back
strike while the iron is hot
sunny south
supreme moment
sure winner

tangled skein
tangled web
tempest in a teapot
tender mercies
tested in the fire
thin as a rail
tip of the iceberg

tired but happy
to all intents and purposes
tough nut to crack
tried and true
truth is stranger than fiction
twinkling of an eye
two-edged sword

undercurrent of excitement
unstinted praise
up in arms

viable alternative
vicious circle [cycle]
vital role

walk a chalk line
walk a fine line
walking on air
walk the line
walk the straight and narrow
wet blanket
when the going gets tough,
    the tough get going
white as snow
work like a dog
work like a horse
wreak havoc

Notes

CHAPTER 1

[1]Roger Angell, "Remembering Mr. Shawn," *The New Yorker,* Dec. 28, 1992/Jan. 4, 1993, p. 136.

[2]John Simon, *Paradigms Lost,* New York, Penguin Books, 1981, p. 18.

[3]Simon, p. 45.

[4]Dennis E. Baron, *Grammar and Good Taste,* New Haven, Conn., Yale University Press, 1982, p. 141.

[5]Rosellen Brown, "His Late Espoused Saint," *New York Times Book Review,* July 11, 1993, p. 24.

[6]David B. Kaminsky, *Aspiration Biopsy For the Community Hospital,* New York, Mason Publishing, 1981, p. 1.

[7]Quoted in E. D. Hirsch, Jr., *The Philosophy of Composition,* University of Chicago Press, 1977, pp. 60–61.

[8]Hirsch, p. 61.

[9]Giovanni Boccaccio, *The Decameron,* Modern Library edition, n.d.

[10]Mary Anne Weaver, "Burying the Martyrs," *The New Yorker,* Dec. 28, 1992/Jan. 4, 1993, p. 106.

CHAPTER 2

[1]Barbara W. Tuchman, "In Search of History," *Practicing History,* New York, Knopf, 1981, p. 20; *Modern American Prose,* 3d ed., New York, McGraw-Hill, 1993, p. 398.

[2]Thomas More, *The Confutation of Tyndale's Answer,* Louis A. Schuster, Richard C. Marius, James P. Lusardi, and Richard J. Schoeck (eds.), New Haven, Conn., Yale University Press, 1973, pp. 20–21.

[3]David McCullough, *Truman,* New York, Simon & Schuster, 1992, p. 829.

CHAPTER 3

[1]Michel de Montaigne, Essays, 3:1. *Oeuvres complètes,* Editions Gallimard, Paris, 1962, p. 767.

❖

[2]Montaigne, 2:10, p. 389.

[3]Erik Larson, "The Story of a Gun," *The Atlantic,* January 1993, p. 48.

[4]Jeannie Ralston, "In the Heart of Appalachia," *National Geographic,* February 1993, p. 116.

[5]William Safire, "Smearing It On, Rubbing It In," *The New York Times Magazine,* Jan. 17, 1993, p. 14.

[6]Philip Langdon, "How Portland Does It," *The Atlantic,* November 1992, p. 134. [Article pp. 134–142]

[7]Brian Fagan, "All About Eve," *Archaeology,* November/December 1992, p. 18.

[8]Garry Wills, "Jefferson's Other Buildings," *The Atlantic Monthly,* January 1993, p. 80. [Article pp. 80–89]

[9]Hugh Sidey, "Last Roll Call for the Reaganauts," *Time,* Jan. 25, 1993, p. 40.

[10]Daniel J. Walkowitz, "The Making of a Feminine Professional Identity: Social Workers in the 1920s," *The American Historical Review,* October 1990, p. 1051. [Article 1051–1075]

[11]Lewis Thomas, "To Err Is Human," *The Medusa and the Snail,* New York, Viking Press, 1979, p. 36.

[12]Thomas, p. 40.

CHAPTER 4

[1]Gilbert Allardyce, "What Fascism Is Not: Thoughts on the Deflation of a Concept," *American Historical Review,* April 1979, p. 367.

[2]Barbara Tuchman, *Practicing History,* New York, Knopf, 1981, p. 23.

CHAPTER 5

[1]Corby Kummer, "Real Olives," *The Atlantic,* June 1993, p. 116.

[2]James Baldwin, "Notes of a Native Son," Boston, Beacon Press, 1955; *Modern American Prose,* 3d ed., New York, McGraw-Hill, 1993, p. 40.

[3]Barbara Tuchman, *The Proud Tower,* New York, Macmillan, 1966, p. 68.

[4]Loren Eiseley, "Charles Darwin," *Scientific American,* February 1956, pp. 62–72.

[5]Loren Eiseley, "The Judgment of the Birds," *The Immense Journey,* New York, Random House, 1956; *Modern American Prose,* 3d ed., pp. 155–156.

[6]William Manchester, *The Glory and the Dream,* Boston, Little Brown, 1974, p. 93.

[7]John McPhee, "The Swiss at War," *La Place de la Concorde Swiss,* New York, Farrar, Straus & Giroux, 1984, *Modern American Prose,* 3d ed., p. 325.

[8]Lewis Thomas, *Late Night Thoughts on Listening to Mahler's Ninth Symphony,* New York, Viking Penguin, 1982; *Modern American Prose,* 3d ed., p. 386.

CHAPTER 6

[1]Robert A. Caro, *The Years of Lyndon Johnson: The Path to Power,* New York, Knopf, 1982, p. 413.

[2]Richard Zoglin, "The Networks Come Home," *Time,* May 31, 1993, p. 62.

[3]Barbara Tuchman, "In Search of History," *Practicing History,* New York, Knopf, 1981, p. 18; *Modern American Prose,* 3d ed., New York, McGraw-Hill, 1993, p. 396.

[4]Stephen Jay Gould, "Evolution as Fact and Theory," *Modern American Prose,* 3d ed., New York, McGraw-Hill, 1993, p. 235.

[5]John McPhee, "The Swiss at War," *Modern American Prose,* 3d ed., New York, McGraw-Hill, 1993, p. 327.

[6]Maxine Hong Kingston, "No Name Woman," *Modern American Prose,* 3d ed., New York, McGraw-Hill, 1993, p. 246.

[7]Barbara Tuchman, "Is History a Guide to the Future?" *Practicing History,* p. 249; *Modern American Prose,* 3d ed., New York, McGraw-Hill, 1993, p. 424.

[8]"Flood, Sweat, and Tears," *Time,* July 26, 1993, p. 30.

[9]Robert W. Creamer, "First Inning: 1876–1901," in *The Ultimate Baseball Book,* Daniel Okrent and Harris Lewine (eds.), Boston, Houghton Mifflin, 1981, pp. 14–15.

[10]Barbara Tuchman, "The Black Death," *Modern American Prose,* third edition, p. 410.

[11]Philip Caputo, *A Rumor of War,* New York, Holt, Rinehart & Winston, 1977, p. 163.

[12]Bruce Catton, *The Coming Fury,* Garden City, N.Y., Doubleday, 1961, p. 247.

[13]William Faulkner, *Light in August,* New York, Random House, 1932, p. 147.

[14]Kirkpatrick Sale, *Human Scale,* New York, Coward, McCann & Geoghegan, 1980, p. 129.

[15]Barbara Tuchman, *A Distant Mirror,* New York, Knopf, 1978, p. 139.

[16]George Orwell, *Homage to Catalonia,* Boston, Beacon, 1955, p. 86.

[17]Norman Mailer, "The Siege of Chicago," *Modern American Prose,* 3d ed., New York, McGraw-Hill, 1993, pp. 622–623.

[18]Tom Wolfe, "Las Vegas," *Modern American Prose,* 3d ed., p. 515.

[19]Malcolm Cowley, *And I Worked at the Writer's Trade,* New York, Viking, 1978, p. 100.

[20]John McPhee, "The Swiss at War," *Modern American Prose,* 3d ed., New York, McGraw-Hill, 1993, p. 325.

CHAPTER 7

[1]Terry Teachout, "The Wrong Kind of Southerner," *New York Times Book Review,* July 25, 1993, p. 22.

[2]"The Collective Behavior of Fads: The Characteristics, Effects, and Career of Streaking," *American Sociological Review,* August 1988, p. 572.

CHAPTER 8

[1]Sophronia Scott Gregory, "'Diss' Is the Word of the Lord," *Time,* July 26, 1993, p. 61.

[2]John Simon, *Paradigms Lost,* New York, Penguin Books, 1980, pp. 17–18.

[3]Quoted in Dennis E. Baron, *Grammar and Good Taste,* New Haven, Yale University Press, 1982, p. 218.

[4]Baron, p. 206.

[5]*Harper Dictionary of Contemporary Usage,* eds. William Morris and Mary Morris, New York, Harper & Row, 1975, p. 312.

[6]Charles Darwin, *Life and Letters,* vol. 8, p. 58 (cited in *O.E.D.*).

[7]N. R. Kleinfield, *The New York Times,* Nov. 23, 1983, p. C-1.

CHAPTER 9

[1]Loren Eiseley, "The Judgment of the Birds," *The Immense Journey,* New York, Random House, 1956; *Modern American Prose,* 3d ed., New York, McGraw-Hill, 1993, p. 155.

[2]William R. Newcott, "Lightning: Nature's High-Voltage Spectacle, *National Geographic,* July 1993, p. 83.

[3]Philip Caputo, *A Rumor of War,* New York, Holt, Rinehart and Winston, 1977, p. 129.

[4]Bertrand Russell, quoted in Ronald W. Clark, *Einstein: The Life and Times,* New York, World, 1971, p. 87.

[5]Norman Mailer, "The Siege of Chicago," *Miami and the Siege of Chicago,* New York, New American Library, 1968, p. 169, *Modern American Prose,* 3d ed., New York, McGraw-Hill, 1993, p. 625.

[6]Joseph Conrad, *Lord Jim,* New York, New American Library, 1965, p. 80; first published in 1899.

[7]Donald Davidson, "What Metaphors Mean," *On Metaphor,* Sheldon Sacks, (ed.), University of Chicago Press, 1979, p. 40.

[8]*The New Yorker,* Dec. 5, 1988, p. 132.

[9]Alexander L. Taylor III, "The Wizard Inside the Machines," *Time,* April 16, 1984, p. 56.

[10]"Block That Metaphor," *The New Yorker,* Dec. 26, 1988, p. 90.

[11]Irving Howe, *World of Our Fathers,* New York, Simon & Schuster, Touchstone Books, 1976, p. 174.

[12]Mailer, "The Siege of Chicago," p. 172; *Modern American Prose,* 3d ed., New York, McGraw-Hill, 1993, pp. 627–628.

[13]Molly Ivins, *Molly Ivins Can't Say That, Can She?* New York, Random House, 1991, p. 107.

[14]John Kenneth Galbraith, *Economics in Perspective,* Boston, Houghton Mifflin, 1987, p. 60.

[15]*Elements of Literature,* Robert Scholes, Carl H. Klaus, Michael Shermon, (eds.), New York, Oxford University Press, 1978, p. 41.

[16]Mike Barnicle, "This Space Not Available—Yet," *The Boston Globe,* June 3, 1993, p. 23.

[17]Michael Kinsley, "The New Politics of Abortion," *Time,* July 17, 1989, p. 96.

CHAPTER 10

[1]Walter Jackson Bate, *Samuel Johnson,* New York and London, Harcourt Brace Jovanovich, 1977, p. 395.

[2]Neil Sheehan, *A Bright Shining Lie: John Paul Vann and America in Vietnam,* New York, Random House, 1988, p. 343.

[3]Stephen Jay Gould, "Women's Brains," *Modern American Prose,* 3d ed., New York, McGraw-Hill, 1993, pp. 226–227.

[4]Robert N. Proctor, *Racial Hygiene: Medicine Under the Nazis,* Cambridge, Mass., Harvard University Press, 1988, p. 187.

[5]Eugene D. Genovese, *Roll Jordan Roll,* New York, Random House, Vintage Books, 1976, p. 249.

[6]"Strollers," *Consumer Reports,* November 1988, p. 723.

[7]Lewis Thomas, "Thoughts on Listening to Mahler's Ninth," *Modern American Prose,* 3d ed., New York, McGraw-Hill, 1993, p. 387.

[8]George J. Church, "The Terror Within," *Time,* July 5, 1993, pp. 24–25.

[9]*Time,* March 4, 1984, p. 47.

[10]"Compact 33mm Cameras," *Consumer Reports,* November 1988, p. 706.

[11]Alice Walker, "A Tribute to Dr. Martin Luther King, Jr.," *Modern American Prose,* 3d ed., New York, McGraw-Hill, 1993, p. 441.

CHAPTER 11

[1]Evan S. Connell, *Son of the Morning Star: Custer and the Little Bighorn,* San Francisco, North Point Press, 1984, p. 231.

[2]Paul Fussell, *The Great War and Modern Memory,* New York, Oxford University Press, 1975, p. 235.

[3]David Donald, *Look Homeward: A Life of Thomas Wolfe,* Boston, Little, Brown, 1987, p. 254.

Index

❖